A BETTER HOPE

A BETTER HOPE

**RESOURCES FOR A CHURCH CONFRONTING
CAPITALISM, DEMOCRACY, AND POSTMODERNITY**

STANLEY HAUERWAS

A Division of Baker Book House Co
Grand Rapids, Michigan 49516

Published by Brazos Press
a division of Baker Book House Company
P.O. Box 6287, Grand Rapids, MI 49516-6287

Printed in the United States of America

Unless otherwise noted, Scripture is taken from the Revised Standard Version of the Bible, copyright 1946, 1952, 1971 by the Division of Christian Education of the National Council of the Churches of Christ in the USA. Used by permission.

Library of Congress Cataloging-in-Publication Data

Hauerwas, Stanley, 1940–
    A better hope : resources for a church confronting capitalism, democracy, and postmodernity / Stanley Hauerwas.
       p.   cm.
    Includes bibliographical references.
    ISBN 1-58743-000-2 (paper)
    1. Christian ethics—United States. I. Title.
    BJ1275.H36 2000
    261'.0973—dc21   00-056426

For current information about all releases from Brazos Press, visit our web site:
http://www.brazospress.com

Contents

■Preface

I WOULD LIKE TO BLAME THIS BOOK on Rodney Clapp. He certainly deserves part of the blame, but unfortunately I had begun to imagine the book before Rodney imagined Brazos Press. I had told myself that *Sanctify Them in the Truth* would be the last book I would publish until I had finished the Gifford Lectures. But then I began to think that some of the essays I had written over the past few years were interconnected. Alex Sider and Richard Church helped me think through those connections. This book is the result of our combined efforts.

I have dedicated this book to those who have thrown in their lot with The Ekklesia Project. Most of you reading this have never heard of The Ekklesia Project, which is one of the reasons I have dedicated this book to them. I want what we are about to be better known, so I have appended the Declaration of The Ekklesia Project to this book. Yet I would not want anyone to assume that The Ekklesia Project and what I am about are one and the same. Those who constitute the Project come from quite different ecclesial backgrounds, some are academics and some are not, and we bring quite different agendas to the work of the group. Yet as the Declaration makes clear, we are united in our commitment to reclaiming the church as an alternative people for the good of the world. At least for me The Ekklesia Project is a reminder that theology is not just another set of ideas to be considered by bored intellectuals.

I am honored that this book is one of the initial publications of Brazos Press. Over the years I have learned the importance of editors. Rodney Clapp is not only a wonderful editor but a friend. The venture he and his friends have begun with Brazos Press is a sign of hope. Another sign of hope for me are the extraordinary graduate students who continue to come to Duke to become theologians. Alex Sider and Richard Church, who helped me with this book, are but representatives of these wonderful people.

Sarah Freedman, the most interesting "secretary" in the world, did the hard work to get this book ready for publication. She never fails to surprise me. Her observations often make my work harder, but the results are worth the extra effort. The divinity school at Duke is a better place because of Sarah Freedman.

I know I am a better theologian because of Paula Gilbert. God has never been just "there" for me. God is "there" for Paula. Her willingness to share that "thereness" with me makes all the difference. God is great.

■INTRODUCTION

ON BEING HOPEFUL

I HOPE A BETTER HOPE will be read as a hopeful book. John Howard Yoder observed that I have maximized the "provocative edge of the dissenting posture with titles like *Against the Nations* or *Resident Aliens*."[1] I do not deny that I love a good fight, but I also know that it is a mistake, at least if you are a Christian, to have your life or theology determined by who you think are your enemies. Christians know we will have enemies because we are told we must love our enemies. That we are commanded to love our enemies is not a strategy to guarantee that all enmity can be overcome, but a reminder that for Christians our lives must be determined by our loves, not our hates. That is why Christians cannot afford to let ourselves be defined by what we are against. Whatever or whomever we are against, we are so only because God has given us so much to be for.

A *Better Hope* is my attempt to make the "for" more determinative than the "against." Of course I should like to think that books like *After Christendom?* and *Against the Nations*, polemical though they may be, are so only because of what I have been for. I have, of course, mounted what I hope are crushing criticisms of political and theological liberalism. I have done so, however, not because I think political liberalism is peculiarly perverse in comparison to other political options. My problem has never been with secular political liberals but rather with the widespread assumption shared by many Christians that political liberalism ought to shape the agenda, if not the very life, of the church. My attacks on liberalism, and in particular the results of liberal practices for the church, but reflect—or at least I hope they reflect—the love that God has made possible in and through the church.

9 ■

I am not suggesting that the reader will find in A Better Hope a kinder, gentler Hauerwas. I am getting older, but I do not think my increasing age is making me more "mellow." A Better Hope is not without polemics. Nor do I think the anger that shapes not only what I write about but how I write is missing from this book. I am still mad as hell at Christians, which certainly includes myself, for making the practice of the Christian faith so uninteresting. Yet I do hope the reader will find in this book, as the title indicates, resources for resisting the powers that threaten our lives as Christians—resources as simple as knowing how, as we grow older, to be friends with ourselves and with one another. To the extent I am able to show that such resources are still available, A Better Hope may appear less polemical and more "positive" than some of my past work.

In truth, as I indicate in the first chapter of this book, I have simply grown tired of arguments about the alleged virtues or vices of liberalism. In the first chapter I again criticize John Rawls's account of liberalism, even though I know my criticisms will only invite the normal response from defenders of liberalism: that is, I have not got Rawls right, or even if I have, he does not represent the most defensible liberal position. That the argument for or against liberalism is interminable does not mean that we cannot learn much from its various mutations. Arguments about liberalism, however, can become a distraction for Christians just to the extent that our agenda is first and foremost set by the church.

We learn from the Book of Hebrews that the church is "a better hope."[2] Our hope as Christians is in an *altera civitas* of which we believe we already have substantive intimations in the church. Unfortunately, many Christians in America have confused the light that comes from the church with America. They have done so because many of the main cultural and political symbols that have shaped American life were "borrowed" from the church. America becomes the intercessor that determines our relationship to God and accordingly shapes our understanding of God. Yet the better hope "by which we draw near to God" is Jesus, who has become the "guarantee of a better covenant" (Heb. 7:18–22). That is why the most determinative criticism of America must be theological. Accordingly I hope the criticism that I mount in this book reflects the great hope that is the church.

THE ARCHBISHOP SPEAKS

I hope the positive character of this book will at least make those who are convinced I am a "sectarian, fideistic tribalist" think twice. I confess I do not expect that hope to be fulfilled. However, it does give me hope that the kind of critique I have tried to mount over the years is now showing up in some quite surprising places. For example, Francis Cardinal George, arch-bishop of Chicago, gave a speech entitled "Catholic Christianity and the Millennium" in the series "Frontiers of the Mind in the 21st Century" spon-sored by the Library of Congress; it exemplifies what I think a theological critique of America should entail. George, and the office he holds, is not usually identified as a representative of "sectarian Christianity." Yet what he says about America and the church's relation to America is quite simi-lar (or at least it seems so to me) to arguments I have made in the past and continue in this book. So I cannot resist rehearsing the main outlines of George's argument: his speech provides a wonderful introduction to what this book is about.

George begins by noting it is fitting that a representative of the church—which traces its history back to Jesus Christ—should have a place on the pro-gram of the Library of Congress. It is fitting because the millennium is not a neutral measure of time but rather is a moment in history that is unintelligi-ble without the "decisive and momentous influence of Jesus Christ."[3] George therefore declares his task to be nothing less than to "hold up the icon of Christ and to show the unique understanding of the world that flows from this picture."[4] George is either oblivious of or chooses to ignore those Catholic theologians who, drawing on modern theories of natural law, argue that if Christians are to speak in the "public" arena they must do so using a "third language" that avoids the "particularities" of the faith.

Without apology George observes that a provocative claim lies at the heart of Christianity: "In Jesus Christ, God has become a creature, with-out ceasing to be God and without compromising the integrity of the crea-ture he becomes."[5] Chalcedon and Nicea are names of the process by which the church thought through the implications of what it means for God to be present in Jesus Christ. The church rejected all attempts to understand Christ as quasi-divine and quasi-human in favor of his being fully divine and human such that the former enhances, without excluding, the integrity of the latter. The "condition for the possibility" of such a claim requires that we understand that God is not *a* being alongside others, God is not in competition with nature, but rather God and God alone can be in Christ, fully human and fully God, without overwhelming created and finite nature exactly because God is not finite.

This understanding of God, rooted in the Jewish faith, is the basis for the peculiarly Christian understanding of creation. "Because God is not one being among others but rather the sheer energy of to-be itself, God does not make the world through manipulation, change or violence, as the gods of philosophy and mythology do. Since there is literally nothing out-side God, he makes the entirety of the finite realm *ex nihilo*, through an act of purest and gentlest generosity."[6] All things therefore "participate" in the power of God's being, which means all that is is related through bonds of

11

ontological intimacy. From this perspective, when St. Francis of Assisi spoke of "brother sun and sister moon" he was not being "poetic" but rather was making a sober and metaphysically realistic remark. All that is exists in communion because all that is is rooted in a more primordial communion with God.

George begins his lecture by rehearsing these christological claims of Christianity to prepare his listeners for his contention that anything Christians have to say about the political and economic realm must flow from this "Incarnational metaphysics." Augustine in *City of God* worked out the politics commensurate to such a christological vision. Refusing to dialogue with the representatives of Roman polity who challenged the legitimacy of Christianity, Augustine is interested neither in accommodating nor in compromising with the Roman system. Rather than turning to Rome to find a social theory or political arrangement compatible with a privatized or interiorized Christian spirituality, he excoriates Rome as an unjust society and, even more outrageously, argues that Christianity is the only basis for a just form of social arrangement. Indeed from Augustine's perspective, Rome—like all the cities of men—is not even a society because there can be no justice in it. There can be no justice in Rome because such societies are but collectivities based on self-love rather than on the shared love of God. Rome's violence and injustice therefore are but correlatives of the false metaphysics on which it is based—a "denial of a metaphysic of participation and *communion* leads to the phony justice of the City of Man."[7]

In contrast, George reminds his hearers, Christians believe in the God of Jesus Christ, "a God of non-violent and creative love," who, unlike the false gods of Rome, enters into competitive relation with no one or nothing. The worship of this God makes possible a society based on love, compassion, and nonviolence because it is based not in the *libido dominandi* but in the love preached and embodied by Jesus. Accordingly Augustine refuses to place his analysis in anything resembling a "church-state" context. There is no distinction in Augustine between a secular state that takes care of the public life and the church that takes care of the spiritual good of people. Rather there is simply "the dramatic difference between the false worship (and hence flawed social arrangement) of the City of Man and the proper worship (and hence life-giving social arrangement) of the City of God."[8] Without romanticizing the past, George suggests that for all their ambiguity the late antique and medieval periods can be characterized by the attempt to find the relationship between worship and social life.

Whatever else the term *modernity* may describe, George argues, "what marks the modern consciousness is a breakdown of this classically Christian participation metaphysics and the consequent emergence of a secular arena at best only incidentally related to God."[9] The impoverishment of discussions surrounding the relation of religion and politics in America is but a

reflection of how national feasts and ceremonies have replaced the liturgical calendar of the church, whose feasts cannot help but become private
observances. According to George "the end of the modern era, however, is
signaled by the inability of the secular calendar to call people out of their private concerns into the rhythm of a shared public life. National holidays have
become primarily occasions for private recreation. Time itself becomes a field
to be personally scheduled, a function of private purpose."[10]

Drawing on the work of John Milbank, Catherine Pickstock, and William
Placher, George believes these results are rooted in Christian theological
mistakes that repudiated the Thomistic understanding of the analogy of
being. The result is an overdetermined distinction between "nature" and
"grace": God is no longer understood as the generous power in which all
things exist but rather that supreme being apart from whom all things exist.
Modernity names that time that assumes a fundamental split between the
divine and nondivine, which stands in opposition to the participation/*communion* metaphysics of the incarnation.[11]

The social and political implications of this change soon manifested
themselves in the work of Thomas Hobbes. His famous description of the
state of nature as "solitary, poor, nasty, brutish, and short" is but an indication that once the worship of God has been lost, "natural man" is left with
no other option than to fight a "war of all against all." The role government plays in such a world cannot help but become what it was in ancient
Rome, that is, "the maintenance of a temporary and ersatz peace on the
basis of coercion and violent control."[12] Because debates about ultimate
ends, particularly in theology, are disruptive of peace, the church must be
kept under tight control, which means whatever role religion may have it
must be subordinated to political ends. Locke softens the essential structure of Hobbes's thought, but like Hobbes he derives individual rights from
antagonizing passions. Given his understanding of the human situation,
for Locke the primary role of government is limited to the protection of
individual prerogatives.

According to George this is the tradition that shaped the minds of the
founders of America. The "self-evident truths" concerning "unalienable
rights" to life, liberty, and the pursuit of happiness are not and cannot be
correlated to moral ends outside of themselves. Government is "instituted
among men" to protect these prerogatives and thus ensure some level of
peace and order, but government so acts because it is assumed that social
and political relations are fundamentally agonistic. The framers of the Constitution seem to distance themselves from Hobbes when they insist that no
one religion will be officially established as well as maintaining that the state
should neither sanction nor prohibit its exercise. But this understanding of
the role of religion is only superficially non-Hobbesian, for it is based on the
assumption of the distinctively modern creation of a secular space untouched

by religious concerns and finalities. America, therefore, is but the institutionalization as well as celebration of what Augustine describes as the City of Man.

Reinhold Niebuhr and John Courtney Murray are often identified as successful attempts by Christians to respond to the challenge of modernity in its American form. George, however, thinks neither Niebuhr nor Murray successfully challenged the metaphysical and social pathologies that constitute America. Niebuhr claimed that he was following Augustine, but George argues that Augustine would have found Niebuhr's distinction between love and justice problematic "precisely because what determines the justice of the City of God is nothing but the quality of its love. The City of God is just only in the measure that it remains a collectivity that loves God (and hence human beings) according to the pattern of Jesus."[13] Moreover, Augustine would have found Niebuhr's privatization of love to be a denial that every Christian claim has a social range and implication.

Catholic attitudes toward the distinctively American polity have been shaped by an immigrant church. Faced with fierce opposition from the Protestant establishment, American Catholics tended to lie low by muting the "political" dimension of their faith. Instead of asserting themselves in the "public" realm with a vengeance, they turned their attention to building a vibrant and institutionally powerful subculture. The American environment seemed so favorable to this Catholic strategy that some Catholic bishops actively promoted the American-styled separation of church and state to the Vatican. Worried that Catholics might be secularized or Protestantized by the nonestablishment clause of the First Amendment, Pope Leo XIII condemned the Americanist heresy at the end of the nineteenth century.

Murray's attempt to reconcile the Catholic faith with the modern political experiment called America must be understood against this background. Murray's insistence that the two articles of the First Amendment are but "articles of peace" was his attempt to show that their purpose is to avoid arguments about ultimate ends in the hope of providing conditions for a peaceful and civil dialogue. He argued the ideological agnosticism of the American "solution" is one Catholics can accept exactly because they are "agnostic." So Murray provided a philosophical justification for the pro-American sentiments of many American Catholics just to the extent he was able to show that a reconciliation between the Catholic and the modern is not only possible but welcome.

George, however, without denigrating Murray's contribution, is not convinced Murray is the way forward. First, Murray assumed a two-tiered conception of nature and grace that is in tension with the *communion* metaphysics of the patristic and medieval periods. Indeed a strong distinction between nature and grace cannot help but underwrite the modern attempt to establish a secular realm untouched by ultimate finalities. The distinction

14

between the "political" in which ultimate ends are bracketed and the "religious" in which such ends can be proclaimed and sought is impossible in the context of a participation metaphysics in which all finitude is grounded and touched by the divine.

Perhaps even more damning, Murray's understanding of nature and grace implicitly accepts the relentless modern view of the person. "If the political or social dimension is essentially untouched by the sacred then the human being is by nature agnostic, even atheist. Whatever is religious in him is added as an extrinsic superstructure to a religiously neutral substructure."[14] Of course American liberalism is not overtly atheistic, but "one could argue," Archbishop George suggests, that it is implicitly or covertly so. Liberalism is atheism inasmuch as the "peace" gained by the articles of the First Amendment is bought at the price of a secularized understanding of the world that assumes the loss of *communion*.

Indeed, George judges that Murray's defense of liberty cannot be made consistent with John Paul II's understanding that liberty flows from the thought world of incarnation and *communion* metaphysics. John Paul II refuses to separate liberty from truth because he rightly thinks the latter is essential to the former. When liberty is separated from love, liberty cannot help but become license, an improperly directed love, a mere "pursuit of happiness." What the pope criticizes in the Western democracies born of the Enlightenment is just this divorce between freedom and truth. When truth is bracketed in the interest of peace, freedom cannot help but be undermined.

> And what indeed are the fruits of this great divorce? When we look at the moral landscape of America at the turn of the millennium what do we see? We see, again to invoke the Augustinian hermeneutic, ample evidence of the triumph of the City of Man. In the millions of abortions annually, the divorce of human reproduction from the embrace of human love, the increased application of the death penalty, the practice of euthanasia, the conviction that hopelessly handicapped people are better off dead, the seemingly indiscriminate and sometimes disproportionate use of the military, the gun violence in the streets of our cities and the corridors of our schools—in all of this we see the fruits of what the Pope has called "the culture of death," a society which allows for the destruction of its weakest members owing to the simple will of the strong. The culture of death is none other than that "world" generated by the separation between freedom and truth; it is a result of the unfortunate compromise between the City of God and the City of Man that stands at the heart of the modern experiment.[15]

George asks what might follow from his critique of modernity. Some, he observes, might think he is advocating a theocracy or confessional state. He denies any such advocacy, noting that the church is opposed to theocracy on two basic grounds: (1) the faith is never to be pressed on anyone through

15 ■

coercive means, and (2) the church should not seek to establish itself officially or juridically outside its own structures. The community of Jesus Christ does not seek political power but rather to create a culture. It does so "simply, boldly, and unapologetically" by being itself. That is why the liturgy is the church's most decisive political act. "The liturgy on earth is an iconic display of the heavenly liturgy of the angels and saints, that community gathered around the throne of God and united in praise. In the way we gather, the way we pray, the way we behave liturgically, we act out the paradigm of the heavenly *communion*, seeking to re-make ourselves in its image. Then, as a liturgical people, we endeavor to shape the world according to this icon, bringing love where there is hatred, forgiveness where there is resentment, compassion where there is animosity and violence."[16]

THE SHAPE OF *A BETTER HOPE*

This book is but a footnote to Cardinal George's address. Some may, with some justification, think it disingenuous for me to claim George as an ally. George, after all, represents a Constantinian church. He is, in spite of his appeals to nonviolence, as far as I know not a pacifist. I am not as convinced that you can draw as clear a distinction between culture and politics as he seems to think you can. Indeed I fear that very distinction may but reproduce the liberal politics he otherwise so acutely criticizes. Yet, I think, it is instructive that in this strange time of the church's existence in America I find an ally in Cardinal George—an alliance he may not welcome. I claim him as an ally, however, because he sees so clearly how our fundamental Christian convictions, what he calls our "Incarnational metaphysics," puts Christians at odds with the presumptions of American democracy. Moreover, he rightly diagnoses how the moral confusions that beset our lives are correlative with the Christian attempt to be "at home" in a society that has made its peace with the presuppositions thought necessary to make America work.

The way I have organized this book, an organization that came to me before I had read Cardinal George's speech, mirrors the way his argument works in "Catholic Christianity and the Millennium." The first chapter, "On Being a Christian and an American," is an attempt to show that the most disastrous result of Protestant attempts to make America "work" has been an attenuated understanding of God. As a result, Christians who believe they are "orthodox" inevitably end up living lives that make sense even if God does not exist or is no more than the god of deism. This essay and the other essays in "The Church in the Time Called America" are diagnostic—they are my attempt to describe, as George does, why the project to make Christianity at home in America cannot help but domesticate not only the church but the God we worship.

In "On Being a Christian and an American" I note MacIntyre's observation that the anti-Americanism characteristic of many in the democracies of the West fails to recognize that you cannot reject America because, if you are honest, you must recognize that America is now the fate of the world. In other words, America is not simply the name of a country but rather names how liberal practices, particularly through the agency of capitalism, now seem to be "global." "The Christian Difference: Or, Surviving Postmodernism," drawing on the work of Nicholas Boyle, is my attempt to show how postmodernism is but the outworking of the logic of capitalism. In other words, the time that is America is a time no longer shaped by the hope made possible by God but rather is the time shaped by quite different presuppositions. As Christians confuse our time with American time we lose the ability to be patient in a world of injustice and war.

"Resisting Capitalism: On Marriage and Homosexuality" is my attempt to make concrete the argument of the first two essays. The capitalist reconstitution of family as individual emotional units devoid of any tradition and thus without duration is one of the fundamental ways our sense of time has been changed. Why we have children as well as how we raise them has accordingly become a matter of subjective preference which makes the activity of child-having increasingly unintelligible. "Resisting Capitalism" tries to show why the capitalist understanding of the family is the background for why arguments over homosexuality are so frustrating. I could have well put this essay in the third section of A Better Hope, but I thought it would make more sense to the reader if it followed the essay on "The Christian Difference."

I confess I am haunted by the question I know some will ask about the essays in this section: what do they say that Hauerwas has not said before? I think it silly to believe that what you write must somehow be "new." Stanley Fish observes that one of the objections about the essays collected in his Doing What Comes Naturally: Change, Rhetoric, and the Practice of Theory in Literary and Legal Studies is that "every essay in the book is the same; no matter what its putative topic each chapter finally reduces to an argument in which the troubles and benefits of interpretive theory are made to disappear in the solvent of an enriched notion of practice."[17] Fish acknowledges the truth of this objection but notes that he can only repeat himself if in fact the argument that "doing what comes naturally" requires no higher theory to be intelligible. In like manner I hope the essays in the first part of this book, if they repeat arguments I have made elsewhere, do so because, given the entrenchment of the position against which I am arguing, I can only say again what I have said before in the hope of establishing new habits that can help us forget what I hope we can learn to leave behind.

17

The essays in "Christian Ethics in American Time" correspond to George's reflections on Niebuhr and Murray. Though I do not have a separate chapter on Niebuhr, the story I tell in these essays provides evidence that George is quite right to think that Protestant Christian ethics was and continues to be theologically inadequate.[18] Christian ethics was and remains a discipline developed largely by Protestant liberal theologians to make America Christian but ended up, at least from my perspective, making Christianity American. I explain in "Christian Ethics in America (and the *Journal of Religious Ethics*): A Report on a Book I Will Not Write" why I abandoned the project of telling the story of the rise and fall of the attempt to make Christianity an ethic to make America Christian. I wrote the chapter on Rauschenbusch for the book I will now not write, but I have included it here not only because I admire Rauschenbusch but because I think the account I give of his life and work documents the argument I develop in chapter 4.

"Not Late Enough: The Divided Mind of *Dignitatis Humanae Personae*" is my attempt to show how the Catholics unfortunately accepted Murray's account of how Catholicism could be reconciled with America. In "Catholic Christianity and the Millennium" Cardinal George acknowledges Murray's insistence on the centrality of religious liberty was affirmed in Vatican II but argues that the Council's defense of religious liberty owes more to the Christian personalism born in France than to Murray's historical and social analysis.[19] George may well be right; but if he is, his account but explains why *Dignitatis* is very close to being an incoherent document.

In the next two chapters on Jenson and Yoder I hope make clear why I think the very development of Christian ethics as an alleged scholarly field divorced from theology has been a mistake. Jenson and Yoder, to be sure in quite different but I hope complementary ways, call into question any attempt to make ethics a field that somehow comes after we have done basic theological work. At the very least I hope these essays make clear how much I have learned from their work.

The essays in the final section, "Church Time," are not meant to build on one another, though I hope the reader will find connections between them. Each of them has been written to suggest the kind of practices the church makes possible if we are to be a people capable of witnessing to God's time. Yet I hope it will be clear that I believe that the practices of forgiveness, peace, praise, enduring, friendship and aging, being sick, and reading mysteries are not the exclusive possession of Christians. Rather I believe what God has graciously called Christians to be makes it possible for those who are not Christians to find that they have the ability to claim such practices as their own. The essays in "Church Time" are meant to show us that these fragments and pieces for recovering moral discourse—be they fragments of memory, sickness, or even reading murder mysteries—still exist as resources that beckon us to a fuller life together.[20]

18

"Why Time Cannot and Should Not Heal the Wounds of History, But Time Has Been and Can Be Redeemed" is not only about the time forgiveness makes but also about what is required if Americans are to come to terms with slavery. In this essay I return to some of the questions raised in the first chapter of this book. The argument of this essay is crucial for the position I take in chapters 11, 12, and 13, just to the extent those essays deal with our ability to endure in a world out of control. That we suffer from growing old, sickness, and death offers us the opportunity to develop the skills to know how to endure and, by enduring, discover gifts otherwise unavailable.

Worship is the practice that sums up or gives direction to all we do as Christians. It is the fundamental performance of faith that, for example, shapes what we talk about and how we talk as Christians. So, "Worship, Evangelism, Ethics: On Eliminating the 'And'" is my attempt to remind Christians that something has gone wrong when we think that worship is something different from evangelism, or ethics, or our politics. Really, all the essays in this section are my attempt to make clear that theology does not just entail a politics but *is* a politics—even when that politics is unacknowledged.

I have included "McInerny Did It: Or, Should a Pacifist Read Murder Mysteries?" just for the hell of it. I wanted to end the book with an essay that I hope many readers will find "fun." I do not mean to suggest that the essay is devoid of serious purpose. Indeed it may be one of the more serious essays in the book. Nonetheless my primary purpose in ending the book with this essay is to provide an example of how an activity as insignificant and entertaining as reading murder mysteries can raise quite interesting theological questions. I am not suggesting that everything we do *must* have some theological significance. Such a view would be at the very least tiring. I only want to illustrate how our most "secular" literature may help us think about the challenge of what it means to see our world as God's creation.

GROWING OLD TOGETHER

Four of these essays were written to honor friends whose work has made my work possible—Robert Jenson, Rowan Greer, Don Saliers, and Ralph McInerny. I suppose it is an indication that I am growing old that I am now asked to write essays for friends who are not that much older than I am. A festschrift article often seems burdensome because you think you will have time to do it, but as the time draws near you discover you do not know when you will be able to write it. But I am not complaining. To write an article for a festschrift at the very least reminds you of the gifts others have made that make your life possible.

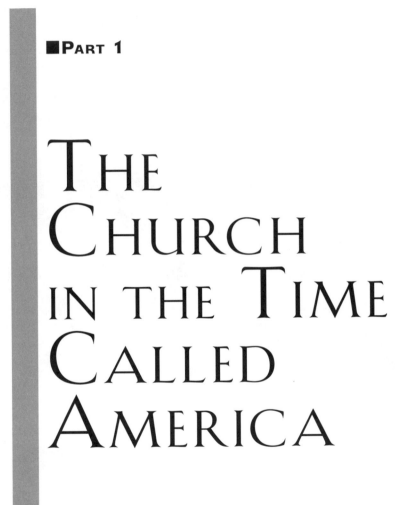

■PART 1

THE
CHURCH
IN THE TIME
CALLED
AMERICA

1

■On Being a Christian
and an American

On Being a Sectarian, Fideistic Tribalist

I have a well-deserved reputation for being an unapologetic Enlightenment basher. I do not believe something called ethics can be shown to exist or to be justified on Kantian-like grounds of reason alone. I have no use for moral or political liberalism in any of their guises. I do not believe in inalienable rights. I tire of the ongoing futile project to show that freedom of the individual can be reconciled with equality. I do not even believe that a good society can or should be egalitarian if that means all hierarchical considerations bear the burden of proof. Accordingly many of my colleagues in that strange field called Christian ethics suggest I am a sectarian, fideistic tribalist.

By this they mean I am trying to convince Christians that we do not have a stake in the "wider world." My oft-made claim that the first task of Christians is not to make the world more just but rather is to make the world the world is interpreted as a call for Christians to withdraw from the world, or at least America. That I should be so understood by those working in Christian ethics is quite intelligible if, as I have argued elsewhere, the subject of

~~Christian ethics in America has always been America.~~ Christian ethicists no longer think, as Walter Rauschenbusch did, that their task is to Christianize the social order, but they continue to share Rauschenbusch's presumption that America is the appropriate subject for Christian ethical reflection and action. My refusal to accept this presumption means I cannot help but be interpreted as a traitor to my class or, at least, my discipline.

I confess I have been tempted, and no doubt at times have succumbed to the temptation, to continue to criticize American liberalism in a manner that only confirms such characterizations of my position. Yet I have grown weary of that game. I simply cannot muster energy for yet one more attempt to show the incoherence of liberal political philosophy or practice. Liberalism, both politically and economically, is doing such a good job of self-destructing it needs no help from me. More important, such a tactic theologically manifests a lack of faith. I believe that the American experiment, as some like to put it, is in deep trouble. Yet Christians are obligated to be a people of hope, not wishing for the lives of our non-Christian brothers and sisters to be worse than they need to be.

Some years ago I wrote an article titled "A Tale of Two Stories: On Being a Christian and a Texan."[1] I wrote the article mainly to please myself and to honor my parents, but also in response to the oft-made criticism that I failed to appreciate that Christians are constituted by stories other than the Christian story—a point a Texan is not likely to overlook. However, my self-description as a Texan was insufficient. I am also an American. As much as I might like—as a Texan or as a Christian—to deny or avoid that I am an American, I know that any such denial would be self-deceptive. Even more important, I have to acknowledge I love the land and the people called American.[2] Of course the issue is not my love of America but rather how such a love should be shaped and governed by the love of God.

So I should like to take this as an opportunity to explore in a more constructive way than is my "normal mode" what positive role the church might have in the project called America. Contrary to the critics of my position, I have no wish to have Christians withdraw from service to their neighbors, even their liberal neighbors. The object of my criticism of liberalism has never been liberals, but rather to give Christians renewed confidence in the convictions that make our service intelligible. In short, I have never sought to justify Christian withdrawal from social and political involvement; I have just wanted us to be involved as Christians.

From my perspective the problem is not liberalism but the assumption on the part of many Christians that they must become liberals or, at least, accept liberal political principles and/or practices in order to be of service in America. When that happens I believe Christians betray their non-Christian neighbors because we rob them and ourselves of exemplification of truthful speech forged through the worship of God. What follows is my

attempt to suggest what I take to be some mistaken strategies for the nego-
tiation of America by Christians. My criticism of these strategies, however,
is meant to make intelligible my claim that Christians have no service more
important than to be a people capable of the truthful worship of God.

THE PROBLEM WITH THE SEARCH FOR FOUNDATIONS

I noted above that the subject of Christian ethics in America was America.[3] The birth as well as the intelligibility of Christian ethics as a discipline drew on institutions we now call mainstream Protestant Christianity. These churches assumed a deep compatibility between Christianity and
American liberal democracy. For most members of such churches it was
unthinkable that being a Christian might in any way render problematic
their full participation in American life. Christian ethics accordingly was
understood as that mode of reflection that helped churches develop policies to make American ideals of freedom and equality more fully institutionalized in American life.

For both internal and external reasons, Christian thinkers learned, as I
suggested above, not to describe their task as Christianizing the social order.
The appeals of the social gospel to Jesus, as well as the movement's opti-
mism about progress, were subjected to the withering critique of Reinhold
Niebuhr. For Niebuhr, the Christian ethical problem became how to
achieve relative justice in a world in which love can never be realized.
Though Niebuhr understood himself to be a theologian, or at least a social
ethicist, his work is almost completely devoid of any account of the church.[4]
Yet I think it also true to say that he continued to assume the viability of
Protestant Christianity as the background for the stance he developed toward
social problems. Such an assumption, of course, has become increasingly
problematic.

The problematic nature of this project is not due to the increasing loss
of membership, social status, and political power of mainstream Christianity.
No doubt such losses are not unimportant for understanding the loss of a
distinctive voice of Protestant Christianity in America. Yet I think more
important has been the increasing recognition that even if such churches
remained socially and politically powerful, they would have nothing distinctive to say as Christians about the challenges facing this society. That
such churches have nothing distinctive to contribute is not surprising, since
their social and political power originally derived from the presumption
that there was no or little essential difference between the church and the
principles of the American experiment. That presumption may, of course,
also help explain the decline of such churches, because it is by no means

25 ■

clear why you need to go to church when such churches only reinforce what you already know from participation in a democratic society.

The increasing loss of social and political influence of Protestant Christianity has not meant Christian theologians and ethicists have abandoned the attempt to make America correspond to some assumed ideal. Faced, however, with America's increasingly diverse population, such an endeavor has been disciplined by the assumption that when Christians enter the public realm they cannot use Christian language. Rather, some mediating language is required and assumed to be justified in the name of a common morality or by natural law reasoning. For those who remain in the tradition of mainstream Protestantism, this often takes the form of trying to show that Rawls, or some Rawls-like account of justice, is the kind of bridge Christians need to justify our participation in the formulation of public policies necessary to govern a diverse society.[5]

I have no intention to be drawn into debates concerning the adequacy of Rawls's account of justice. Yet I want to make clear why the attempt to use Rawls for developing a way for Christians to participate politically in America distracts us from understanding as Christians the contribution we might make. Nicholas Wolterstorff provides a trenchant analysis of Rawls that makes clear why Rawls is such a distraction. Wolterstorff notes the reason Rawls thinks a basis for constitutional democracies is necessary: political issues remain contested in our society. For example, it is not clear how liberty and equality can be expressed in the basic rights and liberties of citizens in a manner that answers the claims of both liberty and equality. From Wolterstorff's perspective, Rawls seeks a way to resolve the conflict in the American tradition between Locke and Rousseau—that is, between freedom and equality—by offering his two principles of justice based on common human reason.

Yet, Wolterstorff asks, how can one possibly move from

a tradition with internal unresolved conflicts, to a pair of principles which resolves those conflicts, by doing nothing other than analyzing that tradition and elaborating the principles embedded therein? How can common human reason, exercised reasonably, propel one across the chasm separating unresolved conflicts from proposals for resolution? The essence of Rawls' strategy is to make do with our common human reason working on the public political culture of our constitutional democracies. Nothing more than that. Of course analysis and elaboration can in principle clarify for us the content and contours of our public political culture. But if there's conflict in our public political culture as to the relative weighting of liberty and equality, then the application of "our common human reason" to this culture will *make clear* to us that there is this conflict. It won't yield a proposal as to how they *ought to be* weighted—unless, perchance, our common human reason is a source of moral principles. But that's the Lockian view which Rawls is trying to avoid, by proposing to extract the relevant moral principles from the extant culture rather than from Reason. If the culture is of different minds as to the relative weighting of liberty and equality, then any proposal as to how they *ought* to be weighted will perforce go beyond what can be extracted from that culture itself.[6]

Wolterstorff, I think, rightly concludes that, contrary to Rawls, we must learn to carry on in a politics without a foundation. We shall have to conduct our political deliberations without a shared political basis—that is, without a neutral or coherent set of principles sufficient to adjudicate conflicts. Which means, according to Wolterstorff, our best strategy is to move from one set of deliberations to another, employing whatever set of considerations we think may be persuasive for the persons with whom we are in conversation. A Rawlsian political unity of overlapping consensus is neither possible nor desirable, but all we need, Wolterstorff argues, is the unity that

> emerges from dialogue among persons each of whom approaches the dialogue with his or her own distinct frame of conviction, and each of whom is willing to live within the confines of a democratic constitution and with the results of fair votes. That's all the unity we have ever had, in these constitutional democracies of ours characterized by religious, moral, and philosophical pluralism. We don't need, and have never had, an ever-present, never-changing foundation of which all of us who are "reasonable" agree and on the basis of which all of us conduct our deliberations. . . . Agreement must be wrought ever anew in ever new ways among ever new parties. For two hundred years now that's been enough for the endurance of pluralistic constitutional democracies. We have no guarantee that it will prove sufficient on into the distant future. Only hope.[7]

I believe one of the great advantages of Wolterstorff's way of understanding our situation is it does not ask Christians to learn some third language in order to participate socially and politically in America. If this is a "pluralist" society, a description I find far too complimentary, then I see no reason that Christians (any more than Jews or secularists) should be asked to put their convictions in some allegedly neutral language in order to talk with one another. Of course "talk with one another" may be a far too innocent way to put the matter in the light of controversies such as those about abortion and assisted suicide. The problem is not that we do not talk with one another but that such talk makes no difference. Yet we will make little progress in even finding our disagreements as long as we search for a "foundation" assumed to be necessary before the conversation begins.

ON TELLING THE AMERICAN STORIES

A more promising way to begin to think about how Christians might contribute to the ongoing American project is that proposed by Martin

Marty in his book *The One and the Many: America's Struggle for the Common Good.*[8] That Marty is a historian rather than a philosopher is why I find the account he provides promising. Rather than looking for foundations, he directs our attention to the stories that constitute the life of that strange entity called America. In this respect he develops a strand of Christian reflection exemplified in H. Richard Niebuhr's *The Kingdom of God in America,* Reinhold Niebuhr's *The Irony of American History,* and the work of Robert Bellah. (No matter how Bellah has tried to distance himself from his early work on civil religion of America, I believe it is to his credit that the kind of analysis he and his colleagues provided in *Habits of the Heart,* as well as *The Good Society,* is in moral continuity with his attempt to name the American civil religion. Bellah's passion has been the attempt to discover the story or stories that can make our common as well as individual lives as Americans morally good.)

One of the virtues of approaches like Bellah's and Marty's is that they have the potential to take account of aspects of American life that are morally richer than any account liberal theory can provide. It is often suggested, for example, that liberalism has worked in America exactly because it has been parasitic on forms of life for which liberalism takes no responsibility or may even undermine. Marty's focus on narratives about this nation, then, provides an opportunity for thicker accounts of such American characteristics as generosity, a thicker account that can in turn help us better understand America's politics.

That I find these historical and sociological approaches more promising for articulating how Christians might make a contribution in the American context does not mean I agree with what Marty, for instance, takes that contribution to be. To his credit Marty has discovered Alasdair MacIntyre. Not only does Marty credit MacIntyre for helping us see how important it is that we discover the narratives we inhabit, but he also takes seriously MacIntyre's judgment that "many citizens in their various competitive groups do inhabit incommensurable universes of discourse, universes that lack a basis of comparison and hence an ability to communicate."[9] Yet Marty thinks MacIntyre's pessimism can be countered by drawing on Felix Frankfurter's contention that this society is not held together by law, creed, or ideology, but by sentiment.

Marty quotes Frankfurter to the effect that "the ultimate foundation of a free society is the binding tie of cohesive sentiment" and observes that such sentiment remains available for us even today in our multicultural society.[10] Indeed Marty, the great celebrator of America, has taken to heart the increasing sense that America is not constituted by one story. Accordingly he criticizes Jefferson and the other founders for using the ideology of the Enlightenment to produce sameness and repress difference. In particular he criticizes the development of the "common school," as well as the texts used in those schools for the repression of difference in the name of creating a common culture. Yet Marty cannot bring himself to abandon the attempt to create a common "sentiment" through what he calls the "commensurable possibilities in storytelling."[11]

He thinks this possible if we learn to think of the nation less as a community and more in terms of Michael Oakeshott's understanding of a "civil association."[12] An association does not demand a credal bond or personal intimacy but rather requires us, like porcupines, to stand at a distance from one another learning the delight in the other that only distance can produce. Drawing on the work of Calvinist social theorist Althusius, Marty suggests that we best understand a commonwealth not as a community of communities but as an association of associations. This would allow people in various groups to live in partly incommensurable universes of discourse and yet to find it valuable to interact in ways other than military force and cultural conflict. Rather than reaching for guns, people will learn to "reach for argument, and the telling of stories from different perspectives is a form of argument. One cannot have a republic without argument."[13]

Marty's story remains the optimistic story of America. He expects the conflicts to continue but believes that, in the longer future,

> every story well told, well heard, and creatively enacted will contribute to the common good and make possible the deepening of values, virtues, and conversation. At the outset I described this book as an effort to contribute to the restoration of the body politic, or, with the many groups in view, the bodies politic. We have been speaking throughout of the "re-storying" of the republic and its associations. The advice for every citizen who wishes to participate in American life and its necessary arguments: start associating, telling, hearing, and keep talking.[14]

In short, Marty seems to think all this will work out if we just learn to be "civil" to one another.

Whatever one may think about the strength or weakness of Marty's account, what I find striking is the absence of any theological justification. Marty, like Reinhold Niebuhr, assumes his task is making America work. The story Marty tells is the story of America in which Christians get to have a role. That such is the case should not be surprising, since Marty represents the discipline of American religious history. Accordingly it never seems to occur to him that he needs to tell the church's story of America. As a result he fails to see how the story of America can tempt Christians to lose our own story and in the process to fail to notice the god we worship is no longer the God of Israel.

In this respect it is fascinating to compare Marty's account of the challenges before American life with MacIntyre's reading of America. What

29

Marty finds admirable about American life—that is, our desire to get along by being likable people—MacIntyre finds our greatest defect. MacIntyre observes:

> This wanting to be liked is one of the great American vices that emerges from this refusal of particularity and conflict. Americans tend under the influence of this vice to turn into parodies of themselves—smiling, earnest, very kind, generous, nice people, who do terrible things quite inexplicably. We become people with no depth, no depth of understanding, masters of technique and technology but not of ourselves. Colonel Tuan of the Army of the Republic of Vietnam, which we so generously aided and then so treacherously betrayed, was once asked by Paul Theroux what he thought of the Americans. He called them "well-disciplined" and "generous." "But we also think that they are a people without culture. . . ." He did not mean by this that they lacked high culture. He meant that he could not recognize what it was about them that made them Americans in the way that he was Vietnamese. And that I think is what happens to people with no story to tell of themselves, people who do not confront their future as a narrative future. They, or rather we, become superficial people, people with surfaces, public relations people.[15]

From MacIntyre's perspective, Marty's account of the role of stories but reproduces the liberal presumption that the "good thing" about America is how being an American makes you aware, alienates you, from your story.[16] That is why, for MacIntyre, what he calls "the American idea" cannot help but be tragic. It is tragic because the conflict between the basic American principles of every person to live, to be free, and to pursue happiness cannot be reconciled with the demand for equality. Slavery is but the most obvious contradiction of the American dilemma. According to MacIntyre, this contradiction represents a conflict so

> deeply embodied in the American character that no care for a surface appearance of consistency or a superficial disguise for hypocrisy could have got rid of it. It is the contradiction between a profound commitment to the principles of equal rights and liberty on the one hand and an equally profound commitment to individualistic practices which generate inequality and unfreedom on the other. American history is the tragic working out of this internalized contradiction.[17]

Marty regrets the general tendency in America for historical amnesia, but he fails to see that a loss of memory is at the heart of the American project. Indeed, as I suggested above, Rawlsian strategies for securing justice require just such a loss of memory. Justice requires the presumption that a genuine break with the past is possible. That is why MacIntyre suggests that

America is not just a country but a metaphysical entity, "an intelligible abstraction always imperfectly embodied in natural reality. It is always *not yet*, it is always radically incomplete; and because the values it aspires to incarnate were from the first seen as *the* essential values, anyone and everyone may be summoned to take part in that completion."[18] Thus America was the attempt to found a historical tradition to connect a particular past to a universal future,

> a tradition that in becoming genuinely universal could find a place within itself for all other particularities so that the Irishman or the Jew or the Japanese in becoming an American did not cease thereby to be something of an Irishman or a Jew or a Japanese. In assuming the burden of this task America took unto itself a genuinely Utopian quality, the quality of an attempt to transcend the limits of secular possibility. America's failures are intimately connected with this grasping after impossibility; but so are its successes.[19]

The tragic character of American history is unavoidable, since rights cannot help but conflict with rights; yet the very moral commitments that shape such a conflict produce a people incapable of recognizing, much less responding to, such conflicts. America is at once the name of an aspiration to liberty and equality of rights and the name of the power that stands in the way of that aspiration. As a result Americans find themselves at war not only with one another but with themselves. MacIntyre observes that "citizens of other nations are free to measure what their government and society does by *external* standards of liberty and right and can choose between their loyalty to these absolutes and their loyalty to their own nature; but the American finds that these absolutes *are* his constitution, that he cannot disown his national allegiance without disowning these moral absolutes or vice versa."[20]

Nothing that MacIntyre has said about America requires him to deny Marty's sense that we need a shared history.[21] MacIntyre doubts we can look to academic historians to supply us with such a story since such a history, through its elimination of evaluative judgments, of heroes and heroines, seeks to abolish history as a story.[22] Our problem is that such history, as well as our political culture, has made us quite literally speechless (though of course we go on talking, but such talking represents no more than the clash of opinion). In a striking illustration MacIntyre offers one exception to our inability to create a common story through public speech—the Vietnam War Memorial. The "Memorial is significant because it both records the names of the dead and also, by style and substance, says that we do not know what to say to or about them. It is a monument to inarticulateness; *both* to our not knowing what to say to and about the dead now, except that

31 ∎

they are our dead and dead because of us, *and* to our inarticulateness at the time of the Vietnam war."[23]

MacIntyre acknowledges that it may seem odd to speak of inarticulateness at the time of Vietnam since so much was said at that time. Yet he argues that we spoke at such length because we could not communicate. The war simply revealed, therefore, that we were not able to speak intelligibly to each other on matters that were so deep. And, of course, it is exactly such inability that we have worked hard to forget by consoling ourselves with rhetorics of consensus and pluralism. Thus projects such as Marty's mask our loss of shared political speech as well as our lack of communal imagination, "deprivations closely related to our inability to master and to make our own the narrative of ourselves."[24] Shared sentiment cannot help but be sentimental without a more determinative narrative that helps name the truth, the tragic truth, that America is constituted by wrongs so wrong that nothing can be done to make them right.[25]

GOD AND AMERICA

If you are schooled in the art of revivals, that should make you attentive to the religious payoff here. For if the analysis I have provided is close to being right, then surely the gospel should have something to say about how to go on as a people who can have a shared past by confessing their sin. Here it seems Christians have something constructive to offer to our politics. We have a story of sin and forgiveness forged in the practices of confession and reconciliation that at least offers the kind of hope Wolterstorff suggests we need. The claim that the first task of the church is to be the church, even in America, could turn out to be good news if the challenge before us as Americans is learning how to be a people who can make our past truthfully ours. That the first task of the church is to be the church, therefore, is anything but a withdrawal strategy.

Yet revival conversions have a well-deserved reputation for not lasting. As tempting as the strategy suggested in the last paragraph may be, I think it would be a mistake to try to make Christianity look good by supplying the substance and practice that the liberal narratives of America cannot supply. The ascendancy of liberal ideology and practice in America could be seen as very good news for Christians. In fact, the very emptiness liberalism creates invites someone to fill the space. That Americans lack a strong moral account to justify or guide their relations to one another seems to make Christianity, or at least a surrogate, all the more necessary. Indeed this can look like the best of all possible worlds as Christianity gets to supply the morality without having to govern. Put in terms of the analysis above, Christianity becomes the master story to sustain a republic that cially can have no master story.

A story not unlike this has been tempting for liberal and conservative Christians alike. Liberal Christians assume that something like a religious appeal is necessary or at least important to sustain the quest for justice; conservative Christians assume that without Christianity people cannot develop the virtues necessary to sustain a free society. Thus the importance of intermediate institutions of which the church seems to be a ready exemplification. Calls for Christians to make the family work are but the outworking of such strategies. The only problem is that the only institution more destructive of the family than capitalism is Christianity.

I am not entirely unsympathetic with some of the suggestions made by those who try to give Christians a role in American society shaped by these strategies. My problem is not that such strategies are wrong; rather, my problem is that this way of conceiving the relation of the church to American society makes the church less than the church. The problem, then, is not as I framed it in the title I first thought to give this paper—that is, "Why Christianity Will Never Work in America." Even though I believe the fundamental presuppositions that shaped much of American life and government were meant to destroy or at least marginalize the church, I believe with God's help the church may even survive in America. Rather, the problem is that when Christians in America take as their fundamental task to make America work, we lose our ability to survive as church. We do so because in the interest of serving America the church unwittingly becomes governed by the story of America that Marty tells. That story is meant to make our God at home in America.

There is no better indication of the Americanization of the church than the god worshiped by Christians in America. For most American Christians, the crucially important things about God are that God exist and that God's most important attribute be love. This is not a recent development; if Thomas Jenkins is right, it began in the late eighteenth century in such figures as Timothy Dwight and was developed in the nineteenth century by such theologians as Noah Porter. In particular Porter, drawing on the Enlightenment celebration of stoicism and modern science, emphasized the importance of emotional restraint and rationality. According to Jenkins:

> This centered on one trait in particular: benevolence. Benevolence was the key emotion emulated by people and ascribed to God. As the historian James Turner put it: "As the archetype of morality, God expressed the most elevated human ethics. He thus above all had to be—perhaps the favorite adjective of enlightenment divines—benevolent: disinterestedly willing the happiness of all his creatures."[26]

33

Jenkins traces the career of this god through the development of liberal and conservative theology and literary figures of the nineteenth and twentieth centuries. We should not be surprised that the result was a vague god vaguely worshiped or at least vaguely considered. For example, the influential liberal theologian, minister, and writer Theodore Munger drew on Thomas Arnold's understanding of God as "a power not ourselves working for righteousness."[27] Such a view finds its most sophisticated expression in William James's suggestion that "God is the natural appellation, for us Christians at least, for the supreme reality, so I will call this higher part of the universe by the name of God."[28]

James's god, I believe, is not remarkably different from Reinhold Niebuhr's understanding of god. Of course Niebuhr's god was a god of judgment, but such judgment was, as Jenkins suggests, the expression of law, history, and the order of the world.[29] Christ was also the symbol of sacrificial love for Niebuhr, but the very language of symbol was used to protect against any need to make classical christological claims that require trinitarian displays of who God is. So in spite of Niebuhr's reputation as one who attempted a recovery of orthodoxy, his account of God remained more theist than Christian—that is, a theism combined with a sentimental Christ. Niebuhr may well be the greatest representative of a theology shaped to make America work. But if that is the case it is a deep judgment on such theology just to the extent that Christians lost the reality of God found in cross and resurrection.

I am not suggesting that the American god Jenkins describes was the result of the Christian accommodation to America, but I think it also undeniable that the attenuated god of American Christianity is necessary for a people who believe they are the future of humankind. I believe, therefore, Christians can do nothing more significant in America than to be a people capable of worshiping a God who is to be found in the cross and resurrection of Jesus of Nazareth. The worship of such a God will not be good for any society that desires a god made in the image of the bureaucrat.[30] A people formed by the worship of a crucified God, however, might just be complex enough to engage in the hard work of working out agreements and disagreements with others one small step at a time.

2

∎THE CHRISTIAN DIFFERENCE

OR, SURVIVING POSTMODERNISM

CAN POSTMODERNISM HAVE A HISTORY?

"Post-Modernism is the pessimism of an obsolescent class—the salaried official intelligentsia—whose fate is closely bound up with that of the declining nation-state."[1] This may sound like a particularly harsh judgment made by Nicholas Boyle in his extraordinary book _Who Are We Now? Christian Humanism and the Global Market from Hegel to Heaney_. Yet I think Boyle is right to so judge postmodernism. That I agree with Boyle may surprise some who have grouped me with the nihilistic, relativistic barbarian hordes who threaten all we hold dear—matters such as objectivity and the family. I confess I have at times taken great pleasure watching postmodernists dismantle the pretensions of modernism, but it is still the case that being an enemy of my enemy does not and should not necessarily make me a friend of postmodernism.

Before I elaborate and defend Boyle's judgment, however, I need to prepare a case for why his understanding of postmodernism is important for those of us who, in an allegedly postmodern time, attempt to do Christian theology. That some may have mistaken me as a sympathetic supporter of postmodernism is understandable. After all, I have playfully used postmodern playfulness to try to remind Christians that we are in a life-and-death struggle with the world.[2] I have thought the playful use of postmodernism was justified because I have found it difficult to take postmodernism seriously as an intellectual position. However, if Boyle is right to interpret postmodernism as the position of those who would make our time the end of history, then I think it is a serious mistake not to take postmodernism seriously.

That I have not taken postmodernism seriously does not mean I have not taken seriously the work of people like Michel Foucault. Indeed as David Toole has shown in his remarkable book *Waiting for Godot in Sarajevo: Theological Reflections on Nihilism, Tragedy, and Apocalypse*, Christians, particularly Christians committed to Christian nonviolence, cannot afford to ignore Foucault's extraordinary work.[3] This is particularly true, as Toole makes clear, for those who have been influenced by the equally remarkable work of John Howard Yoder.

Toole observes that where Foucault's work meets a Yoder-like reading of the New Testament, both step into the glow of a new light that is the product of their convergence. This is particularly the case when considering how similar Foucault's account of power is to that of the "principalities and powers" in the New Testament. Toole rightly defends Foucault against those who suggest he provides no alternative of resistance to the powers; but Toole argues further that it is the cross, as Yoder directed our attention, that gives the hope—a hope Foucault cannot make intelligible—necessary for such a struggle. Responding to his own question of how to characterize the difference between Foucault's tragic politics and Yoder's apocalyptic alternative, Toole observes, drawing on Beckett's *Godot*:

> For Vladimir and Estragon the difference is that Godot will finally arrive. For Nietzsche, the difference lies between Dionysus and the Crucified. John Howard Yoder sums up this difference in a word: Jesus, the slain lamb, the one who took up the cross and not the crown. Of course what this means for Vladimir and Estragon is not only that Godot will arrive one day, perhaps one day soon, but that he has already come and that they can, therefore, wait with confidence and patience; it means that even in Sarajevo they can protest their suffering with dignity.[4]

If Toole is right (and I certainly think he is), Christian intellectuals face an enormous challenge that Yoder's work only signals. In short we theologians must provide an account of our situation that is at least as radical and imaginative as the one Foucault was attempting. In other words, we must challenge the knowledges currently enshrined in the academic disciplines dominating the modern university. Such knowledges provide the theodical accounts necessary to convince us that the way things are is the way things have to be—which is one of the reasons I have had difficulty taking postmodernism seriously. The problem in brief is that postmodernism is a far too comforting story for alienated intellectuals.

Of course, it can be objected that I am being unfair to postmodernism. After all, most postmodern thinkers style themselves as radicals. As a style of thought, postmodernism is allegedly suspicious "of classical notions of truth, reason, identity and objectivity, of the idea of universal progress or emancipation, of single frameworks, grand narratives or ultimate grounds of explanation."[5] Postmodernism seems, in other words, to call into question the Enlightenment project, and surely that is a good thing. Yet I am not convinced that postmodernism, either as an intellectual position or as a cultural style, is post-anything.[6]

For example, Boyle observes that many postmodernists deny or at least remain agnostic about whether *postmodern* is a chronological term at all. Lyotard, according to Boyle, seems to assume that postmodernism runs in parallel with modernism or is even a permanent possibility of the human spirit. Thus Montaigne, in the sixteenth century, is postmodern, but the brothers Schlegel, in the 1800s, are only modern. Boyle notes that the denial of chronology is an understandable ploy for postmodernists just to the extent that modernity depends on some opposition between the present and the past. Thus for the postmodernist, all architectural styles are always simultaneously available.[7]

The Christian difference—why we are not postmodernist—I think is clearly revealed at this point. Christians have a stake in history, which as Boyle (appealing to Hegel) observes is the collective self-understanding of modern Europeans who thought the history of the world, or at least of their "states," to be inseparable from Christianity. They so saw themselves not because of some continuity between institutions but because history, understood as the "meaningful interconnection of *all* events, each of which is invested both with individual uniqueness and absolute importance," is in the bounds of a Christian world.[8] Christians must be able to narrate postmodernism in a manner that postmodernism cannot narrate Christianity. Or more adequately: we must show how Christianity provides the resources for a critique of its own mistakes in a way that modernity or postmodernity cannot provide.

Such narration will require Christians to develop accounts, as I suggested above, that are more powerful than either modernist or postmodernist can muster. Indeed, one of the illusions of postmodernism is to give a far too intelligible and thus comforting account of where we are. Our world and our lives are far too fragmentary and disordered to know where we are, but at least Christians owe it to themselves and their neighbors to confess that such disorder is but a reflection of the failure of the churches to be faithful.

Modernity and its bastard offspring postmodernity are but reflections of the Christian attempt to make God a god available without the mediation of the church.[9] Such a god cannot help but become some "timeless thing" necessary to ensure the assumed truth of Christianity in service to the growth of secular power.

Postmodernism, in short, is the outworking of mistakes in Christian theology correlative to the attempt to make Christianity "true" apart from faithful witness. This is undoubtedly a strong thesis, but one I think we are beginning to appreciate thanks to that extraordinary group of theologians recently clustered at or around Cambridge University. For example, Philip Blond, with the confidence we have come to associate with this theological style, observes that the crucial moment in the surrender of theology to secular reason's account of nature and corresponding understanding of natural theology occurred in England between the time of Henry of Ghent (1217–1293) and Duns Scotus (1266-1308).[10] Blond notes that Henry maintained that any knowledge of a created thing by the human intellect was also knowledge of God. In creatures, however, being was determinable; but God's being is indeterminable. For Scotus the distinction between knowing God in himself and knowing him in a creature was not important. For this reason, according to Blond, when considering the universal science of metaphysics Scotus elevated being (ens) to a station over God in order that being could be distributed both to God and to his creatures. Scotus did this because God could not be known naturally unless being is univocal (univocum) to the created and uncreated.[11]

The univocity of God and creature marks, according to Blond, the time when theology itself became idolatrous. Theologians disregarded what they should have learned from Aquinas, namely, that nothing can be predicated univocally of God and other things. Thus in Aquinas's contention, that which can be predicated of God can be participated in by finite creatures only via analogy. "This analogical mode, whilst it accepts that we only come to have knowledge via His effects, understands that the reality of these effects belongs by priority to God, even though we only uncover God as the source of these effects after having experienced such effects without initially recognizing their antecedent cause."[12]

I am painfully aware that the introduction of these rather obscure remarks about how Christian theologians came to understand God's relation to creation cannot help but appear unrelated to issues raised by postmodernism. I am convinced, however, that in order to grasp the challenge of postmodernism—as Robert Jenson puts it, how "the world lost its story"—we must understand how modernity and postmodernity are the result of mistakes in Christian theology.[13] This means, as I suggested above, Christians must challenge the postmodern narrative that simply forgets that Christianity had anything to do with the world in which we now find ourselves.

I am not suggesting that we need to remind postmodernists that Chris-tianity once was capable of producing cultural and political effects. It is a question not of getting our historical due as Christians, though that is not entirely irrelevant, but rather of our ability to maintain for ourselves an account of the world in which the God we worship matters. The attempt to make God knowable separate from how God has made himself known through Scripture makes a world without God thinkable. God could not help but become another "thing" amid other metaphysical possibilities. Accordingly, Christians robbed the world of its story.

Boyle observes, for example, that Dante's *Divine Comedy* differs in its very manner from non-Christian poetry because, like the Bible, the *Comedy* is about the world of grace and also about the world of history. Dante's poem is about real, datable men and women who at particular times accepted or rejected the grace of God offered them thirteen centuries ear-lier through the bodily life, death, and resurrection of Christ. For Dante, and for the world in which his poem was written, the earthly passing over of the incarnate Word was what constitutes history, "that gives direction and purpose to the time which leads up to Christ and an eschatological expectation to the time after him; that divides the ages into a pre-Christian period of signs and figures and a Christian period of signs and figures and a Christian period of fulfillment; that provides the temporal point of reference by which years are dated and people and their activities made singular and unrepeatable. For Dante it is only in relation to Christ that human doings are part of history, and only as part of history that human doings become the subject-matter of his poem."[14]

Postmodernism, then, names not only the end of the time when poetry like Dante's is possible but a time when such poetry has become unintelli-gible. Modernity, drawing on the metaphysics of a transcendent god, was the attempt to be historical without Christ. Postmodernity, facing the agony of living in history with no end, is the denial of history.[15] In the wake of such a denial, the only remaining comfort is the shopping mall, which gives us the illusion of creating histories through choice, thus hiding from us the reality that none of us can avoid having our lives determined by money.[16] Money, in modernity, is the institutionalization of univocity of being that Scotus thought necessary to ensure the unmediated knowledge of God.[17]

POSTMODERNISM AND THE GLOBAL MARKET

I began by agreeing with Boyle's extraordinary definition of postmod-ernism; his claim is one I think I can defend. I think he is right to suggest that postmodernism is "the pessimism of an obsolescent class." I would

39

emphasize that the most determinative representatives of his "salaried official intelligentsia" are to be found in the universities. That the fate of such an intelligentsia is "closely bound up with that of the declining nation-state" should not be surprising given the fact that universities as we know them were formed to produce and reproduce the knowledges to sustain the ruling classes necessary to maintain the nation-state system. That that system is currently under stress by the developments of global capitalism is reflected in the confusions trumpeted about the universities in the name of postmodernism.

I do not wish to be misunderstood. I am not suggesting that postmodernism is nothing but smoke and mirrors. Rather, I believe that Fredric Jameson rightly identified postmodernism with the cultural logic of advanced capitalism in which the production of culture has been integrated into commodity production, thus creating the urgency of producing ever fresh waves of novelty.[18] As David Harvey observes, "whatever else we do with the concept, we should not read postmodernism as some autonomous artistic current. Its rootedness in daily life is one of its most patently transparent features."[19]

The everyday life in which we are rooted, however, is not easily known, particularly by intellectuals. Indeed, intellectuals (who like to believe their "work" is free from the market) have a stake in hiding from themselves the material factors that make their existence possible. Thus the illusions of a genealogist can be thought to be quite compelling until, as Boyle observes, "the funding dries up and it becomes apparent that the nation no longer has an omnipotent monarch commanding the propagation of Enlightenment (that is, the critique of Church and the bourgeoisie) 'for its own sake' (that is, in the interests of the state)."[20] What the university intellectual cannot face is the socioeconomic truth that in a global market we have all become the proletariat.

It is hard to imagine an intellectual alternative better suited for the elites of a global capitalism than postmodernism.[21] Capitalism is, after all, the ultimate form of deconstruction. How better to keep the laborer under the control of capital than through the scarcity produced through innovation? Capitalism, as David Harvey observes, is necessarily innovative, not because of the myth of the innovative entrepreneur but because of the coercive laws of competition and the conditions of class struggle endemic to capitalism. Of course the effects of such innovation are to make past investments of labor skills valueless.[22]

Obviously such a system produces a self that is fragmented if not multiple. The difficulty in the description of the loss of the unified self by postmodernists is their failure to see that such a self is the result of social and economic developments. Such a causal connection, however, is precisely what "genealogical" deconstructive thinking not only cannot represent—it denies it exists. In so doing it plays the game precisely as the global market wants it played. For the fiction by which the global market commends itself to us and encourages our participation in it is that the human self is purely a consumer. . . .

The self is little more than a formality, the name we give to the principle that consumes options, the transient locus of interpretation. There is nothing outside the text, just as there is nothing outside the market.[23]

The belief that there is no single truth or world but only a multiplicity of mutually untranslatable perspectives, Boyle observes, is strangely analogous to the belief that the market is a boundless medium of perfect competition among an infinite number of ever-expanding commercial identities.[24] It is no wonder that, confronted with such a system, intellectuals discard the idea of totality. "For in a period when no very far-reaching political action seems really feasible, when so-called micropolitics seems the order of the day, it is relieving to convert this necessity into a virtue—to persuade oneself that one's political limits have, as it were, a solid ontological grounding, in the fact that social totality is in any case a chimera."[25]

The recent example of Richard Rorty is surely good evidence for the inability of postmodernism to mount any politics worthy of the name. In his book *Achieving Our Country* Rorty confirms an earlier description of his own position by Terry Eagleton: since all conventions are arbitrary, one might as well conform to those of the Free World.[26] "For purposes of thinking about how to achieve our country," Rorty asserts, "we do not need to worry about the correspondence theory of truth, the grounds of normativity, the impossibility of justice, or the infinite distance which separates us from the other. For those purposes we can give both religion and philosophy a pass. We can just get on with trying to solve what Dewey called 'the problems of men.'"[27]

According to Rorty, that means we must continue to support the nation-state as the only "agent capable of making any real difference in the amount of selfishness and sadism inflicted on Americans."[28] We must do so from Rorty's perspective because since 1909 the only dividing line between the American left and the American right is the former's presumption that the state must make itself responsible for redistributive policies.[29] The cultural left must therefore shed its "semi-conscious anti-Americanism" in order to get back "into the business of piecemeal reform within the framework of a market economy."[30]

Rorty's book, which bears the subtitle *Leftist Thought in Twentieth Century America*, is surely the tombstone that confirms the death of the left in America. His call for a renewed loyalty to the nation-state, at least the nation-state called America, comes just at the time the nation-state, other

41 ■

than as an agency to ensure prosperity,[31] is increasingly undermined by the global market.[32] His "social vision," like that of so many postmodernists, turns out to be but another form of liberalism. That is, the "just state is one neutral in respect of any particular conception of the good life, confining its jurisdiction to furnishing the conditions in which individuals may discover themselves."[33]

I realize that it may be quite unjust to tar postmodernism with Rorty's brush, but too often postmodernists turn out to be liberals in ethics and politics who no longer believe in the philosophical conceits of liberalism but have nowhere else to go.[34] If you want a way to test whether this is true, try to engage a postmodernist in a discussion about abortion or so-called assisted suicide. Eagleton rightly credits postmodernism for putting on the political agenda issues of sexuality, gender, and ethnicity, but fears that these concerns can become a substitute for classical forms of radical politics that deal with class, state, ideology, revolution, and the material modes of production. Questions of sexuality are no doubt political, but they can also be a form of forgetfulness regarding questions about why some people do not get enough to eat. Eagleton notes that perhaps one of the reasons feminism and ethnicity are popular is that they are not necessarily anti-capitalist and so fit well with a postradical age.

Indeed, I fear one of the reasons postmodernism has become such an attractive alternative for many in the contemporary university is that serious work is no longer expected there. The fragmentation of the curriculum into disciplines that are unintelligible even to themselves is surely the breeding ground for postmodernism. The more fractured the university becomes, moreover, the more it is able to act as the institution capable of confirming the postmodernist description of the world. As a result the university becomes a useful place to sequester people who might otherwise get into trouble. But then that is exactly what we should expect, given Boyle's judgment that postmodernism is the pessimism of an obsolete class.

THE CHRISTIAN DIFFERENCE

I obviously think it would be a profound mistake for Christians to side with the postmodernists, although even to think that Christians have a choice to be for or against postmodernism seems to me a far too optimistic account of our situation. If the analysis of postmodernism I have provided is close to being right, it is not a question of choice. Rather Christians are faced—along with our non-Christian sisters and brothers—with the challenge of surviving postmodernism. To survive, moreover, means we must have skills of resistance. I believe God has given us all we need not only to survive but to flourish. But as I suggested above, theologically we have only begun to imagine the knowledges necessary for the task.

To survive will require us to develop practices and habits that make our worship of God an unavoidable witness to the world. By unavoidable I mean that we must help the world discover that it is unintelligible just to the extent that it does not acknowledge the God we worship. That God "is whoever raised Jesus from the dead, having before raised Israel from Egypt."[35] That is the God, who having created all that is, can be known only by way of analogy. Analogy is but the way we name the metaphysical implications that God wills to care for his creation through calling into existence a faithful people.

Commenting on the apocalyptic character of Ezekiel, Daniel, Mark, and John of Patmos, John Howard Yoder observes that these texts are not about either pie in the sky or the Russians in Mesopotamia. "They are about how the crucified Jesus is a more adequate key to understanding what God is about in the real world of empires and armies and markets than is the ruler in Rome, with all his supporting military, commercial, and sacerdotal networks."[36] Postmodernists cannot help but think such a claim to be the grandest of grand narratives, but I cannot imagine Christians saying anything less. Not only saying it, but also truthfully living and thinking that this is the way things are.

For example, consider Yoder's claim that the point apocalyptic makes is not that people who use violence in the name of fostering justice are not as strong as they think, though that is true, but rather

> it is that people who bear crosses are working with the grain of the universe. One does not come to that belief by reducing social process to mechanical and statistical models, nor by winning some of one's battles for the control of one's corner of the fallen world. One comes to it by sharing the life of those who sing about the resurrection of the slain Lamb.[37]

"Working with the grain of the universe" is not a confessional claim peculiar to Christians but a metaphysical claim about the way things are.

Contrary to the oft-made assertion that Yoder-like claims require Christians to withdraw from the world, the opposite (as Yoder constantly stressed) is the case.[38] I think it is important for Mennonites particularly, as well as their fellow travelers—that is, people like myself and John Paul II—to deny they seek only to be a prophetic minority in the wider church or world. Rather we seek to provide an alternative by which the world can see that we are not condemned to anarchy and violence. Rather than withdrawing from the world, even a postmodern world, we are better off siding with those who would "take over" the world.

Gerald Schlabach, a Mennonite theologian who teaches at Bluffton College, sent me criticisms of my work that another Mennonite had posted on an e-mail forum. The critic argued that my work is far too Catholic and thus incompatible with an Anabaptist perspective: "Hauerwas has a Constantinian fear of Christian liberty. He wants the clergy to tell us the story and the church to have the sanctions to enforce it." In his response, Schlabach agreed that this is an accurate (although insufficiently nuanced) summary of my views, but defended my position nonetheless. As Schlabach put it,

> Hauerwas has discovered a dirty little secret—Anabaptists who reject historic Christendom may not actually be rejecting the vision of Christendom as a society in which all of life is integrated under the Lordship of Christ. On this reading, Christendom may in fact be a vision of shalom, and our argument with Constantinians is not over the vision so much as the sinful effort to grasp at its fullness through violence, before its eschatological time. Hauerwas is quite consistent once you see that he does want to create a Christian society (polis, societas)—a community and way of life shaped fully by Christian convictions. He rejects Constantinianism because "the world" cannot be this society and we only distract ourselves from building a truly Christian society by trying to make our nation into that society, rather than be content with living as a community-in-exile. So Hauerwas wants Catholics to be more Anabaptist, and Anabaptists to be more Catholic, and Protestants to be both, and the only way he can put this together in terms of his own ecclesial location is to be a "Catholic" Methodist in roughly the way that some Episcopalians are Anglo-Catholic.[39]

Schlabach's presentation of my own position says what I have been trying to say better than how I have said it. More important, I hope, his suggestion points a way forward if we are not only to survive but to find ways to resist global capitalism. It should surprise no one to discover that I believe any response Christians have to the challenge of the global market will be ecclesial. In particular, I think Christians must find ways to be catholic in a world in which the church is but another international agency—and one that is probably less effective than the many that exist already and the many more that are sure to be created.

Let me try to explain these obscure remarks by returning again to some observations by Boyle, who describes himself as a Catholic humanist,[40] about the international character of the church. He suggests that the international character of the church (and I assume he means the Roman Catholic Church) is likely to be more problematic in the future than it has been for many centuries. In the era of nation-states the international character of the church was one of its most significant features, as the church offered an alternative to the loyalties bred through nationalism. Though the church often failed to challenge nationalism, its very existence at least provided the material possibility for mounting a challenge to the state's pretension to rule over minds and bodies.

44

Yet, Boyle suggests, in the new global order the church's universality may be an even more serious temptation than the temptation of nationalisms since the Reformation. For the new order is a kind of universality whose ambition is to rule minds and bodies just as nations did so effectively in the past. The church may be tempted to collaborate with these worldly powers, celebrating the fact that they have adopted the church's global perspective. But as Boyle notes, the worldly powers have their own purposes, "and if one is disturbed when a papal tour becomes a media event it is because it is becoming unclear in such a case who is using, or paying homage to, whom."[41]

That the church has often imitated the secular rule of its day is no great surprise. In feudalism the popes became feudal lords, absolute monarchs in the age of absolutism, and in the age of nation-states something like presidents for life of a kind of international state. Thus in the First Vatican Council the church "battened down the hatches" to face the totalitarian pretensions of the state in the era of unrestrained nationalism. So in an international age the church, according to Boyle, cannot help but act as one global agency among others, and we should be glad that it does so— just as Christians in the past were glad the church had the strength and presence to speak to the state when men and women were often at odds with their country and had no other friend than the church.

Yet the moral authority the church derived from its past internationalism will have to be drawn from elsewhere if the church in this new age is to continue to be different, to continue to be unassimilated to the secular world. Boyle suggests that such a church will "need to draw its moral strength not from its international presence but from its claim to represent people as they are locally and distinct from the worldwide ramifications of their existence as participants in the global market."[42] Grand narratives continue,

> but the little narratives of the victims of the grand process, the stories of what the big new world is squeezing out or ignoring, they will be told on the small scale, and full of details which the new world will dismiss as superficial and inessential. In terms of church structure, the little narratives will be told at diocesan, parochial, or base-community level.[43]

The church capable of "such little" narratives will need all the resources it can muster—particularly those resources from the past that give us the confidence to counter the false universality of the market with the universality that depends on the fact that Jesus of Nazareth was raised from the dead. The worship of such a God surely requires that the church not forget those who have become expendable, too poor even to be debtors, and therefore from the market's perspective "nonpersons."[44] The worship of such a God means that we must pray and pray fervently for the reconciliation of

Catholics and Protestants, as our very division wounds not only ourselves but the world itself.[45]

Such a church is surely necessary if, as Boyle puts it, we are to learn to see God in the world in which we find ourselves, and not only in some past golden age such as the catacombs or the Middle Ages. Rather we must be at least as courageous and inventive as those Christians who made the Middle Ages possible by living in catacombs. To be such a people in this time we must be sustained by our worship of God who wills himself known in Christ and so known can safeguard "us from self-worship and maintain us in the conviction that nothing we know in this world is ultimate—not the media of communication, nor the system of signs, not even the end of history."[46] Through the faithful worship of a God so known, Christians can not only survive postmodernism but even flourish.[47]

3

■RESISTING CAPITALISM

ON MARRIAGE AND HOMOSEXUALITY

I need to be clear—I am not part of the loyal opposition that would protest the Methodist stated position on homosexuality. I do not think the Methodist position can be opposed, because I think the church is simply too confused on the issue to be able to mount a clear counterposition. I have agreed to write this piece only because I am a Methodist and I feel duty bound to say why we Methodists cannot even get up a good argument about homosexuality.[1]

No process more clearly exemplifies our confusions about homosexuality than the deliberations of the Commission for the Study of Homosexuality established by the General Conference and directed by the Board of Ministry. I was a member of the commission, but I resigned about halfway through our deliberations. There were many reasons for my resignation; one of them was my frustration that no argument was possible in the commission because no one could agree on the appropriate framework for argument. The only authority that was acknowledged was something called "science," and since "science" was inconclusive about whether homosexuality was or was not "innate" no general position was possible.

Early in our deliberations I observed that it was unclear exactly why the church had a stake in the description of "homosexuality," whether justified or unjustified by "science." Under the influence of both Wittgenstein and Foucault, I hoped to remind my fellow commission members that descriptions do not come given but rather are determined by practices that require articulation in whole ways of life. I thought if we could talk about those practices, we might then discover what was at stake in arguments about same-sex sexual relations.

So I suggested rather than begin talking about homosexuality, we should begin by considering a description Christians use that at least suggests we know what we are talking about, that is, promiscuity. I focused on promiscuity because I thought any account of promiscuity required a display of the church's commitment to singleness and marriage as practices that shape how we are called to live as Christians. I thought by focusing on promiscuity we might avoid the unhappy assumption that there is something in general called "sexuality" that is just "there" but must find expression in one way or another. I argued that just as promiscuity is a description produced by the church's practices, sexuality is a description produced by the practices of modernity that separate something called the individual from any thick communal practices. I thought by focusing on promiscuity we might be able to rediscover and reclaim Christian discourse from the cultural formations that were misleading us.

Needless to say, my strategy got no support from my fellow commission members. I suspect the "liberals" thought this might be a very clever way to bring through the back door a condemnation of gays. I suspect the "conservatives" assumed that we so clearly know what promiscuity is and why it is wrong that there is no reason to discuss such a matter. As a result the commission's attention remained fixed on the question whether homosexuality is a good or bad thing. My worries concerning the practices that might make such a question intelligible were not the worries of my colleagues. I had the feeling that most people on the commission had already made up their minds before we began our deliberations. The only question that remained was whether you were for or against it. Since I was neither, I had no place on the commission.

In truth I think the Methodists, as well as most mainstream Protestant churches in America, do not know how to think about homosexuality. They do not know how to think about homosexuality because they do not know how to think about marriage and divorce. The churches have generally underwritten romantic accounts of marriage—that is, you fall in love and get married so that sex is an expression of your love. Such accounts not only destroy any understanding of marriage as lifelong monogamous fidelity but also make unintelligible the prohibition against same-sex relations. After all, the latter are often exemplifications of a loving relation.

I think it would be quite interesting to ask those in Methodism who oppose homosexuality what their views are on divorce and remarriage. Do they think that a marriage is no longer a marriage simply because the people in the marriage no longer love one another? Do they think people who have been divorced can remarry after they have found someone else to love? How should people be examined to discern whether they are capable of making the promises we still ask people to make when the church witnesses their marriage? Should people who have been divorced bear a greater burden of proof if they wish to be remarried?

Let the Methodist people, if they are determined to take a position on homosexuality, first discuss the above questions. I think if we did so, we would discover skills of discrimination and discernment that might reveal why questions about whether we are for or against homosexuality are simplistic. In particular I think we might discover that *love* is far too vague a term to do any work in helping us to discover the disciplines necessary to sustain a marriage, particularly in our cultural context. We might even discover that Christians do not believe that love legitimates sex or even that sex is an expression of love, but rather that marriage names that practice among Christians wherein the *telos* of sex finds material embodiment.

One of those purposes of marriage the church has named is the having of children. That marriage has a procreative end does not entail that every marriage must in fact produce biological heirs, but it does mean that marriage as an institution—that is, an ongoing practice of a community across time—of the church is procreative. Accordingly it would be appropriate as part of the examination of couples desiring to have the church witness their marriages to have their intentions to have children declared. I would think it quite possible to deny marriage to people who refuse to have their marriages open to children. Again, if Methodists would discuss such a claim, the debate about homosexuality might well appear quite different.

I am aware that such suggestions appear "conservative" for many who are supporters of the rights of gays. But that is not necessarily the case. For example, if the church had some understanding of when exceptions might be made for marriages that will not or cannot be biologically procreative, we might have basis for an analogous understanding of some gay relations. Indeed such discussions might help us better understand in what manner all parenting is a form of adoption, and how even "childless marriages" in the Christian community must provide space for children. In the absence of such practices we are simply left with claims and counterclaims about what is and is not loving and/or scriptural.

(I do not intend in this short piece to explore the scriptural issue. Suffice it to say that while there is no question that some scriptural passages condemn something like same-sex relations, I am not convinced that the church's position on these matters can turn on those passages. I am also sure that attempts to historicize those passages in an interest of liberalization is a mistake. Rather, I assume that obscure passages of Scripture should

49

be interpreted in the light of the less obscure. The debate must be framed by the practices of singleness and marriage because they are the practices that clearly are shaped by the scriptural witness and thus can better help us read Scripture.)

If the above suggestions represent an "opposition," they do so only as an alternative to the incoherence of the way this matter is being debated by both sides in the Methodist Church. Indeed, my deepest problem with the current debate among Methodists is that we become one another's enemies and as a result fail to notice who the enemy is—that is, capitalism. We fail to see that the debate about "sexual identities" simply reflects the construction of our bodies by economic forces that make us willing consumers capable of producing nothing.

For example, Nicholas Boyle observes in *Who Are We Now? Christian Humanism and the Global Market from Hegel to Heaney*[2] that he doubts the gay movement will furnish any deep insights into our modern problems of identity. He credits the gay movement with helping us abandon the Puritan pretense that social affections can be anything other than erotic in origin as well as reminding us that much of any human being's affective life has a homoerotic character. Yet he notes that identity is not a matter of our own affective preferences but of the necessities, constructed by choices of others, that build and transform global systems. He continues:

> Sexual preference, once detached from the process of bodily reproduction, loses touch with the necessities and enters the realm of play—it becomes part of the entertainment industry, a choice to be catered for, but not a constraint on producers. Indeed, worldwide consumerism makes use of homosexuality as a means of eliminating the political constraints which regulate our role as producers: if marriage is redefined as a long-term affective partnership, so that it may be either homosexual or heterosexual, the essentially reproductive nature of male and female bodies is no longer given institutional (and therefore political) expression. Bodies are seen as the locus only of consumption, not of production; production is thereby repressed further into our collective unconscious; and producers, particularly women, are deprived of the political means of protest against exploitation. (It becomes more difficult to maintain, for example, that certain working practices are destructive of the family, for "having" a family is treated as the "Choice" of a particular mode of consumption.)[3]

Capitalism thrives on short-term commitments. The ceaseless drive for innovation is but the way to undercut labor's power by making the skills of the past irrelevant for tomorrow. Indeed, capitalism is the ultimate form of deconstruction, because how better to keep labor under control than through the scarcity produced through innovation? All the better that human relationships are ephemeral, because lasting commitments prove to be inefficient in ever-expanding markets. Against such a background the church's commitment to maintain marriage as lifelong monogamous fidelity may well prove to be one of the most powerful tactics we have to resist capitalism.

Again I am aware that these remarks may appear to underwrite the "conservative" side of the debate about homosexuality. That might be the case, except the conservative side too often wants to have marriage and capitalism as well. I am suggesting you cannot have them both. At least, you cannot have both marriage as lifelong monogamous fidelity in which children are desired and capitalism too. Of course conservatives say they want the former, but, in fact, they live and expect the church to practice the kind of romantic conception of marriage I indicated above.

I do not pretend, however, that what I have said here will please those who want the church to acknowledge gay relationships as marriage. I confess my own bewilderment about what can or should be said as a policy. In the meantime I know my life and my church's life are enriched by members of the church who tell me they are gay. I care deeply that their lives may find the support of the church they need and I need. I am not sure if that makes me pro- or anti-homosexual. I hope it just makes me loyal to the church that has produced us both.

Romantic Capitalism?

51

PART 2

CHRISTIAN
ETHICS IN
AMERICAN
TIME

4

CHRISTIAN ETHICS IN AMERICA (AND THE *JOURNAL OF RELIGIOUS ETHICS*)

A REPORT ON A BOOK I WILL NOT WRITE[1]

CHRISTIAN ETHICS IN AMERICA

Twenty-five years ago I began to teach a course at the University of Notre Dame called "Christian Ethics in America." I began the course having the students read Rauschenbusch, then the Niebuhrs, some Catholics such as Murray, Curran, and McCormick, then Ramsey, Gustafson, and finally Yoder. I thought the course was needed because the development of Protestant Christian ethics was still largely a mystery for most of my Catholic colleagues and completely unknown to my students. To be sure some of my colleagues knew something about Reinhold Niebuhr because John Courtney Murray had criticized Niebuhr, but they had little idea how Niebuhr was related to the social gospel or in what ways H. Richard Niebuhr represented an alternative to his brother. I thought it particularly important to read these ethicists "in order" so that the students might appreciate their complex relationship.

Yet it was not just the Catholic context that prompted me to begin to teach Christian ethics in this fashion. I was aware that new people were beginning to come into the field of "ethics" who no longer cut their teeth in ethics by reading Rauschenbusch, much less the Niebuhrs. My generation was the last to assume that if you wanted to do a Ph.D. in theology and/or Christian ethics you first had to go to seminary. Seminary training at least forced us to learn something about Scripture, historical theology, and—particularly important for those of us in ethics—nineteenth-century theology. But now people were coming into the "field" of ethics without this seminary background. They might know about the Niebuhrs, but the training these people received in their graduate programs did not make the Niebuhrs as central for the doing of ethics as the brothers had been for those of us who had seminary training.

I taught the course, therefore, with the hope that I would someday write a book called *Christian Ethics in America*. Jim Childress and I even talked about writing the book together. Distance and different interests I think slowly eroded that plan, but I continued to think I should write such a book. Moving to Duke reinforced my view that such a book was needed. Protestant seminarians were as innocent of the history of the field as Catholics. If Rauschenbusch and the Niebuhrs were to be read, surely a book was needed that would help students understand the complex relation between their thought. Moreover, how could you understand Ramsey, Gustafson, and even Yoder if you had no sense how their work was positioned in relation to the Niebuhrs?

Of course my interests in such a book were not disinterested. It was not just a matter of whether you could understand Ramsey, Gustafson, or Yoder without the Niebuhrs. It was how could you understand what I was trying to do without such a history. Given my critical relation to Reinhold Niebuhr, some may find it odd I think it so important to maintain his significance, but such a view fails to appreciate that criticism is finally the deepest form of appreciation. I can only think the way I think because Reinhold Niebuhr made such important mistakes.

Yet how I thought about the book changed over the years. Such changes, moreover, have everything to do with what the birth of the *Journal of Religious Ethics* represented and the effect it has had on the field. Let me try to explain. The *Journal of Religious Ethics* began at Harvard because that is where Charles Reynolds went to do his Ph.D. in ethics. Jim Childress and I were at Yale at the same time Charlie was at Harvard. Due to Charlie's wonderful gift for building community, Yale and Harvard graduate students in ethics were meeting yearly to read papers and compare notes with one another. I remember those of us at Yale were dependent on Charlie for securing the ever-revised mimeographed copies of Rawls's A *Theory of Justice*. In effect I believe the *Journal of Religious Ethics* began during those years, because that was the time that Christian ethics was becoming more a graduate school discipline than a manifestation of seminary culture. The Niebuhrs were impressive intellectuals, to be sure, as was Paul Ramsey, but their work remained rooted in church culture and particularly seminary education. I am more than willing to argue that the fact that Ramsey taught at Princeton University does not require me to qualify this claim. It was Charlie Reynolds's great gift to sense the significance of the relocation of ethics from the seminary to the university that led him to imagine the *Journal*. Of course he had also gone to teach in a religious studies department at the University of Tennessee. He understood, I think, sooner than many of us that what we had learned to call Christian ethics at the very least had to be reformed if it was to be taught as a subject in the contemporary university. No matter how impressive the intellectual accomplishments of the Niebuhrs may have been, their "ethics" was still far too theological if ethics was to be recognized as well as secure a place in the curriculums of universities and, in particular, religious studies departments.

The *Journal* was the attempt to give ethics legitimacy. A journal that required rigorous review standards was at least the first step if the fledgling discipline was to "make it." Of course most of us who supported the *Journal of Religious Ethics* were the products of Protestant liberalism and accordingly had been trained to be Christian rather than religious ethicists. Yet Protestant liberalism was in many ways a wonderful preparation for some to assume the allegedly nonparticularist description "religious." What defined the differences between those of us who supported the *Journal* was not our "religious backgrounds" but rather where we went to graduate school. Whatever theological convictions we may or may not have had were more the result of where we went than from where we came.

In 1980 there was a symposium on the development of religious ethics at a meeting of the AAR in New York. In preparation for writing this paper I searched for the paper I had written for that occasion. Finding the paper was not easy because, contrary to the general impression that everything I have written I have published, that paper had not seen the light of a journal. I vaguely remember there was some plan to publish those papers, but I do not remember why that did not take place. Do not despair, gentle reader, that you have no access to my paper. Adhering to Paul Ramsey's self-description, "never waste a word Paul Ramsey," I now impose that AAR paper into this narrative. I do so because I think it describes, to be sure in a less than serious mode, the differences that I thought were emerging due to our graduate school training. Moreover, what I said then helps make clear why I once thought it important to write an account of the development of Christian ethics in the past century and why I no longer plan to write that book. My account, I believe, will also help place the kind of articles that appeared in the early years of the *JRE*. The *Journal* was often used to explore and develop the implications of what we thought the field ought to be about given the differences we developed in and throughout the kind of training we received in our respective graduate schools.

WHERE WE WENT IS WHAT WE DO: A NOSTALGIC INTERLUDE OR, NOT MUCH HAS CHANGED OVER THE LAST FIFTEEN OR SO YEARS

Max Stackhouse observes that if religious ethics is to be characterized by any one dominant mood, "it is the quest for the central organizing tenet or method which can give focus and coherence. Some are peeling the onion to find the pure core, others seek integrative principles which can comprehend the diversity."[2] I think he is right about the mood, but I think the project radically mistaken. Religious ethics has not been, is not, nor should be a discipline. At best, it is an area of study, but even that is unclear. This is our dirty little secret, which some, I think, hope to keep hidden until they come up with an account of "religious ethics" that will make it appear as an intelligible intellectual activity or, failing that, at least coherent enough to deserve a faculty slot in departments of religious studies. In contrast, my recommendation is for us not to worry about being an "intelligible intellectual activity" and have some fun at what we can do.

But if there is no central organizing tenet, it is difficult to know how to characterize directions in current ethics. It is tempting to try to come up with conceptual machinery that will help us pull it all together à la Reeder,[3] or at least some sociological categories that will help us see what is going on like those of Stackhouse[4] or Everett.[5] However, being short on both skills, I want to share with you an insight I had during a retreat of the theology department at Notre Dame.

We were having our usual discussion on the same old topic—namely, what does it mean to be "an ecumenical department in a Catholic context"? Some of my colleagues described how they understood what it meant to do systematic theology in the Catholic tradition, or what difference being a Calvinist made for how pastoral theology was done, or how being a Lutheran shaped one's work in historical theology. The discussion made me very uncomfortable since I could not think how being a Methodist made a difference for how I did Christian ethics. I suddenly thought, *I am not a Methodist, I went to Yale!* Accordingly I do not represent any identifiable religious tradition, but rather I do ethics, or better, I am concerned about the kind of problems we were taught to think of as ethics at Yale.

■58

I think this insight not unimportant to help understand that any attempt to account for the past and future direction of religious ethics turns on where we went to graduate school. You need only to add the qualification that our graduate school agendas may be modified by where we end up teaching. Yet it is the graduate school, rather than identifiable religious traditions, that determines the way most of us understand or do ethics. If we are what we eat, then insofar as any of us are ethicists, we are where we went.

That where we went to be trained to be ethicists is so important provides an interesting contrast to the training for moral theologians in the Catholic tradition. At least this was true until recently; but now Catholic moral theologians are coming to the graduate schools of the mainline to become Christian ethicists. Prior to that development, where Catholic moral theologians went to study did not constitute anything like the difference for their work that it did for those of us in Christian ethics. I am not suggesting it made no difference, but rather that difference was contained within a larger set of institutional practices. Accordingly the "ethics" that Catholic moral theologians produced was not personalized in the way Protestant ethics has tended to be. There were no Niebuhrs or Barths in the Catholic tradition exactly because they were part of a tradition. That tradition was rationally coherent within the presuppositions and practices of Catholicism. Indeed, I take it that part of the difficulty of current Catholic debates about ethics is that those who call for revision do so presupposing the same neoscholastic nature-grace structure for moral theology of their opponents. As Alasdair MacIntyre observes, this gives the impression that Roman Catholic moral theologians are not very interested in God or Jesus Christ, but they are passionately interested in other Roman Catholic moral theologians.[6]

The other exception to my thesis about the importance of graduate schools for shaping different accounts of ethics is the conservative Protestants. Yoder[7] seems to me to provide a singular example of someone working in this tradition. Not only is his work a model of clarity, but the substantive issues he raises about how ethics is to be done are enriching for those who share and do not share his views. And it is important to remember that Yoder does not write primarily for other ethicists, but for Mennonites and, in particular, church Mennonites.[8] Along with Yoder I would mention Vernard Eller,[9] George Forell,[10] Richard Mouw,[11] some Calvinists in Michigan, and a few Lutherans and Baptists everywhere.

Once you put yourself up against the Catholics and conservative Protestants, I think you can feel why graduate school is the "religious ethicist" tradition.[12] But if that is true, then accounts of the direction of religious ethics will turn on characterization of our various graduate programs. I cannot pretend the characterizations I am going to provide are accurate; I put them forward in half seriousness. But like most stereotypes I think they contain some truth. I should also say I cannot deal with all the places that turn out Ph.D.'s in religious ethics. The ones I fail to name I think are partly captured by characterizations of others.[13] A good deal of cross-fertilization has taken place between schools that has resulted in some children that, while not clearly illegitimate, are at least of doubtful parentage.

Each of the graduate school traditions I describe has been marked by the work of a major figure. Thus Yale graduates continue, like H. Richard Niebuhr, to have so many agendas they are not sure what they are doing; but whatever it is, they are sure it involves a great deal of ambiguity. Union people, like Reinhold, know what they are doing and wonder why you are not doing the same thing. Harvard graduates, like James Luther Adams, are not sure what they are doing but know all the sources you ought to read to do whatever you are doing. Princeton folk spend the rest of their lives arguing, as Ramsey does, with Ramsey; and Chicago graduates, at least until recently, continue to develop theories for understanding why people cannot understand Winter's theories of understanding. Of course these are matters of style, but as in so many things, style is substance.

Yet the importance of these individuals is not sufficient to characterize the differences between these graduate schools. What each of these schools represents is a story into which graduate students are lured by the promise of being a participant in an extraordinary adventure in which they may be able to play a heroic role. Thus at Harvard your task is to help the rest of the world understand the historic and conceptual significance of voluntary institutions and along the way develop an ethical theory, or perhaps more accurately defend a Rawlsian or ideal observer theory, that will be sufficient to defeat relativism and utilitarianism. In the process you discover that you now have a theory that satisfactorily accounts for the relation of religion to morality, the priority of obligation to virtue, and why it never rains in Albuquerque. Even more helpful, you also learn you can do ethics in a manner that requires no reference to positive religious beliefs about Christ, Torah, or other irrational or at least nonrational commitments.

At Yale you learn the problem is, Why is religious ethics religious? The challenge is how to preserve the integrity of theological ethics while acknowledging that all positions different from your own are probably more true. Of course you are still interested in something called "social ethics," but you are not sure you know what that means. Therefore you spend a great deal of time analyzing normative discourse and correlative political theories in hopes you can provide a more disciplined argument about complex personal and social questions. As a result, Yale graduates are clear that clarity is the most important thing.

Graduates of Union have less time for interminable and irresolvable philosophical issues, wanting as they do to get on with the business of making the world more just or at least less evil. The ethicist's task is to be where the action is, not simply to analyze arguments. Of course you ought to do some theory, but not take it so seriously that it might change your mind about positions you already hold. Ethics is an aid for action and criticism, which means you suspect that those who emphasize the importance of conceptual clarification (that is, those people from Yale) are really conservatives in disguise. You either join the liberated or you do not, and only by taking part in the fight can you learn what the world is like.

Students at Chicago, like those at Union, believe in advocacy ethics. But at Chicago you must know more about the social sciences and social theory, believing as they do that you cannot find out what kind of world needs changing just by reading the signs of the time in the *New York Times*. And even more important, you understand—unlike those folk at Union—that you need a metaphysics to provide a foundation for any adequate social theory or action. So sometimes you feel more comfortable with the Yale philosophical types, but unfortunately from the perspective of those at Chicago, the Yale people read the wrong philosophers. As a result those trained at Chicago are more likely to make common cause with Harvard graduates, as the latter understand the need for an adequate social theory to explain why Union graduates are often on the right side though people at Union do not understand why.

Princeton *is* Ramsey leading his troops into battle under the flag that displays the deontological symbol.[14] The task of the ethicist is nothing less than recovering and developing a normative ethics sufficient to save the moral capital deposited by Christianity and thus rescue what is left of Western civilization from the barbaric relativists and utilitarians. Therefore, with the people from Harvard and a few from Yale, Princeton graduates seek to form coalitions on the basis of a modified natural-law theory that can hopefully provide an adequate common morality. However, those at Princeton are not as convinced as those at Harvard that you need all that social theory; nor are they sure you need to worry about those funny philosophical and theological problems those people at Yale worry about.

In spite of these differences, however, the graduate school tradition of religious ethics shares the important assumption that the subject of study and/or action is America. The academic pretensions of religious ethics cannot hide the fact that in this respect it remains in continuity with the social gospel, now shorn of the theological and ecclesial commitments of the social gospel.[15] The graduates of these different graduate programs may have divergent views about the basic strengths and weaknesses of America; they may differ about what social and political theories best help one characterize the nature of, as well as the current stresses in, the American society; they may differ about what historical interpretation is appropriate for helping us understand the American experience: but they all agree the subject of Christian ethics in America is America. Some ethicists may be more concerned about social policy, others about an ethos sufficient to sustain a

61

discriminating public discourse; others attempt to develop radical critiques of American economic structures; but all remain concerned about America and understand "ethics" to be about making America work. That such is the case should not be surprising, since universities must be funded by someone and graduates even in religious ethics need jobs.

Of course America was assumed to be the primary subject of ethical analysis and action by those who created and represented the subject called Christian ethics in seminaries. Yet they assumed that to do ethics for America still required or, better, presumed the importance of the church (and Scripture) as important for ethical reflection. Yet the church as a necessary institution to make intelligible the work of ethics simply makes no sense once Christian ethics is transformed into the graduate school tradition of religious ethics. Of course the disappearance of the church had already begun, particularly in the latter work of H. Richard Niebuhr in which the church at best had an ambiguous presence.[16] The church is almost nonexistent in Reinhold Niebuhr's corpus; and though Adams's Troeltschian framework meant some account of the church was required, more important was the framework itself—i.e., the social presuppositions that provide for the flourishing of voluntary institutions.

Oddly enough, the loss of the church for naming the set of practices necessary to make ethical reflection intelligible for Christians makes it more, rather than less, difficult for Christians to engage other traditions. For example, Judaism does "ethics" not for a nation but for the sustaining of a people within diverse nations. As Christians and Jews seek a deeper understanding of one another, we must do so on ground that enables us to appreciate how an ethic works in such particularistic traditions. Not to do so seems to involve reductionistic accounts of "morality" that give the impression that such a morality is more fundamental than the actual beliefs and practices of the tradition itself. Unless we take the particularity of our convictions seriously, we have no way to even know what it means to claim them as true or false.

That, as they say, is a subject for another time. It remains for me to test my thesis that religious ethics represents a shift from seminary to graduate school culture by suggesting how some of the directions and developments in religious ethics manifest our graduate school training. Without question the most important development in religious ethics in the last three decades has been the influence of philosophical ethics on the field. Issues such as the relation between religion and morality, normative ethics, the relation of virtue to obligation have been discussed primarily in terms borrowed from philosophical sources. There are many good reasons for this development, the most important being that philosophical resources seem to provide a clarity often lacking in more strictly theological discussions. However, in the process it is often hard to say, especially for graduates from Harvard and Yale, what makes them theological ethicists.[17]

Some no doubt will object to Gustafson's judgment that many trained in Christian ethics abandon the theological side of the discipline by noting that they no longer desire to do Christian ethics but rather want to contribute to the emerging field called religious ethics. But as I suggested at the beginning, it is by no means clear what that is. At the very least it can mean several things. A religious ethicist may be someone who does what philosophers do; only the religious ethicist retains the concern for social reform or at least hopes to help clarify moral issues in and for the public. Those who specialize in medical ethics, legal ethics, business ethics, and professional ethics can be understood in this way.

Another way to be a "religious ethicist" is just beginning—that is, to develop comparative religious ethics. Many aspire to do ethics in this fashion, but as yet we have few who can claim to be adequate practitioners. Little and Twiss[18] and Green[19] have made a beginning. But it remains to be seen if any "method," which usually looks like some version of Kant, develops to give this endeavor coherence and intelligibility. Certainly I think it is fair to say that those working in comparative religious ethics are more interested in philosophical questions than in historical investigation of the actual practices of another tradition—thus the concentration in books such as Little and Twiss as well as Green on "beliefs" abstracted from their liturgical and cultural settings.

I am not suggesting that the rise of religious ethics has meant no one is any longer trying to do theological ethics. That work still goes on, but it is hard to characterize the endeavor. Certainly Jim Gustafson, Fred Carney, Gene Outka, and Tom Ogletree provide notable examples. Their work is also increasingly philosophical as they attempt to use tools of philosophical analysis to clarify the claims implicit in religious affirmations. Much of Gustafson's work, especially in his occasional essays, reads this way; and Outka's *Agape*[20] is certainly more a philosophical analysis of a theological motif than an attempt to do first-order theological work. Ogletree's attempt to make issues of interpretation central to theological ethics is promising, but as yet he has not developed beyond his phenomenology far enough for evaluation. However, he and Gustafson hold out the possibility for doing Christian ethics in a constructive manner—that is, to show how the very nature of Christian convictions may transform and be transformed by seeking to unravel their moral significance.

Particularly important for this constructive task is the attempt by some to open up the significance of history and historical understanding for Christian ethics. Not only Ogletree's work but also the suggestions made by James Johnson and Dennis McCann point in promising directions. It is my suspicion we will understand how Scripture should work for ethical reflection only when we recover the importance of history for ethics. (It is interesting that most of the work on the ethical significance of Scripture is being done by Scripture scholars who do not think of themselves as doing "ethics.")

But the way I have told the story of how Christian ethics moved from seminaries to graduate schools to become religious ethics cannot help but reveal the bias of my account. The way I have told the story makes clear I cannot muster much interest in whether an intelligible account or justification for religious ethics can be given. What I think is important is that people who received the strange training called Christian ethics find ways to show how matters of human significance involve questions of God's creative and redemptive purposes. But then that is what you should expect a Yalie to say!

WHY I WILL NOT WRITE A BOOK ON CHRISTIAN ETHICS IN AMERICA

The book I had planned to write on the development of Christian ethics in America was meant to be a response to the development of religious ethics. I wanted to tell the story such that Christian ethics might be understood as a compelling way to develop a constructive theological agenda. I sought to show through such a telling that ethics could be and should be theological without sacrificing the methodological self-consciousness represented by the *Journal of Religious Ethics*. Critical though I was of the liberal political and theological presumptions that had given birth to Christian ethics, I would argue that for all its limits the story of the development of Christian ethics from Rauschenbusch to Yoder constituted a recognizable set of skills worthy to be called a discipline. Such a discipline, moreover, was inescapably theological even if the theology that was inescapable was liberal.[21]

The more I reflected on the development of Christian ethics, the less sure I became about whether the very idea of Christian ethics as a distinguishable discipline in theology was a good idea. Accordingly I began to think of the book less as a defense of the development of Christian ethics as a discipline, less as an introduction to those figures I thought were in danger of being lost, and more as an archaeology of how the very idea of Christian ethics had come about. I now thought of the book as organized by the question: how did a tradition that begins with a book called *Christianizing the Social Order* end with a book called *Can Ethics Be Christian?* My answer was simple. The subject of Christian ethics in America had always been America. Just to the extent that we got the kind of social order Rauschenbusch wanted, that is, a democratic social order, that accomplishment made Christianity unintelligible to itself. Of course that way of putting the matter is overly simple, but the complexity could be worked out through the presentation of the factors that drove the construction of the discipline.

To be sure, it is hard to separate the construction of Christian ethics from the spirit of Protestant progressivism. America in fact became the great experiment, in what Max Stackhouse happily describes as constructive Protestantism.[22] Stackhouse argues that Rauschenbusch and the progressive Protestantism he represented in fact constituted a new Christian social philosophy, which Stackhouse calls "conciliar denominationalism." Following Ernst Troeltsch's account in *The Social Teaching of the Christian Churches*, Stackhouse states that only two major Christian social philosophies have ever been developed—the Catholic and the Calvinist. The former was a vision of an "organic, hierarchical order sanctified by objectified means of grace," while the latter centered on the ideal of "an established theocracy of elect saints who are justified by grace through faith."[23] Both these forms of "Christendom" have now ended, never to be resurrected.

Yet Protestantism in America, according to Stackhouse, provided a third alternative that combines two conflicting motifs from the Calvinist and Catholic visions: sectarianism and Christendom. These came together in the life of Rauschenbusch, who on the one hand came

> from an evangelical background from which he gained a sense of intense and explicit faith that could only be held by fully committed members. On the other hand, Rauschenbusch lived in the age of lingering hope for a catholic "Christian culture" and in an age that, especially through the developing social sciences, saw the legitimacy of secular realms. He, like the developing "conciliar denominations," saw the necessity of the select body of believers anticipating the Kingdom in word and deed in good sectarian fashion, and of taking the world seriously on its own terms, as did all visions of Christendom. These motifs conspire in his thought to produce a vision of a revolutionized responsible society for which a socially understood gospel is the catalyst.[24]

Protestants would thus come to dominate American civilization, particularly in the nineteenth century, but without a sense that they were ruling. As Robert Handy observes in his wonderful book *A Christian America: Protestant Hopes and Historical Realities*, although American Protestants had hoped from the beginning that someday American civilization would be fully Christian, that hope gained its most characteristic expression only in the nineteenth century. Indeed, "such expressions usually assumed that while the primary concern of true evangelicals would be for religion itself, devotion to the progress of civilization followed closely. Committed to the principle of religious freedom and to the voluntary method, the leaders of the thrust to make America Christian usually failed to sense how coercive their efforts appeared to those who did not share their premises."[25]

That Protestants failed to see the coercive nature of their attempt to create a Christian civilization was partly due to the presumption that what they wanted was not significantly different from what anyone would want for America. As George Marsden points out, they were proud of the civilization they were sure was being created in America. The United States represented a model society where people of many nations could live in peace and economic prosperity. "Whatever injustices, discriminations, and poverty were in the United States, one could find far worse in other quarters of the globe. Among the essential premises of the dominant American thought of the era were: (1) the superiority of Western civilization, (2) that Anglo-American democratic principles were the highest political expression of that civilization, (3) and that these principles were bound to triumph throughout the earth."[26]

The presumption of "American exceptionalism" that shaped so much of the story of the development of Christian ethics as a discipline found a parallel in the discipline of American church history. In fact, throughout much of this period it is difficult to separate "ethics" from "history." Rauschenbusch thought of himself as a historian. H. Richard Niebuhr's *The Kingdom of God in America* is as influential among those writing the history of religion in America as it is among "ethicists."[27] Reinhold Niebuhr's *The Irony of American History* was equally, if not more, influential.[28] It should not be surprising, therefore, that Reinhold Niebuhr becomes the paradigmatic "public theologian" in Martin Marty's historical account of the relationship between religion and the republic.[29]

The close relationship between Christian ethics and American church history is not surprising insofar as they were both given birth by the same spirit of progressivism. James L. Ash traces the beginnings of American church history to the deanship of Shailer Mathews at the Divinity School of the University of Chicago (1907–1933). Ash notes that Mathews, in his *Spiritual Interpretation of History*, asserted that history manifests a general trend toward spiritual progress. Accordingly, he sought to attract scholars to Chicago who shared his views "that religion was an integral part of society and therefore ought to be studied in the context of its social environment. He also believed that the empirical and inductive methods of 'scientific' history, when properly pursued, would separate the essential elements of the Christian faith from their particular manifestations in individual societies and would enable modern people to use them most fruitfully. Mathews's 'socio-historical method' became the hallmark of what is now known as the 'Chicago school' of historians and theologians, a remarkably prolific and gifted group of scholars."[30]

Central to the narrative of the book would have also been the personal histories and interrelation of the figures addressed. For example, the fact that Rauschenbusch and Reinhold Niebuhr could read German, and particularly that they read Ernst Troeltsch, is significant. For if the subject of Christian ethics in America has always been America, it is nonetheless equally true to say that the script, as is evident even in Stackhouse's account above, was written by Troeltsch. It is no doubt wrong, though instructively wrong, to suggest that the history of Western philosophy is a footnote to Plato; it is certainly closer to the truth to suggest that Christian ethics in America is a footnote to Troeltsch.

Likewise, I hoped to show how Paul Ramsey in many ways remained the last great representative of the social gospel precisely because he thought the Christian ethicist had a responsibility for sustaining as well as shaping the ethos of America. From my perspective, Ramsey was more a student of Reinhold Niebuhr even though his teacher had been H. Richard Niebuhr. H. Richard Niebuhr represented the professionalization of Christian ethics that was in some ways carried forward by Ramsey; but Ramsey in an odd way remained an activist more than a thinker. For example, Ramsey never worried, as H. Richard did, about what would be required for Christian ethics to account for itself. That task became the lifework of James Gustafson as he sought to help us understand the various alternatives for how Christian ethics might be done if one ever got around to doing any. In effect, Gustafson became the great cartographer, our own William Frankena, of the field.

That Christian ethics had become its own subject matter would have dumbfounded Rauschenbusch. Christian ethics was born of the desire to transform the social order but in the process became, as I suggest above, just another discipline in the university.[31] That I intended to end my narrative with Yoder was meant to revivify the tradition through the energy represented by an outsider. Yoder in many ways represents the diverse strands of the tradition in their most powerful form. Like Rauschenbusch he makes Jesus unavoidable for how one thinks about ethics; he shares Reinhold's profound realism; he is as theocentric as H. Richard; he is as serious about the ethics of war as Ramsey; and he strives for Gustafson's clarity.[32] So Yoder was to climax my story as the one who gathered up the good while helping us to go on.

I no longer plan to write this book, even though I have written an overview chapter as well as a long chapter on Rauschenbusch.[33] The more I read for the book, the less enthusiasm I could muster for writing the book. I think one of the reasons for my hesitation was I did not want to write so critically about people I so deeply admire. I had begun thinking about the book as an exercise in memory, but I increasingly found I was telling the story as an argument for forgetting. Every remembering, of course, is a forgetting, but the kind of forgetting entailed by the way I increasingly came to think I had to tell the story was too sad.[34]

Put differently, I find it hard to write a book about a history that I believe has come to an end. I realize such a judgment seems extreme. Ethics, after all, is a flourishing business. But the ethics that is flourishing seems to me to have little connection with the story I was going to tell. Who, for example, represents the continuation of the kind of work Paul Ramsey did? Of course there are many people who would claim to be influenced by Ramsey, but where is there a Ph.D. program that is shaped by his way of doing theological ethics?[35] The same question, I believe, can be asked about the Niebuhrs or James Luther Adams or Paul Lehmann. Of course their books may be read in this or that course, but I suspect such reading is now more an exercise in historical placement than an attempt to encourage students to imitate their work.

In short, the politics that made their work intelligible and important is gone. They depended on the viability of mainstream Protestantism in America as well as the generalized Christian civil religion that pervaded American life.[36] Those politics, particularly in the American academy, simply no longer have the power to sustain Christian ethics as an intelligible enterprise. This creates the problem that even if I still wanted to write the book, who would want to read it? Such a book might be useful to graduate students to refresh their memories before comprehensive exams; but as useful as that might be, it hardly justifies writing the book. Academics are often tempted to ignore questions of audience; but when we do so, we fail to attend to the material conditions that make our work possible in the first place.

An observation that invites a criticism about the very way I conceived the book I will not write: the absence of women and African-Americans from the story I was going to tell is glaring. That is particularly the case given the importance of the work of women and African-Americans in the field in recent times.[37] Yet what I find so interesting about much of their work is how little it draws on the work of the ethicists who were to be the center of my story. Liberation themes, with the possible exception of Rauschenbusch and Yoder, simply do not comport with the theological and ethical frames of the Niebuhrs, Ramsey, and Gustafson. I am not suggesting that some feminist and African-American thinkers have not drawn on the Niebuhrs, Ramsey, and Gustafson, but rather that the use of their work has not been an attempt to develop their intellectual agendas.

Which brings me back to how the *Journal of Religious Ethics* fits into my decision not to write the book on Christian ethics in America. The audience as well as those who write for the *JRE* remain largely people trained in the graduate school traditions I described above. The *Journal* has tried to attract articles as well as readers from traditions other than those left over from the Protestant mainstream. Some quite good articles by Jews and Muslims have even been published, but I do not think the *Journal* is read by Jews and Muslims. At least the *JRE* is not read by them because they are a Jew or a Muslim. For to the extent they are a Jew or a Muslim, with a few exceptions, they are not products of the graduate school traditions that produced the people who read and write for the *JRE*.

The *Journal of Religious Ethics* is neither fish nor fowl.[38] It continues to draw on the intellectual capital left over from Protestant liberalism. But if the story I was going to tell about Christian ethics in America is close to being right, then the *Journal* is drawing on the principal of that capital at a time when there is little capital left. Of course ethics is a boom industry in America, and no doubt the *JRE* can and no doubt will benefit from that development. But it is by no means clear that will provide the *JRE* with the kind of ongoing readership and, even more, intellectual justification required.

The same reasons that have led me to abandon the project to write the story of Christian ethics in America force me to ask why I should continue to support or even read the *JRE*. The reason I continue to care about the *JRE* is the history of friendships it represents for me. I care about its future for the same reason. I want to continue the conversations the *Journal* has made possible. But I have no way to know if and why those conversations are sufficient to attract a continuing readership given the diversity in graduate training today.

Of course there are quite pragmatic reasons for continuing to support the *JRE*. Not only has it provided a space for me to publish, but, equally important, it has published Yoder, McClendon, Milbank, and many others on whose work I have come to rely. Where else could the issues on Ramsey and Gustafson have been published? The *Journal*, moreover, represents a good place for the graduate students I have trained to continue to have a place to publish.

Yet I worry that the conventions that determine what a good article should look like to appear in the *JRE* will force my students to mute their theological commitments. The *JRE* was born at a time when modernist presumptions reigned supreme in philosophical and theological work. Carefully wrought articles by analytic philosophers became the models for how to "do ethics." I do not wish to be misunderstood: I am deeply indebted to the analytic tradition. But it is nonetheless true that the analytic style can become an end in itself in a way that inhibits fuller forms of discourse.

Questions of style, however, do not go to the heart of the matter for me. The more my theological agenda has developed over the years, the more I have thought it important to support the *JRE*. There is no reason the *JRE* cannot become the site for exploring the difference theological claims make for how religious communities and lives are ordered. Such an exploration will not and cannot be sufficient to make something called "religious ethics" a self-justifying activity. What it may be able to do, however, is attract readers who read the *Journal* not because it represents a disciplinary subset but because the articles the *Journal* publishes are about matters that matter.

5

■Walter Rauschenbusch and the Saving of America

THE LIFE OF AN EVANGELIST

Walter Rauschenbusch never aspired to be an "ethicist." Such an ambition he would have thought far too modest. He sought nothing less than the saving of America. Ethics was an aid for that task, insofar as ethics named the ideals constitutive of salvation. In short, Walter Rauschenbusch was engaged in a continuous camp meeting designed to reclaim the "sinner," America, for the kingdom of God.[1]

In his adulatory biography of Rauschenbusch, Dores Robinson Sharpe recounts an experience in Chicago in 1912 that wonderfully confirms Rauschenbusch's own understanding of his evangelical task. Sharpe tells us that, exhausted from having just delivered a lecture, Rauschenbusch bought two boxes of strawberries, a bottle of milk, and some crackers and led the way to the shore of Lake Michigan:

There on the beach, as the water lapped at our feet, we had our meal. For me it was an hour of holy communion. We talked of spiritual values and things pertaining to the Kingdom of God. Rather abruptly he turned his steady, penetrating gaze on me and asked: "How do you think of me and my work?" My reply was: "I think of you as an evangelist and of your work as evangelism of the truest sort." The effect was electric for he threw his arms around me and, with deep emotion, said: "I have always wanted to be thought of in that way. Your testimony gives me new fighting power." That he considered himself such may be adjudged from his own words: "I have always regarded my public work as a form of evangelism, which called for a deeper repentance and a new experience of God's salvation."[2]

It seems odd for us who now read Rauschenbusch to think of him except as an evangelist, but of course that was not the case for Rauschenbusch's contemporaries. His "public work" was considered to be something other than Christianity. Most assumed that Christianity was about the saving of souls, not about the saving of "society." The latter was politics, which was clearly separate from "religion."

Such a view of the relation, or lack of relation, between religion and politics was simply accepted as a given. That such an apolitical account of Christianity was so commonly assumed is apparent from Rauschenbusch's own account of how he became one of the prominent figures of the social-gospel movement. We have his account because a reporter from the *Rochester Democrat and Chronicle* was fortunately present when Rauschenbusch was giving an informal talk to a Sunday school class in Rochester in 1913. We do not know how the reporter happened to be present, but it is surely an indication of Rauschenbusch's status both nationally and in Rochester that what he said in a Sunday school class was thought worth reporting in the paper. He is reported to have said:

I was born and brought up in a religious way, and when I was about sixteen or seventeen my religious experience began to come to me. At this time, it had no social expression in it. I felt that I ought to do something for people, but I didn't know how. After a while, I became a minister and my idea then was to save souls in the ordinarily accepted religious sense. I had no idea of social questions. Then I began to work in New York and there, among the working people, my social education began.

I began to understand the connection between religious and social questions. I had no social outlook before. I hadn't known how society could be saved. When I began to apply my previous religious ideas to the conditions I found, I discovered they didn't fit. At this time, my friends were urging me to give up this social work and devote myself to "Christian work." Some of them felt grieved for me, but I knew the work was Christ's work and I went ahead, although I had to set myself against all that I had previously been taught. I had to go back to the Bible to find out whether I or my friends were right. I had to revise my whole study of the Bible. Then I began to write for the newspapers. That is where my ideas began to clear up.

People didn't want to hear my message; they had no mind for it; they would take all I said about religion in the way they had been used to it, but they didn't want any of this "social stuff." All my scientific studying of the Bible was undertaken to find a basis for the Christian teaching of a social gospel. I kept on that way for eleven years in New York. I lived among the common people all the time. Before I went there for $600.00 and I never got more than $1,200 a year. Then I came to the seminary here and took up my work as a teacher of church history.[3]

We are in debt to this anonymous reporter for being at the right place at the right time, as few quotes tell us as much about Rauschenbusch as this one.[4] "Then I began to write for newspapers" is an innocent enough statement, but its significance should not be lost. Not only does this statement indicate Rauschenbusch's extraordinary ability to extend the social gospel as a popular movement, but it also signals his ability to write in a compelling and eloquent manner.[5] Equally important is his declaration of salary and his claim that he returned to the seminary to teach church history. They are important because, as we shall see, in an interesting way they quite innocently give the wrong impression. The church he served was poor, but he and his wife, Pauline, maintained a cordial relationship with Aura and John D. Rockefeller.[6] He did teach church history, which I will make much of below, but he first returned to Rochester to teach in the German department, which in its own way is equally important.

To understand Rauschenbusch we must understand something of the progression of his life. That is not true of many who in his wake became Christian ethicists. You cannot understand Rauschenbusch unless you understand his life because Christian ethics for him had not yet become a position separable from his life. He was not an academic but rather a figure of what might be called a "church" or "seminary" culture. He did not just "think"; he was an activist. In spite of their differences, Rauschenbusch and Reinhold Niebuhr were products of the same kind of Protestant church and seminary culture.

Rauschenbusch was, of course, many things, but in all the things he was he was German. His father, August Rauschenbusch, was born in Germany in 1816. He was a sixth-generation Lutheran pastor who had been tempted toward theological rationalism while a university student, but in 1836 he underwent a dramatic conversion and assumed a conservative religious stance for the rest of his life.[7] No doubt Rauschenbusch's father was a complex figure, which is but another way of saying that he was difficult. Unhappy with his ministry in Germany, he became a missionary to America in 1846. Working among the German-speaking population of Missouri, he became convinced that the New Testament required believer's baptism and thus became a Baptist.[8]

August Rauschenbusch was obviously a person of strong conviction. He was invited to join the faculty of the newly founded (1850) Rochester Theological Seminary in 1855 but refused to leave the Germans of Missouri, whom he feared might otherwise be destroyed by worldliness or the errors of Roman Catholicism. Yet in 1857 he was enticed to come to Rochester Seminary to direct the German department. Rochester was a center of German immigration, and in particular of German Baptist life. It was amidst that peculiar German pietistic ethos that young Walter Rauschenbusch was raised in America.

Yet even that was not sufficiently German for August Rauschenbusch. In 1865 he sent his wife Caroline, son Walter, and daughters Frida and Emma to Germany for four years in an effort to ensure that they did not lose their German roots. August joined them only in the fourth year, bringing them back to Rochester in 1869. Walter was raised in a home of outward Victorian respectability and marital turmoil. His mother and father were obviously so incompatible that the turmoil could not even be hidden in Rochester. One of the results was that August found increasing excuses to spend more and more time in Germany away from the family.

We have no basis to suggest that Walter, as the only son, was favored, but there can be no question that he was given every educational advantage. After graduating from the Rochester Free Academy in 1879 at the age of seventeen, he was taken to Germany by his father and enrolled at the *Evangelische Gymnasium zu Gütersloh*. By the time he returned to enter Rochester Seminary in 1883, he not only had benefited from a classical German education but also felt part of his German family.

Rauschenbusch was impressed by what he had learned in Germany. He was proud of Germany's intellectual tradition and culture. His German heritage, as well as his commitment to all things German, would break his heart as he tried to negotiate World War I. I suspect, however, that one of the most lasting influences Germany had on Rauschenbusch was his extraordinary sense of the beauty of nature. Rauschenbusch's work is full of metaphors derived from the created order. It comes as no surprise, therefore, that his view of society is fundamentally organic. While there were obviously romantic sources in America that could have influenced him in this respect, he attributes his aesthetic sensibilities to his stay in Germany. Writing of a trip along the Rhine, he confessed that he was "intensely happy when I can drink in with full draughts the beauty that God has poured with a prodigal hand over this earth of ours." He regretted that Americans had not learned to "cultivate the perception of the beautiful" as much as Europeans.[9]

Rauschenbusch's attraction to "nature" was not simply an interesting aspect of his personality. Though seldom noticed, it lies at the heart of his understanding of the social gospel. His fascination with science, particularly social science, his "activism," his desire to "engineer" society, are such prominent themes in his work that the essentially romantic and conservative forms of his thought can be overlooked.[10] There can be no doubt that he reacted against the "injustice" of capitalism, but, as I hope to show, equally important for Rauschenbusch was the ugliness of the society that he saw around him. I do not mean this critically, since I think ugliness may well be a more damning indication of a corrupt society than injustice.

Rauschenbusch returned from Germany to finish his education at Rochester Seminary, which by that time had become, like most seminaries in America, a battleground for emerging issues raised by the historical criticism of the Bible. Rauschenbusch went against many of his professors' deep distrust of this development. His theology was, of course, "liberal," but like many Protestant liberal theologians, he was equally pietistic. That liberalism and pietism might be at odds is a later development that is inappropriately applied to Rauschenbusch and his social-gospel friends. Their "social work" was but a continuation of their understanding of the significance of their experience of Christ.[11]

Graduating from seminary in 1866, he accepted a call to the Second German Baptist Church, which lay just beyond the "Hell's Kitchen" area of New York City. This was a German-speaking congregation numbering 125, most of whom were factory laborers. He brought two things with him from Rochester: (1) a decline in hearing that finally resulted in his becoming virtually deaf and (2) his mother, since she and his father had finally agreed to separate.[12]

Rauschenbusch's account above suggests that there was a deep discontinuity between his early ministry and his taking up the "social questions." No doubt it felt that way to him, but there are also deep continuities. Paul Minus characterizes his early preaching as "resembling what one would have heard from most other recent seminary graduates in Baptist churches across the United States. It was a Calvinist version of the gospel, modified by a pietist-Evangelical heritage in the direction of Arminianism, with only a touch of his nascent theological liberalism apparent. The central theme of his sermons was the human journey from sin to salvation."[13] Yet as Minus also observes, even the young Rauschenbusch's account of that journey from sin to salvation was a corporate one. *Salvation* names a process in which the world is moving from evil to the kingdom of God. Rauschenbusch's turn to social questions did not require him to fundamentally change his theological outlook.

In his 1917 Taylor Lectures at Yale Divinity School, published as *A Theology for the Social Gospel*, Rauschenbusch, perhaps somewhat disingenuously, argues that the social gospel effected no significant change to any fundamental Christian doctrine. For example, the social gospel was often criticized for having an inadequate view of sin. In response, Rauschenbusch observes that when the social gospel undertook to define the nature of sin, "we accepted the old definition, that sin is selfishness and rebellion against God, but we insisted on putting humanity into the picture. The definition of sin as selfishness gets its reality and nipping force only when we see humanity as a great solidarity and God indwelling in it. In the same way the terms and definitions of salvation get more realistic significance and ethical reach when we see the internal crises of the individual in connection with the social forces that play upon him or go out from him."[14]

Yet there can be no doubt that the poverty that Rauschenbusch saw around him "burned into his soul the conviction that poverty and its causes must somehow be overcome."[15] Rauschenbusch was deeply influenced by Henry George and Richard Ely, but his perspective was always that of a pastor.[16] He tells a story in *Christianity and the Social Crisis* that I think encapsulates his reaction to the poverty around his church in New York. The story is about an elderly working man, "a good Christian man," who had been run down by a New York City streetcar. He had been inadequately cared for in the city hospitals, even being shipped to a charity hospital on Blackwell's Island. Rauschenbusch had to help the man's wife and daughter locate their husband and father, as well as get them across to the island. The man died of gangrene.

The streetcar company offered the man's family one hundred dollars in settlement. Rauschenbusch once more intervened and saw the manager of the company on behalf of the wife and daughter, hoping to get a more equitable settlement. The manager informed Rauschenbusch that five thousand dollars would be the maximum allowed by New York laws, but since the man's earnings were small the amount the courts would allow would also be small. Moreover, even if the family sued, the streetcar company with its paid lawyers would appeal to a higher court, wearing out the resources of the family with slight expenses to the corporation. The widow submitted to the company offer and was given the hundred dollars in single dollar bills to make it seem more than it actually was.

The president of the company, "a benevolent and venerable-looking gentleman," had explained to Rauschenbusch that the streetcars of New York traveled thousands of miles each day and people were always being run over. People needed the streetcars, and if the company was to remain viable it could not afford to be more generous. Rauschenbusch acknowledges that the officers of the streetcar company were not bad men. "Their point of view and their habits of mind are entirely comprehensible. I feel no certainty that I should not act in the same way if I had been in their place long enough. But the impression remained that our social machinery is almost as blindly cruel as its steel machinery, and that it runs over the life of a poor man with scarcely a quiver."[17]

Rauschenbusch learned much from George and Ely, but I suspect that they only served to confirm as well as give expression to what he was learning as a pastor. Experiences like the above confirmed his conviction that redemption of people required the redemption of the social order. In *Christianizing the Social Order* he observes, "An unchristian social order can be known by the fact that it makes good men do bad things. It tempts, defeats, drains, and degrades and leaves men stunted, cowed, and shamed in their manhood. A Christian social order makes bad men do good things. It sets high aims, steadies the vagrant impulses of the weak, trains the powers of the young, and is felt by all as an uplifting force which leaves them with the consciousness of a broader and nobler humanity as their years go on."[18] Such passages were surely written with men like the president of the street-car company in mind.

Rauschenbusch's social vision was also shaped in the parish, but he lacked a theological expression of that vision. In 1891 he announced his resignation, explaining to his congregation that he was going to study in Germany for a year in anticipation of beginning a literary career.[19] Church leaders and members, however, begged him to remain as their pastor and offered him a sabbatical with pay. They even offered to retain an interim pastor who would be hired during his absence and kept on after his return to lighten his load. Rauschenbusch agreed.

The year in Germany Rauschenbusch spent studying and writing. Some of what he wrote during that time no doubt later became *Christianity and the Social Crisis*. He tells us in *Christianizing the Social Order* that he spent the year studying the teaching of Jesus and sociology—"a good combination and likely to produce results."[20] He reports that through such research and reflection he discovered Christ's conception of the kingdom of God, which "came to me a new revelation. Here was the idea and purpose that had dominated the mind of the Master himself. All his teachings center about it. His life was given to it. His death was suffered for it. When a man has once seen that in the Gospels, he can never unsee it again."[21]

With the discovery of the centrality of the kingdom in Jesus' teaching, Rauschenbusch felt a new security in his social impulses. Tellingly, he notes that the spiritual authority of Jesus would have been sufficient to offset the "weight of all the doctors," but he now knew that he had history on his side as well. Grasping the significance of the kingdom united the old and new elements of his religious life. "The saving of the lost, the teaching of the young, the pastoral care of the poor and frail, the quickening of starved intellects, the study of the Bible, church union, political reform, the reorganization of the industrial system, international peace,—it was all covered by the one aim of the Reign of God on earth."[22]

Rauschenbusch returned to Second German Baptist Church in New York and remained the church's pastor until 1897. During those six years two important developments transpired—the forming of the Brotherhood of the Kingdom and his marriage to Pauline Rother of Milwaukee in 1893.

Their marriage was as happy as his father and mother's marriage had been miserable. A girl, Winifred, was born to them in 1894 and a boy, Hilmar Ernst, in 1896. They eventually had three more children. From all reports Rauschenbusch was a loving and devoted husband and father. Like so many late Victorian figures, Rauschenbusch considered the love between a man and a women resulting in a family the quintessential form of Christian love.

In 1914 he published a small but elegant book on Christian love called *Dare We Be Christians?*[23] Not only does Rauschenbusch refuse to ignore the erotic character of love, but he highlights its physical character as one of love's essential capacities to enlarge human community.

> The attraction between man and woman is indeed the most striking and stirring form of love. We can gauge its force by the intense joy of its satisfactions, and the agony when love is unrequited or its trust wronged or its faithfulness broken. Two persons, at opposite poles in their physical tastes, their aesthetic habits, their aims in life, perhaps strangers to each other until recently, break away from their family bonds of a lifetime and enter into a physical and mental intimacy of life which binds them in a lasting social partnership of work and mutual care. If it were not an old story it would be a miracle. Even its reflected sensations are so charming that we never tire of reading love stories or discreetly watching them in real life.[24]

Rauschenbusch observes that this love is but a specialized form of the larger love that "pervades our race." That is why if there is nothing but sex-desire, love can be a vice. Sexual love must be formed by love of the family, for such love is essential to the very existence of human society. "These family affections are the most striking and powerful forms of human love. They have the support of physical nearness and of constant intercourse and habit. But the social impulse of the race is just as truly at work in the keen interest we take in a chance-met stranger, in the cheer we feel in meeting a boyhood friend, in the sense of comradeship with those who work or play alongside of us. Every normal man has uncounted relations of good-will, and the mobility of modern life has immensely increased the contacts for most of us."[25]

The "sense of comradeship" was as concrete in Rauschenbusch's life as were his marriage and family. In 1892 Rauschenbusch joined with other like-minded young ministers to create an organization to meet periodically for study and mutual support in their efforts to serve the kingdom. This group of like-minded men proved to be one of Rauschenbusch's most enduring primary commitments, particularly after his return to the seminary in Rochester after his year in Germany. The "manly" character of this group is apparent: they pledged to "give their support to one another in the public defense of the truth, and jealously guard the freedom of discussion for any man who is impelled by love of the truth to utter his thoughts."[26]

These men needed one another because they thought they were fomenting a revolution. They were trying to change at once the church and society. Because the church had abandoned the idea of the kingdom of God, a false and one-sided conception of Christianity developed. Rauschenbusch observes that personal salvation has been substituted for the kingdom, with the result that

> men seek to save their own souls and are selfishly indifferent to the evangelization of the world. Because the individualistic conception of personal salvation has pushed out of sight the collective idea of a Kingdom of God on earth, Christian men seek for the salvation of individuals and are comparatively indifferent to the spread of the spirit of Christ in the political, industrial, social, scientific, and artistic life of humanity, and have left these as the undisturbed possessions of the spirit of the world. Because the Kingdom of God has been confounded with the Church, therefore the Church has been regarded as an end instead of a means, and men have thought they were building up the Kingdom when they were only cementing a strong church organization.[27]

That is the "social gospel" in a nutshell. Advocacy on its behalf consumed the rest of Rauschenbusch's life.[28] No doubt such advocacy gave Rauschenbusch and his fellow members of the Brotherhood a sense of representing a radically different kind of Christianity. Yet they remained deeply embedded in the practices of Protestant pietism.[29] Of course the social gospel was about social reform, but it was equally about prayer, hymns, and devotional practices. The social gospel was meant to be a popular movement, and in particular a movement of the spirit.[30] You cannot understand Rauschenbusch by reading only *Christianity and the Social Crisis*. At least as influential, if not more so, were his *Prayers of the Social Awakening* and *The Social Principles of Jesus*.[31] "Ethics," at least the ethics of the social gospel, were as much about prayer and the singing of hymns as they were about the transformation of the economic order. More accurately put, for Rauschenbusch the transformation of the economic order was prayer.[32]

In 1897 Rauschenbusch finally accepted a call to head, as his father had before him, the German department at Rochester Seminary. He believed that his deafness would be less a problem in teaching than it had been in the pastorate, but equally important was the knowledge that Pauline would be happier in Rochester. Moreover, he believed that by training the denomination's future ministers, he would have more influence than came from pastoring a single church.[33] Officially Rauschenbusch's denomination was American Baptist, but it was the aim of the German department at Rochester to sustain those congregations that continued to speak German, particularly in their worship services.[34]

79

Though he was called to the German department as professor of New Testament, he also taught natural sciences, civil government, zoology, English, and other subjects.[35] Such a wide array of courses were required because his students were German-Americans trying to combine college with seminary studies. He was a captivating teacher in spite of, or perhaps because of, his deafness. In 1902 he became professor of church history in the English department of the seminary. This move was in many ways natural, since Rauschenbusch's first love had always been church history. But it also indicated his increasing awareness that his commitment to the church's social mission simply did not have a home among German Baptists.[36]

As we shall see, Rauschenbusch's ethics were done primarily as historical reflections. Indeed, for Rauschenbusch there could be no sharp distinction between history and theology, since history is the outworking of Jesus' influence. He observes in *The Righteousness of the Kingdom*, for example, that Jesus sought to duplicate himself in his disciples and in great measure he succeeded. "Their hearts were plastic to his touch. They loved him. They found the chief good of their lives in him. His thoughts became their thoughts. His sympathies and antipathies were theirs. Christ was formed in them. . . . Since then there has been a long, long series of Christ-like lives on earth, of men and women in whom Christ has taken form. History has recorded some of them; but history itself is slowly being christianized; it is only gradually learning to apply Christ's standards of greatness."[37]

Rauschenbusch wrote a quite interesting article, "The Influence of Historical Studies on Theology," that makes explicit his methodological presuppositions about the role of history.[38] He begins the article by observing that the dominance of historical studies in the theological curriculum is recent. In the Middle Ages systematic theology dominated, and after the Reformation theology became primarily the study of the Bible. History entered with exegesis, yet it would be a mistake to limit the significance of history to the study of the Bible. For history has an essential place in all the theological sciences, since it "irrigates and fertilizes all other departments."[39] Rauschenbusch observes that because a biblical book gets its significance "only" in connection with its historical environment, the more penetrating and fruitful will be the interpretation the greater the interpreter's knowledge of contemporary history.[40]

The phrase "contemporary history" is, of course, ambiguous. It can mean the history that we are currently experiencing or the way we now write history. Rauschenbusch probably conflated both meanings, since he believed that the development of "scientific history" was an advance peculiar to our living in a "modern" time. For example, he assumes that "human life is continuous, and a subsequent period of history is always the most valuable interpreter of an earlier period."[41] For Rauschenbusch, history is a moral science that allows us to recover the "real" intent of the prophets and Jesus without the qualifications of later developments. "When we have been in contact with the ethical legalism and the sacramental superstitions of the Fathers, we feel the glorious freedom and the pure spirituality of Paul like a mighty rushing wind in a forest of pines. When we have walked among the dog-matic abstractions of the Nicene age, the Synoptic Gospels welcome us back to Galilee with a new charm, and we feel that their daylight simplicity is far more majestic and divine than the calcium light of the creeds."[42]

The sense of continuity and development characteristic of historical studies is therefore essential for all the theological sciences. Indeed "it is interesting to imagine how the course of Christian history would have been changed if the leaders of the early church had only had a modern training in history."[43] That was, in effect, the great insight of the Reformers, as they appealed to original historical sources against the falsifications and legends produced by the church.[44] The scientific study of history is the necessary means for training the scientific temper and critical faculty of theologians. Ancient and medieval civilizations had no "real" natural science or train-ing in historical criticism, and consequently theology was dogmatic and credulous. Fortunately we are obviously not so limited, benefiting as we do from the development over the last century of modern history.

The importance of history is no less significant in the work of Reinhold and H. Richard Niebuhr, but what they mean by "history" will certainly be different. They do not share Rauschenbusch's confidence that the scientific study of history can only confirm Christian convictions. For Rauschenbusch,

> the fundamental fact in the Christian revelation was that the Word became flesh. Therewith Truth became History. Christianity was first a single life, then a collective life, then a stream of historical influences, and always a healing saving power. Let us not reverse God's process. Let us not be ratio-nalists and turn the flesh into words and history into dogma. The future of Christian theology lies in the comprehension of Christianity in history. The future of Christianity itself lies in getting the spirit of Jesus Christ incarnated in history.[45]

Christian ethicists after Rauschenbusch will never write a line like that.

In 1907 Rauschenbusch published *Christianity and the Social Crisis*. Rauschenbusch thought he had written a "dangerous book" that would anger people. Indeed he believed it might even cost him his job.[46] The vol-ume appeared just as he and his family sailed to Germany for a sabbatical. To his great astonishment, he returned to find that not only was he not to be fired, but he had become famous. Published by Macmillan, *Christianity and the Social Crisis* had gone through thirteen printings by 1912, selling fifty thousand copies.[47] That it was so popular should not be surprising, since it was an eloquent revivalist sermon meant to reclaim the sinner.

81

Rauschenbusch's main thesis was that "the essential purpose of Christianity was to transform human society into the kingdom of God by regenerating all human relations and reconstituting them in accordance with the will of God."[48] Why that did not happen, of course, was the problem for which Rauschenbusch needed to provide a convincing account. According to Rauschenbusch, such a reconstruction of human relationships was impossible in early Christianity because of state hostility as well as the general breakdown of the social order. Also contributing to Christianity's social impotence was the apocalypticism of the early church, a debased form of prophetic hope. Moreover, the influence of pagan "otherworldliness" resulted in a concentration on the future life as well as ascetical disciplines that could only distract Christians from the task of social reconstruction.[49] Monasticism, ritualism, sacramentalism, dogmatism, the churchliness of Christianity, and the subsequent subordination of the church to the state all combined in a manner that resulted in loss of hope in the kingdom.

In the next chapter, "The Present Crisis," Rauschenbusch described the imminent collapse of our Western civilization. The crisis began with the Industrial Revolution, in which the very discovery of the instruments that promised to raise humanity from fear of want has resulted in submerging people in perpetual want and fear.[50] The alienation of the people from the land through the institution of private property; the division of society into owners and workers, with the latter's wages in no way allotted by sharing in the profits of what is produced; the resulting loss of morale of the workers who now take no pride in what they produce; the physical decline of workers; and, in particular, the degradation of women and children[51] all conspire to threaten our political democracy.[52] According to Rauschenbusch, we are facing the end of our civilization, a civilization in which Christianity has been the salt and in which it must now become the preservative. Everything depends on the moral forces that "the Christian nations can bring to the fighting line against wrong, and the fighting energy of those moral forces will again depend on the degree to which they are inspired by religious faith and enthusiasm. It is either a revival of social religion or the deluge."[53]

The last chapters of *Christianity and the Social Crisis* in effect constitute Rauschenbusch's "altar call." "Repent and be saved." Such a saving begins by awakening individuals from their complicity with the sins of society and a renewed commitment to social reform.[54] But equally important, the church, which is now too controlled by the wealthy,[55] must join forces with the "common people" so that the salvation of the political order through democracy can be extended to the industrial and economic order.[56] A saved church is the beginning of the salvation of the nation. Or, better put, for Rauschenbusch the saving of the nation and the saving of the church are one inseparable whole.[57] If the gospel is to have power over an age, it must be "the highest expression of the moral and religious truths held by that age. It cannot afford to have young men sniff the air as in a stuffy room when they enter the sphere of religious thought. When the world is in travail with a higher ideal of justice, the Church dare not ignore it if it would retain its moral leadership."[58]

Like any good altar call, Rauschenbusch's book ends with a chapter on "What to Do." We must repent of our social sins;[59] see through the fictions of capitalism, such as the claim that the poor are poor through their own fault; follow the mind of Christ by taking the side of the poor; turn the spiritual forces of Christianity against materialism and mammonism; and create laws, institutions, and customs that will mitigate social hardships. Among the customs Rauschenbusch thought particularly important were the elimination of alcoholic liquors from the home, Sunday rest, summer holidays, and the creation of public parks. Finally, a recovery of fraternal communism is necessary, which would require the public ownership of enterprises essential for public life, such as utilities and transportation.[60]

This was bracing stuff that appealed to the "manly" spirit of many as well as tapping into the progressive spirit of American life at the turn of the century.[61] For the next ten years Rauschenbusch was in constant demand as a speaker and writer.[62] *Prayers of the Social Awakening* was published in 1910, *Unto Me* in 1912, and *Dare We Be Christians?* in 1914.[63] In 1912 he published *Christianizing the Social Order*, which was well received but added little to what he had done in *Christianity and the Social Crisis*. The book is organized quite differently than *Christianity and the Social Crisis*, as he begins by reporting on the present social awakening. In the second part he goes over much of the same material as appeared in *Christianity and the Social Crisis*, explaining why the social transformation Jesus intended did not take place. The last parts of the book are more "practical," suggesting what is wrong with society and what needs to be done. I do not mean to suggest that *Christianizing the Social Order* is without interest, only that Rauschenbusch's theological and ethical position remained relatively unchanged from *Christianity and the Social Crisis* until his death.

From the perspective of the argument I am developing in this book, however, he does take up an issue of great importance in *Christianizing the Social Order*. He denies that he wants to put "Christ into the Constitution," nor is he seeking to set up a theocracy.[64] Rather,

> Christianizing the social order means bringing it into harmony with the ethical convictions which we identify with Christ. A fairly definite body of moral convictions has taken shape in modern humanity. They express our collective conscience, our working religion. The present social order denies and flouts many of these principles of our moral life and compels us in practice to outrage our better self. We demand therefore that the moral sense of

humanity shall be put in control and shall be allowed to reshape the institutions of social life. We call this "christianizing" the social order because these moral principles find their highest expression in the teachings, the life, and the spirit of Jesus Christ. Their present power in Western civilization is in large part directly traceable to his influence over its history.[65]

Rauschenbusch observes that, of course, many like himself regard Jesus as the unique revelation of God, but even those who do not hold this belief in a "formulated way" or feel compelled to deny it, "including an increasing portion of our Jewish fellow-citizens," will still consent to the claim that in Jesus "our race has reached one of its highest points, if not its crowning summit thus far, so that Jesus Christ is a prophecy of the future glory of humanity."[66] To say that we want to moralize the social order is too vague and powerless. In contrast, "Christianizing the social order" is at once concrete and compelling.

That Rauschenbusch could write in this manner is but an indication that he assumed a generalized Christian social order. He feels no need, as later Christian ethicist do, to appeal to natural law to justify Christian participation in social policy. Rauschenbusch is vaguely aware that not everyone in America is Christian, but he cannot imagine they would not support Jesus' ideals. Yet there is a tension even within Rauschenbusch's understanding of these matters, since it is not clear how the moral ideals integral to Jesus' personality can be abstracted from that personality. Those who follow after Rauschenbusch in the name of Christian social ethics see the need to leave Jesus behind.

Almost as quickly as fame came to Rauschenbusch, it left him. It is probably an exaggeration to say that he was killed by World War I, but it is close to the truth. His close family ties and his admiration for all things German prevented him from celebrating the war *against* Germany. It was not war itself that so disturbed him, but the war against Germany. Rauschenbusch is sometimes described as a pacifist, but his position was certainly not that clear.

In *The Righteousness of the Kingdom* Rauschenbusch argues that one of the defining characteristics of Jesus was his refusal to use force to establish the kingdom. Jesus chose truth, not the sword, since it is truth that makes us free. Rauschenbusch used his considerable rhetorical power to make the point:

It is true that, like Christ, we wield no sword but the truth. But mark well, that truth was a sword in his hands and not a yard-stick. It cut into the very marrow of his generation. It was mighty to the casting down of strongholds. So it has proved itself wherever it has been used in dead earnest. It reveals lies and their true nature, as when Satan was touched by the spear of Ithuriel. It makes injustice quail on its throne, chafe, sneer, abuse, hurl its spear, tender its goal, and finally offer to serve as truth's vassal. But the truth that can do such things is not an old woman wrapped in the spangled robes of earthly authority, bedizened with golden ornaments, the marks of honor given by injustice in return for services rendered, and muttering dead formulas of the past. The truth that can serve God as the mightiest of his archangels is robed only in love, her weighty limits unfettered by needless weight, calm-browed, her eyes terrible with beholding God.[67]

Rauschenbusch, moreover, insisted that whenever Christianity shows an inclination to use violence in its own defense it has become a thing of the world. "Coercion is in religion what rape is in love."[68] But such sentiments do not mean that Rauschenbusch was a pacifist. He was critical of the idealization of war that hides the "maggots of the battle-field," he thinks few wars have been fought for justice or the people,[69] but he never disavows war as an instrument of national policy.

In fact, Rauschenbusch could be quite militaristic. Though he later expressed regret for his enthusiastic support of the Spanish-American War,[70] he gave a Thanksgiving Day sermon in 1898 that is remarkable:

Again and again in the course of the War we have had the awed feeling that these events were not to be explained by human bravery and skill alone, but that an unseen hand was guiding and a higher will controlling. . . . There is in the heart of our people a deep sense of destiny, of a mission laid upon us by the Ruler of history. As a nation we feel the call of God just as truly as a young man chosen by God for a great work.

God thinks in acts. He speaks in events. He has made clear his will by the irrepressible force of events. We shall have to accept and obey. We may well view this new task with bated breath. If we rejoice at all in our new imperial domain, we rejoice with fear and trembling. But it is not of our seeking. We did not enter this war with the intention of annexing Puerto Rico and the Philippines. We did not even want Hawaii that begged to come in. And yet by a higher guidance than our own we now stand charged with duties the scope of which we hardly surmise. . . . The American people has but one superior. It is for us to obey. We may look back regretfully at the long period of history during which we lived in the safe isolation of our ocean walls, enjoying the undisputed supremacy of the Western hemisphere, busy in conquering our domain and building up a great nation. God calls us forward. The growth of our youth at home is elided. The life-work of manhood lies before us. The pillar of fire has lifted and moved. We must break camp and follow.[71]

What is important about this sermon is not that Rauschenbusch gave too enthusiastic support to the war but that the structure of the argument expresses one of his most fundamental theological convictions—God is using American Christianity to move all the world to a higher stage. For example, in *Christianizing the Social Order* he observes that at one time the demand for men and money to support foreign missions was based on the assumption that heathen souls were dying without the saving knowledge of Christ. But with the development of social conceptions of Christianity,

> today the leaders of the missionary movement are teaching a statesmanlike conception of the destiny of Christianity as the spiritual leaven of the East and the common basis of a world-wide Christian civilization. On the foreign field the Christian Church is not yet a conservative force, but a power of moral conquest. There it really embodies the finest spiritual purposes of the Christian nations in the effort to uplift the entire life of the backward people. There is no doubt that the influence of the English and American Protestant missions was one of the chief forces at work in the Turkish and Chinese revolutions.[72]

When the war in Europe began Rauschenbusch was devastated. He wrote letters to Baptist periodicals urging that financial support be sent to Baptists on both sides.[73] He wrote articles trying to help Americans appreciate Germany's point of view. This resulted in a withdrawal by Canadian Methodists of an invitation to speak at several of their conferences in 1914. He also lost support and allies in Rochester and in the seminary. In 1915 he opposed the beginning in America of "preparedness"; this only increased his isolation. He was confronted by a public letter from Algernon Crapsey, an Episcopal clergyman and his former ally, demanding that he answer questions to clarify his views on the war. Rauschenbusch poignantly ended his reply confessing, "I am glad I shall not live forever, I still trust that good will be the final goal of ill, and that the wisdom of the Eternal does not end where my little understanding ravels out. I can see only a step ahead, and that little step consists in keeping our nation within the area of peace."[74]

Rauschenbusch endured from 1914 to 1917, but his health deteriorated. With the American entry into the war he was pressured to make his views known. He finally agreed to issue a public statement in the form of a letter to Cornelius Woelfin, a former colleague at the seminary. He was gravely ill and was helped by Paul Strayer in drafting the letter. He begins by noting that he was born an American citizen and had never dreamed of being anything else. He confesses his great love for Germany, though the American ideals of democracy have dominated his intellectual life; accordingly, he opposes the antidemocratic forces in Germany and their desire for war. It would be a disaster for there to be a German triumph, though he is not convinced that a victory by the Allies will free the world of imperialism. He ends the letter noting that his son Hilmar has volunteered for ambulance service in France.[75]

Three months later he was dead. He had been diagnosed as having pernicious anemia but in June 1918 had surgery to have a tumor removed from his large intestine. The tumor was malignant. He died on July 22.

During his illness he wrote a number of moving pieces, some of which were poetic in form. One reads:

> In the castle of my soul
> In a little postern gate,
> Whereat when I enter,
> I am in the presence of God.
> In a moment, in the turning of a thought,
> I am where God is. . . .
> The world of men is made of jangling noises.
> With God is a great silence.
> But that silence is a melody,
> Sweet as the contentment of love,
> Thrilling as a touch of flame.[76]

In his dying he reminds us of his deafness, but the silence that surrounded him did not silence him. In fact, in his last years he wrote what many consider his finest book, A Theology for the Social Gospel. The book comprised the Taylor Lectures delivered at Yale in 1917. In the first chapter Rauschenbusch observes that the Great War had dwarfed the agenda of the social gospel. Yet he denies that the social gospel was lost; it was simply being redirected. Prior to the war the social gospel dealt with issues of the social classes, but now it was being translated into international terms. For the cause of the war was the same lust for unearned gain that created the social evils under which every nation suffers. "The social problem and the war problem are fundamentally one problem, and the social gospel faces both. After the War the social gospel will 'come back' with pent-up energy and clearer knowledge."[77]

It did not come back, but Rauschenbusch was not wrong that the agenda would shift to the international arena. The name that would embody that shift is Reinhold Niebuhr.

WALTER RAUSCHENBUSCH THE THEOLOGIAN

For Rauschenbusch theology was history. Accordingly, Christianity and the Social Crisis and Christianizing the Social Order might be characterized as historical commentaries. The only exception is Theology for the Social Gospel, where he explicitly endeavors to present a "systematic theology" to support the social gospel.[78] Christianity and the Social Crisis therefore begins with a chapter on "The Historical Roots of Christianity." By "historical roots" Rauschenbusch means the Old Testament, and in particular the prophets, "because they are the beating heart of the Old Testament. Modern study has shown that they were the real makers of the unique religious life of Israel. If all that proceeded from them, directly or indirectly, were eliminated from the Old Testament, there would be little left to appeal to the moral and religious judgment of the modern world."[79]

The study of the prophets therefore is not just of "historical interest" but indispensable for any "true comprehension of the mind of Jesus Christ." In Jesus the prophetic spirit rose from the dead. Like the prophets, Jesus was indifferent to the "ceremonial aspects of Jewish religion," focusing instead on social transformation.[80] The prophets, according to Rauschenbusch, challenged the assumption that "the traditional ceremonial" was what God wanted of Israel. As long as people thought such worship is what God wants, they would be indifferent to the reformation of social ethics. Amos and Jeremiah denied that God had commanded sacrifices when God constituted the nation after the exodus. Obedience, not sacrifice, is what God requires. The prophets are thus the heralds of the "fundamental truth that religion and ethics are inseparable, and that ethical conduct is the supreme and sufficient religious act."[81]

The prophets, of course, drew on Israel's early experience as an "organic people." They were not religious individualists but spoke of Israel as a virgin, a city, a vine, in order to express the corporate character of the nation. "In this respect they anticipated a modern conception which now underlies our scientific comprehension of social development and on which modern historical studies are based."[82] The prophets, moreover, were on the side of the poorer classes, condemning the land hunger of the landed aristocracy and the venality of the judges who took their bribes. This dominant trait in their moral feeling shaped their theology, so that it "became one of the fundamental attributes of their God that he was the husband to the widow, the father of the orphan, and the protector of the stranger."[83]

There were, of course, good historical causes for the prophets' condemnation of riches. Israel had begun as an agricultural people, and its development toward civilization was rooted in "ideas that long protected primitive democracy and equality."[84] In fact, the absence of social caste and fair distribution of the means of production in early Israel were much like the early times in America. "America too set out with an absence of hereditary aristocracy and with a fair distribution of the land among the farming population. Both the Jewish and the American people were thereby equipped with a kind of ingrained, constitutional taste for democracy which dies hard. In time Israel drifted away from this primitive fairness and simplicity, just as we are drifting away from it. A new civilization arose, based on commerce and mobile wealth."[85] The championship of the poor by the prophets was not, therefore, due to a new set of ideas, but rather was the result of their unwillingness to let go of the nobler expressions of the community from former times.

Rauschenbusch unrelentingly ties the prophets' social witness to their re gious commitments. They are the great representatives of "ethical monothe ism," which is Israel's invaluable contribution to the religious life of human ity. He quotes George Adam Smith's characterization of prophetic religion: "Confine religion to the personal, it grows rancid, morbid. Wed it to patri otism, it lives in the open air, and its blood is pure." Rauschenbusch thinks Smith's generalization about purely private religion may not be entirely just, but he thinks Smith is right to remind us that the entire religion out of which Christianity grew took shape through a divine inspiration that found its high est organ in a series of political and social preachers.[86]

Jesus incarnated the spirit as well as the social teachings of the prophets, but he was more than a teacher of morality. Even if all our economic wants are met, a person may still be haunted by a sense that life is meaningless. Beyond the question of economic distribution, beyond moral questions, lies the question of religious communion with the spiritual reality in which we live and move—"with God, the Father of our spirits. Jesus had realized the life of God in the soul of man and the life of man in the love of God. That was the real secret of his life, the well-spring of his purity, his com passion, his unwearied courage, his unquenchable idealism: he knew the Father."[87]

The center of Jesus' message for Rauschenbusch was, of course, the king dom of God. Jesus placed his own distinctive stamp on the hope of the king dom that the prophets had prepared. In particular, he repudiated the use of force for the kingdom's realization; he universalized the kingdom, see ing it as a human ideal not limited to a select group of Jews; he freed the kingdom from the monarchical expression of the past by democratizing the law of service; he set the kingdom in the secular and moral domain rather than limiting it to the ceremonial and ecclesiastical; and, perhaps most important of all, he rejected the apocalyptic accounts of the kingdom in favor of the "law of gradual growth."[88]

Jesus' teaching was important, and it was Jesus' teaching that Rauschen busch emphasized in *Christianity and the Social Crisis*, but what is important is not the teachings in the abstract but their embodiment in Jesus. Rauschenbusch had little interest in the "theological dogmas of the later church" that assert the "highest things concerning the person of Christ."[89] He acknowledges that certain qualities in the social gospel may create an apathy toward such speculative questions. Such speculation draws on the atomistic desert of individualism and fails to give us the Christ who is truly personal.[90]

What makes Jesus more than the prophets is his personality. In him the kingdom of God got its first foothold, making him the initiator of the king dom. "This great personality, Jesus Christ, has entered humanity as a force. He threw himself with all his strength into the history of our race. And we assert that he is now a revolutionary force, changing individuals and revolutionizing nations. We assert that the personality of Christ has in a few nations overcome the inertia and retrogression everywhere else visible and has started them upon that series of revolutionary eras by which they are hewing their way toward the perfect society."[91] This "Word made flesh" is the necessary ingredient for Christianity to be a universal religion capable of serving all nations, times, and grades of spiritual development.

The ethical monotheism Jesus inherited from the prophets was transformed by his new experience of God into something far lovelier and kinder. Jehovah, the covenanting and judging God, became for Jesus the Father in heaven who forgives sins, welcomes the prodigal, whose sun shines on the just and unjust, who asks for nothing but love, trust, and cooperative obedience. Jesus needed an "overpowering consciousness of God" to accomplish the centers of spiritual strength necessary to sweep evil from our social life. Such a center is constituted by love, thus becoming the highest idealistic faith ever conceived and the greatest addition ever made to "the spiritual possession of mankind."[92] Rauschenbusch's "Christology" obviously reflects developments in Protestant liberal theology in the nineteenth century. He seldom mentions the Trinity, and if he does it is usually dismissively. God is the "father," but not as the first person of the Trinity. Rather, when Jesus "took God by the hand and called him 'our father,' he democratized the conception of God."[93] Jesus disconnected the idea of God from monarchical conceptions and transferred it to family life, which is the chief embodiment of solidarity and love. Accordingly Jesus "not only saved humanity; he saved God."[94]

Rauschenbusch does treat the "spirit of God," but that spirit is never identified with the third person of the Trinity. In *The Righteousness of the Kingdom* the spirit is characterized as a revolutionary force that frees "the enslavement of our ethical and spiritual nature under the cravings of our animal nature."[95] According to Rauschenbusch, we all feel the moral demands within us are higher and ought to rule, but we know too often we are overpowered "by brutal instincts" and do not do what we should. Such a servitude is broken by the revolutionary power that comes from God's indwelling spirit.[96] The spirit also acts as a revolutionary force emancipating people from superstition as well as breaking the power of priestcraft.[97]

In A *Theology for the Social Gospel* he discusses revelation, inspiration, and prophecy in connection with the Holy Spirit. Modern conceptions of inspiration, he suggests, have rightly moved beyond the old mechanical and individualistic views of the tradition. We are now able to see the free operation and contributions of the psychical equipment of the inspired person, but even better we are now able to see the inspired persons in their social setting. This is particularly important for understanding the Scripture, as it has been "the great work of biblical criticism to place every biblical book in its exact historical environment as a preliminary to understanding its religious message."[98]

The social gospel therefore does not deny the need for inspiration but rather emphasizes the need of living prophetic spirits to lead humanity toward the kingdom. "The social order cannot be saved without regenerate men; neither can it be saved without inspired men."[99] Such men of spirit are the result of a sense of antagonism between the will of God and the present order of things. When such men arise they all tend toward the same kind of Christianity: "strong fraternal feeling, simplicity and democracy of organization, more or less communistic ideas about property, an attitude of passive obedience or conscientious objection toward coercive and militaristic governments of the time, opposition to the selfish and oppressive Church, a genuine faith in the practicability of the ethics of Jesus, and, as the secret power in it all, belief in an inner experience of regeneration and an inner light which interprets the outer word of God."[100]

I have presented Rauschenbusch's theology following the pattern first established in *The Righteousness of the Kingdom*, though that book was unknown by his contemporaries, and continued in *Christianity and the Social Crisis* and *Christianizing the Social Order*. The pattern exemplified in those books is clearly historical in form. As I have noted, in *A Theology for the Social Gospel* he tried to present a systematic theology "for" the social gospel. I am not suggesting that his presentation was in discontinuity with his earlier work, as is apparent from my use of that book in my account to this point, but rather it is important to note that it is not as if he had not been doing theology in his earlier work. What is new about *A Theology for the Social Gospel* is not that it is theology but that from Rauschenbusch's perspective it is "systematic."

He used the occasion of the Taylor Lectures at Yale, and the book that resulted from those lectures, to mount a defense of the theological assumptions of the social gospel. He claimed that the social gospel was not some radical new innovation in Christianity but rather was in continuity with Christianity at its best. As I noted above, Rauschenbusch responds to the oft-made criticism that the social gospel was "soft on sin" by pointing out that sin is selfishness and rebellion against God. Yet the social gospel insists on putting "humanity into the picture," since sin gets its reality only when humanity is seen as a great solidarity in which God dwells.[101]

Rauschenbusch's great gift was his ability to put "humanity into the picture." That project reflected his deepest conviction that the progress of religion is marked by a close union of religion and ethics and the elimination of the nonethical in religion. The union of religion and ethics had found its highest expression in the life and mind of Jesus, but after him Christianity had returned to a pre-Christian stage. Yet "it is clear that Christianity is most Christian when religion and ethics are viewed as inseparable elements of the same single-minded and whole-hearted life, in which the consciousness of God and the consciousness of humanity blend completely."[102]

Rauschenbusch set out, therefore, in A *Theology for the Social Gospel* to show that he could "out orthodox" the orthodox, be as conservative as the conservatives, on theological matters. Accordingly, he begins the book with an account of consciousness and the nature of sin. Though such a beginning was meant to show that he did not downplay the significance of sin, in fact he was simply following the path well trod by Protestant liberal theologians for whom sin was a surer reality than Trinity.[103] Moreover, it is not with sin that Rauschenbusch begins but with the consciousness of sin, which "is the basis of all doctrines about sin."[104] Sin matters for Rauschenbusch, but the sin that matters is anthropologically displayed.[105]

Like most liberal theologians, he wants to at once maintain that sin is an unavoidable reality, given the nature of the human condition, and yet insist that we can mistake what makes us sinful. It never occurred to him that the very descriptor *sin* depends on "doctrine" that is not grounded in "consciousness."[106] Yet he attacked the individualistic notions of sin created by "the old religious teaching," that is, the sense of sin associated more with personal holiness than with social wrong. With his characteristic gift for example, Rauschenbusch tells the story of a Mennonite dairyman who swore because his milk cans had been marked for containing cow dung. He was shunned because he had sworn an oath. According to Rauschenbusch, when his church has digested the social gospel they will treat the case this way:

> Our brother was angry and used the name of God profanely in his anger; we urge him to settle this alone with God. But he has also defiled the milk supply by unclean methods. Having the life and health of young children in his keeping, he has failed in his trust. Voted, that he be excluded until he has proved his lasting repentance.[107]

This example embodies Rauschenbusch's fundamental insistence that "sin is essentially selfishness,"[108] for the sinful mind is the unsocial and anti-social mind. A clear vision of the kingdom of God alone can make this clear. Our ability to see unrighteousness, in other words, depends on there being a "reign of organized righteousness."[109] Rauschenbusch begins with sin, but finally it is sin that can be known only because we first know the kingdom. In this Rauschenbusch represents, at least structurally, the orthodox Christian view that the order of redemption precedes the order of sin. Of course, the redemption that precedes sin is that determined by Protestant liberalism.

"Salvation is the voluntary socializing of the soul."[110] Complete salvation, which is not possible in this life, consists in an attitude of love in which one person's life is freely coordinated with another, creating a divine organism of mutual service. This is the kingdom of God, divine in its origin since it was initiated by Jesus Christ. Because Christ "revealed the divine worth of life and personality, and since his salvation seeks the restoration and fulfillment of even the least, it follows that the Kingdom of God, at every stage of human development, tends toward a social order which will best guarantee to all personalities their freest and highest expression. This involves the redemption of social life from the cramping influence of religious bigotry, from the repression of self-assertion in relation of upper and lower classes, and from all forms of slavery in which human beings are treated as a mere means to serve the ends of others."[111] Such is the reign of love that frees us from the use of force and legal coercion and makes possible the free surrender of life, property, and rights. Such a reign of love "tends toward the progressive unity of mankind, but with the maintenance of individual liberty and the opportunity of nations to work out their own national peculiarities and ideals."[112]

This kingdom, the kingdom of God, is a reality progressively growing through history. Opposing this kingdom is the kingdom of evil. Just as the kingdom of God is not made up of our individual willing, neither is the kingdom of evil. This is the substance of truth in the old doctrine of original sin. Sin is transmitted racially and through social customs, habits, and institutions.

> The popular superstitious beliefs in demonic agencies have largely been drained off by education. The conception of Satan has paled. At the same time belief in original sin is also waning. These two doctrines combined,— the hereditary racial unity of sin, and the supernatural power of evil behind all sinful human action,—created a solidaristic consciousness of sin and evil, which I think is necessary for the religious mind. Take away these two doctrines, and both our sense of sin and our need of redemption will become much more superficial and will be mainly concerned with the transient acts and vices of individuals.[113]

The power of sin and evil can be seen in their idealizations and our willingness to let them become "the way things are." We are ashamed of our ordinary sins, but when sin becomes the source of great wealth "it is no longer a shame-faced vagabond slinking through the dark, but an army with banners, entrenched and defiant."[114] Equally destructive is the acceptance of sin through custom, such as the acceptance of alcohol. "Intoxication, like profanity and tattooing, is one of the universal marks of barbarism."[115] Yet alcoholic drinking customs continue to prevail because they thrive on the authority of custom, even being praised in song and poetry. In short, the "super-personal forces" of evil can only be known as well as defeated by a force as powerful as the kingdom of God.

In the last chapter of A *Theology for the Social Gospel,* titled "The Social Gospel and the Atonement," Rauschenbusch draws on this understanding of the solidarity of the sin and the kingdom to develop a quite innovative account of the atonement. As would be expected, he rejects individualistic accounts of the atonement. To be sure our personal sins contribute to the existence of the public sins that killed Jesus, but to reduce such sins to the "personal" is to fail to understand Jesus' bearing of sins as well as his defeat of them. The forces that combined to kill Jesus were religious bigotry, graft and political power, corruption of justice, mob spirit and mob action, militarism, and class contempt.[116] These realistic forces killed Jesus, and the guilt of those who did it spreads to all who reaffirm the acts that killed him.

According to Rauschenbusch, "theology has made a fundamental mistake in treating the atonement as something distinct, and making the life of Jesus a mere staging for his death, a matter almost negligible in the work of salvation."[117] Jesus' death was of one piece with his life, his death being his dying to those forces that he opposed with his life. In his life and death therefore he revealed the power of sin in human life, but he equally revealed the power of love. "His death effectively made God a God of love to the simplest soul, and that has transformed the meaning of the universe and the whole outlook of the race."[118] The atonement is thus the symbol and basis of a new social order based on love and solidarity.

The kingdom of God, not the church, is clearly at the center of Rauschenbusch's theology. The church is usually treated more as a problem requiring transformation than as a resource for social transformation. Nonetheless, Rauschenbusch maintains that the "Church is the social factor in salvation. It brings social forces to bear on evil. It offers Christ not only many human bodies and minds to serve as ministers of his salvation, but its own composite personality, with a collective memory storied with great hymns and Bible stories and deeds of heroism, with trained aesthetic and moral feelings, and with a collective will set on righteousness."[119] The criticism of the church by people who stand for the social gospel is a form of compliment. In fact they may well turn out to be the best apologists for the church, as they are best suited to see the influence that the church can have on society.[120]

The saving power of the church, however, can never be identified with the institution of the church or with church order. Like the wider social order, what matters is that the church is the embodiment of the kingdom of God. The church becomes a problem only when it is thought to be the kingdom rather than a witness to the kingdom. The kingdom breeds prophets; the church breeds priests and theologians concerned with traditions and dogmas rather than the boundless horizons of the kingdom.[121] So Rauschenbusch ends where he began—with the kingdom of God that knows no bounds.

94

WALTER RAUSCHENBUSCH'S "ETHICS"

There is no clear line in Rauschenbusch between his theology and his ethics. His whole task was to deny the separation of theology and ethics.[122] Yet the question remains: from where does Rauschenbusch draw the content of the kingdom of God? I suspect he would find the question puzzling, since he assumed that the answer is obvious—the kingdom is present in every social order that guarantees each personality their freest and highest development.[123] Moreover, that content is drawn from the teaching and consciousness of Jesus.

Harlan Beckley confesses that his major discovery in doing the research for his *Passion for Justice*

> was a historical Rauschenbusch far different from the rather superficial optimist whom I thought I had read and heard about. Rauschenbusch was not, in my judgment, a liberal Protestant who thought the difficult problems of justice could be solved by applying a sentimental version of Jesus' love to social institutions in order to bring about the kingdom of God. His sociologically informed interpretation of Jesus and the kingdom of God led him to appreciate natural limits on the capacities of human agents, limits that Niebuhr's ideal of love defies. His conception of justice is inferred, in part, from a divine ordering of nature and social relations that Niebuhr's understanding of God rejects. As I began this project, I did not imagine finding similarities between Rauschenbusch's view of justice based on the kingdom of God and Ryan's understanding of justice based on Catholic natural law theory. As my analysis progressed, I found that Rauschenbusch and Ryan both emphasized that justice requires an equal opportunity for persons to develop their natural interest toward realized excellences of personality.[124]

Beckley rightly challenges the characterization of Rauschenbusch as an "optimist,"[125] but I am not convinced he is right to suggest that justice is the "foundation for the Kingdom of God" in Rauschenbusch. Rauschenbusch seldom uses the language of justice, and he certainly never provides any substantive account of justice. He does have one chapter on justice in *Christianizing the Social Order*, in which he briefly discusses the importance of the law being justly administered and why unjust privilege must be destroyed if the social order is to be Christianized, but it seems never to occur to him to make justice the overriding concept for Christian ethics.[126] Beckley notes that Rauschenbusch never proposed any universal principles of justice; rather his emphasis on the importance of, as well as his understanding of, the content of justice was grounded in his analysis of socio-historical circumstances.[127] That is certainly the case, but I think what must be said further is that justice does not play a central role in Rauschenbusch's work. This may appear a scholarly quibble, but it is important if we are to understand the significance of Reinhold Niebuhr. *Justice* becomes the overriding term for Niebuhr, and for many who follow Niebuhr, exactly because they no longer share Rauschenbusch's account of Jesus. Put simply, and in a manner that is simplifying, once you no longer have Jesus all you are left with is the dialectic between love and justice. For Beckley to narrate Rauschenbusch's ethics as an ethic of justice is, even given his criticism of Niebuhr, to make Rauschenbusch a creature of Niebuhr.

If there is any one concept that suggests the nature of the ethics of the kingdom, it is democracy. Rauschenbusch was as enthusiastic about democracy as he was unclear about its nature. Democracy for Rauschenbusch was not a political system external to Christianity but rather the very nature of the gospel. As I noted above, Rauschenbusch thought Jesus had "saved God" by teaching us that God is a "democratic father," but *democracy* also names a movement in history.[128]

Of course democracy cannot be limited to a changed conception of God, but rather *democracy* is a reality in history. "Where religion and intellect combine, the foundation is laid for political democracy."[129] That is the difference between "saved and unsaved organizations"—the one is democratic and the other is autocratic.[130] The state, at least a democratic state, can be saved from the use of coercion to crush offenders by dealing with those who have erred by way of teaching, discipline, and restoration. The politics of America, Rauschenbusch thought, had been saved. The challenge before the church is to secure for the economic realm the same kind of cooperative life that had been achieved in American politics.[131]

Yet I think it would be a mistake to make too much of Rauschenbusch's concentration on democracy as *the* defining characteristic of his ethics. To be sure, democracy stood for his general commitment to a fraternal and cooperative social order that would ensure the flourishing of each individual, but he never attempted to define or justify in a more detailed manner what he meant by "democracy." He did not do so because he simply assumed it was obvious to anyone what democracy is and why it is preferable to any other form of social organization.

Rauschenbusch's ethics were essentially theologically and morally informed journalism. He narrated the social realities of his day by redescribing them Christianly. That was his great genius and why it is so hard to characterize his "ethics" using any one concept or set of formal characteristics. In an interesting way Reinhold Niebuhr worked much in the same fashion, even though Niebuhr appears to be clearer about the nature of "ethics" in distinction from theology. Yet the assumed deep differences between Rauschenbusch and Niebuhr appear less "deep" once their common mode of narration of social questions is recognized.

Christianizing the Social Order is probably the most concentrated example of Rauschenbusch's journalistic mode of ethical commentary. For example, in part 3 of that book Rauschenbusch describes "our semi-Christian social order." In his characteristic fashion he describes "Christianized" aspects of our social order—the family, church, education, and politics to the extent the latter has been democratized.[132] He then begins an extraordinary account of business, since it is the seat of so much of our current problems.

According to Rauschenbusch, nothing calls for more discussion than the unsatisfactory relation between economic life and the "higher laws of humanity."

> This book is part of this collective effort to understand. I propose throughout to think from the point of view of a Christian man. The tests that I shall apply are not technical but normal. Does our business system create sound and noble manhood? Does it make it fairly easy to do right and hard to do wrong? Does it call men upward or tempt them downward? Does it reward or penalize fraternal action? Does it furnish the material basis for the Reign of God on earth? As a Christian man I shall have to judge more patiently and forbearingly than if I were inquiring why high prices are making it hard for me to feed my family and rear my children. I shall also have to probe more incisively and condemn more sweepingly than if I were arguing as a lawyer or an economist.[133]

This is an admirable account of the way Rauschenbusch proceeds to display the problems with modern business. For he is as much concerned with what the "system" does to the businessman as he is with the effects on those who are not in power. He begins by drawing on his own experience working on farms prior to their transformation by machinery, as well as working in a tailor's shop prior to mass merchandising. He clearly prefers those ways of economic life, but he does not romanticize them. He recognizes that the development of modern enlarged and diversified economic orders is not an evil but a good.

Though Rauschenbusch was a "socialist," he did not think capitalism was an unmitigated evil. He recognized that capitalism was the most efficient system for the creation of wealth that had yet appeared. Moreover, the technical efficiency of capitalism indicates that as a system it has powerful moral forces within it.[134] Capitalism was revolutionary in its youth, as it was the cry of freedom against feudal privilege, but unfortunately now when capitalists cry for freedom it is an attempt to defeat some movement for real liberty and a defense of mammon.[135]

The moral problem with the modern economic world is not its size and complexity but that the immense powers of production have put ownership into the hands of a few. This group is always changing, but as a group it is permanent. Such an uneven apportionment of power cannot help but lead to injustice and frustrate "the Christian conception of human fellowship."[136] Such a system puts workers and owners at odds, since the interests of the workers revolve around their jobs and the interests of the owners revolve around their profits. As a result, both are condemned to the "law of tooth and nail," unable to embody their instincts for cooperation. "Every man is taught to seek his own advantage, and then we wonder that there is so little public spirit."[137]

Our economic life cannot help but be a reign of fear that makes children lie and adults cheat. Competition can be quite good, as it gives life zest, but in a world of fear it becomes a "leaden weight" as businessmen become paralyzed before a vanishing profit margin they are helpless to control. Moreover, the competitors in the game of business do not all start with vast accumulations of capital. As a result, the "game of competition," which some forget is more than a game, becomes murderous.[138]

Just as capitalism perverts competition as an important part of our lives, so it also corrupts the significance of leadership in human society. We cannot live without good leadership, but leadership can become tyrannical and despotic. This is particularly the case with capitalism, since all the power is on the capitalist side, enabling the control of consumer and worker alike. Such disequilibrium of power is nothing less than an invitation to sin, since the economic man capitalism creates cannot help but become "a covetous machine."[139] If we are to be a free society, such power inequities must be alleviated by a movement toward industrial democracy.

Rauschenbusch's narrative is not a demonization of the businessman in favor of labor. Indeed he is quite sympathetic to business as a "network of fiduciary relations."[140] The problem is that business owners are under the law of profit. They would prefer to sell good and wholesome things, but the law of competition forces them to sell "flashy goods at a heavy profit."[141] Rauschenbusch notes, for example, that in the Middle Ages the poisoning of rich men was one way to become wealthy, but now rich men, through the liquor trade, poison the poor because it pays. Capitalism depended on the self-restraint grounded in its origin in Calvinism, but now capitalism is destroying that which gave it birth.[142] Nothing indicates this development better than the lying and dishonesty that are now accepted as integral to business practice. Lost is any account of honor capable of sustaining the self-sacrifice involved in our necessary service to one another.[143]

I am not trying to make Rauschenbusch an early proponent of "narrative ethics," particularly since I do not think any such ethic exists or should exist. Rather, I am suggesting that in a quite remarkable manner Rauschenbusch was able to provide a Christian reading of his world. It was an extraordinary achievement that dwarfs the easy criticisms of Rauschenbusch as naive and unrealistic. That he insisted that the political, social, and economic world was open to moral construal was remarkable enough given the reigning presupposition at the time, but how he did that is no less important.

Moreover, that "how," as I have already suggested, was imitated not only by Reinhold Niebuhr but by many who, under Niebuhr's influence, thought they had left Rauschenbusch far behind.[144] Thinking of Christian ethics as a form of journalism may well embarrass some who seek a more "academic" stance, but I suspect that any serious ethics requires the kind of readings in which Rauschenbusch excelled. Ethics could never become "applied" for Rauschenbusch (or Niebuhr), because the very way they understood their task meant that they were engaged in a project of social transformation or challenge at the beginning of their work, not as "implications" to come later.

That Rauschenbusch's ethics worked in this manner also indicates the "churchly" nature of his work. Nothing he did could make sense if he had not been presupposing, even in his criticism of the church, the indispensability of the church as a community necessary to sustain the story he was telling about social life. That such was the case is important for understanding later developments that try to make "Christian ethics" intelligible without the presupposition of the church. That Rauschenbusch's account of the church and Christianity is thin, or at least liberal, is less important than that it was unavoidable if his ethics and theology were to make any sense.

WALTER RAUSCHENBUSCH AND THE SOCIAL-GOSPEL MOVEMENT

We can now see that Rauschenbusch was the climax of the social-gospel movement. He had not intended that to be the case. Though he was in fact at the end, he assumed that he was at the beginning.[145] The vibrancy and energy that surrounded the social gospel and Rauschenbusch are part of the story, however, that cannot be overlooked. Reinhold Niebuhr inspired few to write hymns, but you could and can still sing the social gospel.[146] For example, *The Book of Hymns* of the United Methodist Church contained this hymn until 1989:

> 1. God send us men whose aim 'twill be
> Not to defend some ancient creed,
> But to live out the laws of Christ
> In every thought and word and deed.

> 2. God send us men alert and quick
> His lofty precepts to translate,
> Until the laws of Christ become
> The habits of the state.

3. God send us men of steadfast will,
   Patient, courageous, strong and true,
   With vision clear and mind equipped
   His will to learn, his work to do.

4. God send us men with hearts ablaze,
   All truth to love, all wrong to hate;
   These are the patriots nations need;
   These are the bulwarks of the state.
   Amen.[147]

Such hymns exhibit the social gospel's unique ability to combine social vision and Protestant piety. That combination is what made the social gospel a movement rather than just another "academic position." No book better exemplifies these elements than Charles Sheldon's *In His Steps*. *In His Steps* was published in 1898; by 1933 Sheldon estimated that twenty-three million copies had been published in English, and the book had been translated into twenty-one foreign languages.[148] It tells the story of the transformation of the First Church of "Raymond," occasioned by the testimony of a young man who died after telling his story of social woe. He had ended his appeal before the congregation with the question "What would Jesus do?"

This question galvanized the minister and church in a manner that led to a transformation of many lives. A singer refused an offer to go on tour and instead dedicated her life to rescue-mission work; the editor of a newspaper resolved to make his paper a "Christian daily" that would reject sensational features and less than worthy advertising; a railroad superintendent resigned his position after he discovered his company was engaged in illicit behavior; the college president ran for mayor on a Prohibitionist platform but lost due to the power of the liquor interests; a merchant set his business on a new footing of "intelligent unselfishness" by providing for profit sharing. Although much of this activity led to losses, there were also "positive" stories. For example, an heiress and her brother were converted and discovered that they could use their wealth to aid these social transformations as well as invest their now-consecrated wealth in rebuilding the tenement district of the town. The effects resulting from the question "What would Jesus do?" became widely known and "spread to other churches with the result that a national revival of social religion seemed imminent."[149]

In his *Christianizing the Social Order* Rauschenbusch paid tribute to Sheldon for reviving, like St. Francis, the thought of following Jesus in daily conduct. Sheldon, according to Rauschenbusch, set forth this ideal with a winning spirit that has influenced thousands of young people. The only problem was that this is so high a law that only the most consecrated individuals can follow it permanently. "To most men the demand to live as Jesus would, is mainly useful to bring home the fact that it is hard to live a Christ-like life in a mammonistic society. It convicts our social order of sin, but it does not reconstruct it."[150]

Rauschenbusch, no less than Sheldon, aspired to write in a manner that would be of use to thousands of people. In 1909, at the urging of Pilgrim Press, he published *For God and the People: Prayers of the Social Awakening*. The book was extraordinarily successful, going through many printings. Precisely because these prayers gave voice to many, Sheldon and his family used Rauschenbusch's prayers in their home morning and evening.[151] Rauschenbusch began the book with an exposition of the "social meaning" of the Lord's Prayer, reminding his readers that the first three petitions of the prayer express Jesus' faith in the possibility of the reign of God on earth and our solidarity with one another. Thus as we ask together for our daily bread, facing common needs, we "ought to feel the sin and shame of it if we habitually take more than our fair share and leave others hungry that we may surfeit. It is inhuman, irreligious, and indecent."[152]

There are fifty-eight prayers in *Prayers of the Social Awakening*, ranging from morning and evening prayers to prayers for children who work, for all true lovers, for Big Sister Clubs; prayers of wrath against war, alcoholism, servants of mammon; prayers against impurity; and, finally, prayers for the progress of humanity. A representative prayer of the latter category is titled "For the Cooperative Commonwealth":

O God, we praise thee for the dream of the golden city of peace and right-eousness which has ever haunted the prophets of humanity, and we rejoice with joy unspeakable that at last the people have conquered the freedom and knowledge and power which may avail to turn into reality the vision that so long has beckoned in vain.

Speed now the day when the plains and the hills and the wealth thereof shall be the people's own, and thy freemen shall not live as tenants of men on the earth which thou hast given to all; when no babe shall be born without its equal birthright in the riches and knowledge wrought out by the labor of the ages; and when the mighty engines of industry shall throb with a gladdened music because the men who ply these great tools shall be their owners and masters.

O God, save us, for our nation is at strife with its own soul and is sinning against the light which thou aforetime has kindled in it. Thou hast called our people to freedom, but we are withholding from men their share in the common heritage without which freedom becomes a hollow name. Thy Christ has kindled in us the passion for brotherhood, but the social life we have built, denies and slays brotherhood.

We pray thee to revive in us the hardy spirit of our forefathers that we may
establish and complete their work, building on the basis of their democracy
the firm edifice of a cooperative commonwealth, in which both government
and industry shall be of the people, by the people, and for the people. May
we, who now live, see the oncoming of the great day of God, when all men
shall stand side by side in equal worth and real freedom, all toiling and all
reaping masters of nature but brothers of men, exultant in the tide of the
common life, and jubilant in the adoration of Thee, the source of their bless-
ings and the Father of all.[153]

This prayer contains most of Rauschenbusch's characteristic themes—
joint ownership of land and industry, freedom from domination, the inequity
of want amid plenty, the importance of democracy as a cooperative commonwealth, the progressive overcoming of sin—yet those themes are given
new power through prayer. Rauschenbusch assumed that the structure and
style of prayer common to Protestant pietism but gave that form an unex-
pected content. That he did so was not a strategy but a natural expression
of his deepest religious habits. That he was not calculating in his prayers is
why they were so effective. For it is impossible to miss the genuine piety
that shapes them and the sincerity with which they are written.

They are, moreover, characterized by a candor and directness often missing from prayers. Nothing is covered over, as if we could hide sin from God.
The "everyday" is lifted up as part of our life with God, giving it new significance. For example, in a prayer "For Consumers," Rauschenbusch
reminds us of our interdependence on one another and how that same interdependence can be used for injustice:

O God, thou Father of us all, we praise thee that thou has bound humanity
in a great unity of life so that each must lean on the strength of all, and
depend for his comfort and safety on the help and labor of his brothers.

We invoke thy blessing on all the men and women who toiled to build and
warm our homes, to fashion our raiment, and to wrest from sea and land the
food that nourishes us and our children.

Grant us wisdom to deal justly and fraternally with every man and woman
whom we face in the business of life.

May we not unknowingly inflict suffering through selfish indifference or the
wilful ignorance of a callous heart.

Since the comforts of our life are brought to us from afar, and made by those
whom we do not know nor see, grant us organized intelligence and power
that we may send the command of our righteous will along the channels of
trade and industry, and help to cleanse them of hardness and unfairness.

May the time come when we need wear and use nothing that is wet in thy sight with human tears, or cheapened by wearing down the lives of the weak.

Speak to our souls and bid us strive for the coming of thy kingdom of justice when thy merciful and saving will shall be done on earth.[154]

Rauschenbusch's prayers, like his "ethics," created through their very form the community he sought. They could be prayed alone, but their very form prevented the one praying from being alone. Rather, they implicated the one praying in a network of relations that required at once a confession of sin and a hope for the transformation of those relations. To be sure, Rauschenbusch's prayers could often be sentimental and romantic, such as his "For All Mothers" and "For All True Lovers," but that he was not afraid of being sentimental was his power.[155] Through his prayers Rauschenbusch shaped emotions and judgments by teaching people how to speak a new language. Such prayers were no doubt his most powerful ethical tool. "I shall always regard it as one of the best gifts of God to me," he said, "that he led my mind to these prayers."[156]

Nowhere is Rauschenbusch's passion to shape his reader clearer than in his book *The Social Principles of Jesus*. That volume was written as part of a series of books designed for college students. Indeed, we are told on the front page of *The Social Principles* that the book was "written under the direction of sub-committee on College Courses, Sunday School Council of Evangelical Denominations and Committee on Voluntary Study Council of North American Student Movements." *The Social Principles* was designed to be read during the students' fourth year. The course of study was voluntary but serious, requiring daily Bible readings as well as group discussions directed by questions in the text.

Rauschenbusch divided his book into four main sections: (1) the axiomatic social convictions of Jesus, (2) the social ideal of Jesus, (3) recalcitrant social forces, and (4) conquest by conflict. Each of the four sections is divided into three parts, consisting of a Bible reading for every day of the week, a small essay to direct the student's study, and finally a set of suggestions and questions for thought and discussion. Rauschenbusch's *Social Principles* is a textbook designed to change those using it.

Rauschenbusch's book begins with a chapter on the value of life, asking how Jesus viewed the life and personality of the people around him. The student is then asked to read Mark 10:13–16, which recounts the story of Jesus summoning the little children to come to him and concluding with Jesus' proclamation that one can enter the kingdom only as a little child. According to Rauschenbusch, in a child we see humanity reduced to its simplest terms, which explains why Jesus was indignant with his disciples who seemingly thought of children as not important enough to command his attention. The reading ends with the following questions: "Can the moral standing of a community be fairly judged by the statistics of child labor and infant mortality? What prompts some young men to tyrannize over their younger brothers? How does this passage and the principle of the sacredness of life bear on the problem of eugenics?"[157] A similar pattern is followed over the readings for the next six days.

Rauschenbusch tried to make each passage particularly relevant to the college situation. For example, on the third day he uses Matthew 5:21–22, in which Jesus suggests that anyone who is angry, and thus in danger of judgment, should ask, "How is the self-respect and sense of personal worth of men built up or broken down in college communities?"[158] On the fourth day, employing Luke 15:1–10, in which God rejoices in one sinner who repents, Rauschenbusch challenges his readers by asking what social groups in college towns are spoken of with contempt by college men and why they do so. The questions are clearly meant to be exercises to challenge the "natural habits" of college life.

In the short essay for study that follows Rauschenbusch observes that from these passages we cannot doubt that Jesus had a spontaneous love for his fellow people that grew from his sense of the sacredness of each human personality. "This regard for human life was based on the same social instinct which every normal man possesses. But with Jesus it was so strong that it determined all his viewpoints and activities. He affirmed the humane instinct consciously and intelligently; and raised it to the dignity of a social principle. This alone would be enough to mark him out as a new type, prophetic and creative of a new development of the race."[159]

He acknowledges that too often we lose the power of the social instinct through class differences, war, and prostitution.[160] Moreover, the study of science can chill the warm sense of human values because of the enormous waste of life that seems exemplified by the impassiveness of nature. The detached attitude of science can combine with our natural egoism to create a cold indifference toward the less attractive masses of humanity. We need the "glow of Christ's feeling for men" if we are to avoid such intellectual temptations.[161]

Some will no doubt object that it is not in the interest of the future of the race that the weak should be coddled so that they can multiply and assume control of society. But Jesus did not want the weak to stay weak. He wanted for each person what he was himself—a powerful and free personality. Because Jesus was strong, he demanded for others the right to become free and strong. Rauschenbusch ends his short essay quoting Harnack, Kant, and Fichte in support of the necessity of treating each person as an end in themselves.

The first chapter includes a series of questions such as: "On what basis do we ordinarily value men?" "Which source passages in the daily readings seemed to put the feeling of Jesus in the clearest light?" "Is the tendency in modern life toward a lower or higher valuation of the individual? To what extent is this due to the influence of Christianity?" "What connection was there between the Wesleyan revival and the rise of the trade union movement in England?" "Describe the class lines drawn in your home town." "Does college life tend to make us callous or sympathetic?" "Have your scientific studies, and especially evolutionary teachings, increased your regard for humanity in the mass?"[162]

Rauschenbusch is clearly concerned to help his readers acquire a character benefiting the kingdom and the social gospel. In chapter 10, on "The Conflict with Evil," he notes that character is formed by action, but after it is formed it determines action. "What a man says and does, he becomes; and what he has become, he says and does. An honest and clean-minded man instinctively does what is kind and honorable. But when a man for years has gone for profit and selfish power, you can trust him as a general thing to do what is underhanded and mean."[163] *The Social Principles of Jesus* was Rauschenbusch's attempt to shape a new generation so that it might have a character sufficient for the social gospel. He sought not to clarify students' ethical choices; on the contrary, he wanted to change their lives.

Moreover, he had an institutional basis for that project. It is not by accident that the copyright for *The Social Principles of Jesus* was held by the International Committee of the Young Men's Christian Association. The YMCA and other broadly based Christian movements were the natural home for Rauschenbusch's message. The social gospel also created institutions that would "outlive" the social gospel, at least as expressed by Rauschenbusch. Not the least of these was the Federal Council of Churches, which we now know as the National Council of Churches.[164]

From its beginning in 1894, the Federal Council was committed "to bring the Christian bodies of America into united service for Christ and the world. To secure a larger combined influence for the Churches of Christ in all matters affecting the moral and social conditions of the people, so as to promote the application of the law of Christ in every relation of human life."[165] A Commission on the Church and Social Service was established by the Council and initiated close relations between social-workers groups as well as the American Federation of Labor.[166]

The influence of the social gospel on the Federal Council is most apparent in the adoption, in 1912, of the "Social Creed." There it was claimed that the churches must stand

1. For equal rights and complete justice for all men in all stations of life.
2. For the protection of the family, by the single standard of purity, uniform divorce laws, proper regulation of marriage, and proper housing.

3. For the fullest possible development for every child, especially by the provision of proper education and recreation.

4. For the abolition of child labor.

5. For such regulation of the conditions of toil for women as shall safeguard the physical and moral health of the community.

6. For the abatement and prevention of poverty.

7. For the protection of the individual and society from the social, economic, and moral waste of the liquor traffic.

8. For the conservation of health.

9. For the protection of the worker from dangerous machinery, occupational diseases, and mortality.

10. For the right of all men to the opportunity for self-maintenance, for the safeguarding this right against encroachments of every kind, and for the protection of workers from the hardships of enforced unemployment.

11. For suitable provision for the old age of the workers, and for those incapacitated by injury.

12. For the right of employees and employers alike to organize for adequate means of conciliation and arbitration in industrial disputes.

13. For a release from employment one day in seven.

14. For the gradual and reasonable reduction of the hours of labor to the lowest practicable point, and for the degree of leisure for all which is a condition of the highest human life.

15. For a living wage as a minimum in every industry, and for the highest wage that each industry can afford.

16. For a new emphasis upon the application of Christian principles to the acquisition and use of property, and for the most equitable division of the product of industry that can ultimately be devised.[167]

Such a "creed" appears unremarkable to us, but it was certainly not seen so when it was written. Each of the clauses challenged the presumption that the market was self-regulating or that owners had the right to do what they wanted with their property. The advocacy by the Federal Council of Churches of the social-gospel agenda certainly did not mean that the majority of Christians agreed or even more supported these aims, but at the very least it suggests that Rauschenbusch and his social-gospel colleagues had been able to define the challenges for the mainstream Protestant denominations. Of course they could hardly be satisfied with the transformation of the churches, since their object was the transformation of America.

Oddly enough, the very fact that the "Social Creed" no longer seems remarkable is an indication that Rauschenbusch and his social-gospel colleagues were successful in their desire to transform America. Of course many factors contributed to that transformation, but certainly Rauschenbusch and the movement he eloquently represented made a considerable contribution to the changes that were perhaps inevitable. Yet in the process, what had made them what they were, namely the church, became increasingly irrelevant for the project of changing America. Reinhold Niebuhr, also a product of a church culture not unlike that of Rauschenbusch, represents the development of Christian ethics that no longer needs to understand itself as a movement sponsored by the church.

I noted above that part of the difficulty in telling Rauschenbusch's story is that the narrative has been so strongly shaped by Reinhold Niebuhr's influence. I have tried to resist Niebuhr's account by providing a sympathetic presentation of Rauschenbusch as intelligible only because he was deeply rooted in the church and, in particular, the pastoral ministry. His evangelical mission to convert America, as well as his criticisms of the church, can give the impression that he only "used" the church. Yet only a man as embedded in Christianity and the church as Rauschenbusch could write a book like *Christianizing the Social Order*.[168]

The irony is that the very society—democratic—that Rauschenbusch desired made his account of Christianity and the church unintelligible. He assumed that there was a significant relation between Christian belief in the kingdom of God and his social vision. That assumption would become increasingly problematic.[169] Indeed, in some ways the rise of "ethics," understood as the project to state more explicitly the conceptual connections between "theology" and "behavior," was the attempt to remedy Rauschenbusch's failure to see that no one ethical position follows from Christianity. However, despite the fact that many "ethicists" see their task as clarifying and/or redefining the relations between ethics, theology, and social vision, they continue to yearn, like Rauschenbusch before them, to have a public impact. Only now they no longer speak of "Christianizing the social order" but of providing ethical analysis of "policy options."

Finally, Rauschenbusch's liberal theology begins to appear surprisingly conservative. After all, he still thought that Jesus mattered.[170] He assumed that being a Christian required a transformation and conversion. Such a conversion, moreover, involved practices like prayer and study of the Bible. Those who follow Rauschenbusch will often be as "personally religious" as he was, but such practice will not be as integral to their theology and ethics as it was for him. None of the figures that follow Rauschenbusch make sense without Rauschenbusch; but he would not have been able to make sense of them. That, of course, is the final irony of Rauschenbusch's life.

6

■NOT LATE ENOUGH

THE DIVIDED MIND OF DIGNITATIS HUMANAE PERSONAE

John Courtney Murray, in remarks that preface the text of *Dignitatis Humanae Personae* in *The Documents of Vatican II*,[1] observes that it can hardly be maintained that the declaration is a milestone in human history. He notes that the principle of religious freedom has long been recognized in constitutional law, to the point that even Marxists pay lip service to religious freedom. Murray concludes, "In all honesty it must be admitted that the Church is late in acknowledging the validity of the principle."[2] To which I can only respond, "Not late enough."

All life, as has been often observed, is timing. Sometimes you get lucky and sometimes you are not. The timing of *Dignitatis* was distinctively unlucky. Written at the height of modernist presumptions about "man," the document—under the influence of Murray—unfortunately betrays an anthropology that has come under increasing attack since the time of the council. The high humanism that informs the Declaration on Religious Freedom has unfortunately been exposed as a correlative of the atheism that goes hand in hand with modern political regimes. Indeed, the very progressivist presumptions that inform Murray's assessment of the development of liberal political regimes can now be better understood to betray a naive view of history.

In Murray's defense it can be observed that at the time he was working he seemed to represent the most progressive alternative. After all, he thought he was defending the integrity of the human person against the far too "pessimistic" view of Reinhold Niebuhr. Recent philosophical developments that decenter the human subject at least make clear that this side of the "postmodern divide" Murray and Niebuhr shared far more than they disagreed. Both sought to underwrite liberal versions of democracy on anthropological grounds that lacked appropriate theological warrant.

I do not want to tar *Dignitatis* with John Courtney Murray's brush. Murray's influence on the document is unmistakable, but Murray, so to speak, did not "win." By that I mean Murray was not able to make the declaration "his": he had to compromise with the French, who were arguing for a more determinative theological view.[3] The result, of course, is that the final draft of *Dignitatis* is incoherent, but I want to argue that such incoherence is a very good thing. Better a divided mind than the mind of John Courtney Murray.

The two chapters of the document nicely illustrate the divided mind of the declaration. The document begins with the "General Principle of Religious Freedom," to which is then added "The Light of Revelation"; but why we need "revelation" is never clear. The candid admission that begins the second chapter, that "revelation does not indeed affirm in so many words the right of man to immunity from external coercion in matters religious," is to say the least something of an understatement.[4] One almost hears in the background the neoscholastic mantra "Grace does not deny but fulfills nature," thus ensuring the need for the second chapter but with no good reason why it is needed.

Of course questions about the incoherence of the document cannot be restricted to the issue of the relation between the first and second chapters. The discussion of the general principle of religious freedom is shot through with tensions, if not outright contradictions. The chapter begins asserting that the human person has a right to religious freedom.[5] The grounds of such a "right," however, are quite ambiguous. We are told that the right to religious freedom lies not in the subjective disposition of the person but in the very nature of what it means to be a person, but the document seems to be of two minds about what constitutes "very nature."

The "two minds" result from the document's wanting to underwrite the modern understanding of rights based on the inherent dignity of the person being at the same time abstracted from a teleological understanding of our nature.[6] The declaration clearly seems to be committed to the latter view while accepting the results of the more liberal understanding of rights. Thus appeal to human participation in the divine law is made to supply the necessary background to justify the appeal to "rights." "Hence every man has the duty, and therefore the right, to seek the truth in matter religious, in order that he may with prudence form for himself right and true judgments of conscience, with the use of all suitable means."[7]

This strikes me as a good and right account of the priority of accounts of duty necessary to make sense of any appeal to rights. But such a view also entails the presumption that any strict appeal to rights qua rights, even the "right to religious freedom," at best can be only a qualified right. Put more strongly, the appeal to the "right to religious freedom" becomes more a matter of prudential judgments depending on contingencies of a social order than a hard and fast policy for which we should work irrespective of a society's history and culture. Yet the Declaration on Religious Freedom clearly seems committed to the latter as (in principle at least) a policy decision on grounds that "the right to religious freedom" is in no way governed by the duty to seek the true and the good.

In order to sustain this latter view, the declaration has to resort to a distinction between the internal and external actions of the moral subject. By its very nature the exercise of religion is alleged to consist in "those internal, voluntary, and free acts whereby man sets the course of his life directly toward God. No merely human power can either command or prohibit acts of this kind."[8] In the next paragraph we are informed that, of course, the "social nature of man" requires that the internal acts should be given external expression, but how such an expression is anything other than arbitrary is not explained. Clearly what seems to be "really religious" is "internal."

I confess I remain amazed that the council approved the declaration with the distinction between the internal and external allowed to stand. It almost tempts one to speculate that Protestant moles disguised as Catholic theologians wrote this document. The Catholic insistence that the Christian faith is necessarily mediated seems lost entirely in these claims about "faith." It may in fact be true that religion, whatever that is, consists in such internal acts, but it is hard to conceive how the Catholic faith could be so understood. The very assumption that there exists an "internal act" that the "social nature of man" requires to be expressed "externally" is the kind of presumption we rightly associate with various forms of Protestant pietism and liberal theology. But such a view has seldom been accepted in Catholicism.

It is one thing to say that the faith cannot be coerced. It is quite another to say that the reason the faith cannot be coerced is that it is "internal." In modernity Protestantism has been the form of Christianity tempted to gnosticism about the body. Catholics, and not just Italian Catholics, have rightly maintained the materiality of the faith, and in particular the significance of the body, that renders problematic the distinction between internal and external we find in the Declaration on Religious Freedom.[9] Moreover, if the body matters and the body is part of the body politic, then the question of

111

the political and legal establishment of Catholicism cannot be excluded in principle on grounds of freedom of religion.

That Catholicism can be so established is, moreover, rightly acknowledged by the declaration. Because religious acts are meant by their nature to direct our lives to God and thus transcend the order of terrestrial and temporal affairs, governments "ought indeed to take account of the religious life of the people and show it favor, since the function of government is to make provision for the common welfare. However, it would clearly transgress the limits set to its power were it to presume to direct or inhibit acts that are religious."[10] Of course, the last sentence presupposes there must be some unproblematic agreement about what constitutes the distinction between religious and nonreligious acts. For example, it would have been very instructive to have heard John Courtney Murray try to convince a Hindu that the eating of meat is a purely secular matter.

Obviously the declaration is trying to have its cake and eat it too. Religious freedom is a very good idea when Catholics are in the minority, but such freedom does not rule out the societal or legal establishment of Catholicism (or Islam or Hinduism) if "peculiar circumstances" obtain among certain people.[11] Indeed such an establishment might well be required if one takes seriously the presumption that the duty to seek the truth has precedence over the right of religious freedom. Thus we are told that "government is also to help create conditions favorable to the fostering of religious life, in order that the people may be truly enabled to exercise their religious rights and to fulfill their religious duties, and also in order that society itself may profit by the moral qualities of justice and peace which have their origin in man's faithfulness to God and to His holy will."[12]

Of course the declaration soon follows this wonderfully candid advice with the qualification that "the right of all citizens and religious bodies to religious freedom should be recognized and made effective in practice."[13] Yet I do not think the council fathers assumed that such a right might extend, for example, to allowing Latter-Day Saints to practice polygamy or other religious groups to engage in animal sacrifices. The declaration observes that society has the right to defend itself against "possible abuses" done in the name of religious freedom, but we are given no hint how we might know what a possible abuse might look like. All we are told is that governments are not to act in arbitrary fashion or in an unfair spirit of partisanship.[14] This is a suggestion with all the power of asking Israel and the PLO to love one another.

A potentially useful test for discriminating between the rightful exercise of a religion and abuse might be found in the declaration's calling attention to the significance of the family. The family is said to be a "society in its own," which means that parents have the right to determine the kind of religious education their children are to receive. The declaration even suggests (one hopes with an eye to the public education system in America) that the freedom of choice of schools should not impose an unjust burden on parents who seek to have their children educated in their own faith.[15]

There is no question, I believe, that the declaration is right to insist on parents' duty to educate their children in a manner that renders secondary those children's loyalty to the state. The difficulty, however, is that in liberal societies—that is, those that provide for freedom of religion in principle—too often parents begin to think they have no right to "impose" their religious beliefs on their children. Put differently, the great problem of Catholic schools in America is not that they provide an alternative to the state-run schools but that they do not. Children are taught, I suspect, the same story of "freedom" in parochial schools that reigns in public education, with a religious twist. As a result Catholics presume that they believe what most Americans believe about the state—namely that any state that provides religious freedom in principle is to be obeyed because by definition such a state must be "just." So Catholics become in America our most enthusiastic "citizens," ready to go to war against other states that do not provide freedom of religion.

I wish I could say the incoherence of the Declaration on Religious Freedom was resolved by the second chapter on revelation, but I fear that things only get worse. It may be, as the declaration asserts, that one of the major tenets of Catholic doctrine is that human response to God in faith must be free, but it is not clear why such a claim is a matter of "revelation," given the declaration's own unclarity about what is actually revealed in revelation.

This may appear to be a harsh judgment, given the declaration's claim that "the act of faith is of its very nature a free act. Man, redeemed by Christ the Savior and through Christ Jesus called to be God's adopted son, cannot give his adherence to God revealing Himself unless the Father draw him to offer to God the reasonable and free submission of faith."[16] This seems to me to have great potential: free response to God is located in the very life of the Trinity. The problem, however, is that the declaration fails to provide an account of the complexity our response to God's free act entails.

Think, for example, of Augustine's account in his *Confessions* of accepting God's pursuit of him. Of course his coming to faith was "free," but such freedom becomes the acknowledgment that God refuses to abandon us even in our willfulness. Under the condition of our sinfulness, God's refusal to abandon us may seem to be anything other than "free." To be wrenched from sin is appropriately described as an act of freedom, as we see from the very character of Augustine's *Confessions*, only retrospectively.

I am aware that such an observation can invite quite dangerous practices. For example, some drawing on such logic have provided justifications for

113 ■

torture in order to "free" a soul from sin. Such torture, moreover, even "works" since those tortured can come to love their torturer for giving them new "life." I have no desire to underwrite such practices, but that I do not is not because I think freedom is a possession of the agent that gives us the power to decide for or against God. God refuses to be trumped by human sin.

What is wrong with torture is not that it violates another person's dignity but that Christians are called to live lives of nonviolence. Christian nonviolence does not gain its intelligibility from a high humanism presupposing that freedom is the absence of "coercion." Rather, Christian nonviolence gains its intelligibility from the cross, where we see our God suffering so that we might be freed from the violence that grips our lives. To be freed from such violence requires an alternative politics to the politics of the world. The name for that alternative politics is church.

I am well aware that the insertion of my "pacifism" into this discussion may seem an irrelevant incursion. After all, Catholics are not pacifists— at least they are not as a church pacifist. Yet I think the introduction of nonviolence into the discussion of questions of religious freedom is crucial to understand why I think the declaration is not only incoherent but theologically deficient in its account of revelation. Put differently, the revelational claims in the declaration are muted in favor of assertions such as "God has regard for the dignity of the human person who He Himself created; man is to be guided by his own judgment and he is to enjoy freedom."[17] Surely the last clause of this sentence does not follow from the acknowledgment of our created status.

The declaration rightly notes that Jesus did denounce unbelief in some who listened to him, but he left vengeance to God on the day of judgment.[18] But acknowledgment of Jesus' nonviolence does not justify the claim that Jesus "refused to be a political Messiah ruling by force; He preferred to call Himself the Son of Man, who came 'to serve and to give his life as a ransom for many' (Mark 10:45)."[19] If Jesus was not "political," then one surely has a very hard time explaining the "misunderstanding" that resulted in his death. The appeal to satisfaction accounts of the atonement in this context only confirms the declaration's general tendency to "privatize and internalize" salvation. As a result the Declaration on Religious Freedom plays into the hands of one of the most violent and virulent forms of politics, that is, liberal political arrangements that require our lives be shaped by the distinction between the public and the private.

Such a criticism of the declaration may be unfair given the time the council fathers were working. After all, liberation theology was not yet a force, and even if it had been, it is by no means clear the Europeans and Americans would have had the intellectual resources to understand what those "Southern theologians" were about.[20] Nor had Yoder's The Politics of Jesus appeared with its quite different alternative to those accounts of Jesus enshrined in German biblical scholarship that so influenced the council.[21] Unfortunately such scholarship too often reproduced the practices of the Lutheran two-kingdom views under the guise of objectivity.

Claims about the alleged apolitical character of Jesus' proclamation of the kingdom result in not only making Jesus a "personal savior" but also forcing the "political" to be the realm of violence. Such an account of politics, to be sure, seems "natural" in modernity, but such an assumed givenness is surely no reason that Christians should accept such a view. We are, as the declaration claims, God's good creatures, and as such we are not created to have our lives ruled by violence. What is required is not acquiescence to the presumptions of liberal political theory but rather for Christians to help ourselves and those who do not share our practice to imagine a peaceable politics.[22]

In this respect, at least, the Declaration on Religious Freedom does not ignore the politics of the church. "The Church should enjoy that full measure of freedom which her care for the salvation of men requires. This freedom is sacred, because the only-begotten Son endowed with it the Church which He purchased with His blood. It is so much the property of the Church that to act against it is to act against the will of God. The freedom of the Church is the fundamental principle in what concerns the relations between Church and governments and the whole civil order."[23] Here we have the kind of claim we should expect from a church that has over the centuries done battle with kings and emperors.

The crucial question, of course, is what the church is about that would make the question of its freedom so threatening to worldly powers. A church that maintains the right of freedom of religion, at least as that freedom is understood in the declaration, is surely not a church that would so challenge the secular powers. But a church constituted by the practices necessary to free us from the violence that grips our lives could not help but be a church to which the world would not willingly grant "freedom." For such a church to claim against the world the freedom to be the church is surely how a politics is created that also requires those who are not Christian to be protected from state coercion.

I am aware that my reading of the Declaration of Religious Freedom may be thought uncharitable. After all, the declaration was written at a general level, trying to provide the most general principles to help the church in quite different contexts negotiate the complex relations between church, society, and the state. So to ask it to say when an abuse of the principle of religious freedom takes place is to ask it to do what it manifestly cannot do. If that is the case, however, I think the Vatican Council would have been wiser to have attempted no general statement about these matters, for the declaration as we have it cannot help but put the church on the side of liberal political practices designed to make it politically impotent.

In fact, I think my reading of the declaration is quite charitable. To suggest that the declaration is incoherent, or at least of two minds, is a charitable reading. At least the document was not entirely evacuated of theological substance in the interest of underwriting the sense of the dignity of the human person that "has been impressing itself more and more deeply on the consciousness of contemporary man."[24] The "conservatives" got their sentences, and we should be grateful they did so. That they got their sentences means there is no way the declaration can be read as a consistent theological politics, and we should be very glad for its incoherence.

7

■ONLY THEOLOGY OVERCOMES ETHICS[1]

OR, WHAT "ETHICISTS" MUST LEARN FROM JENSON

HOW THEOLOGY BECAME ETHICS IN AMERICA

I have been asked to write on Robert Jenson's "ethics"—a straightforward request that should elicit a straightforward response. There is, however, one small problem. Jenson does not "do" ethics. "Ethics" is not listed in the index of topics in either volume of the *Systematic Theology*. To be sure, Jenson, who seems to share my view that it is better to have views than not, declares himself often on matters that many might consider to be "ethics." Yet he does not seem to think his declarations about abortion or politics or how they are connected constitute "ethics." The one time Jenson uses the description "Christian ethics," he does so only to express doubt whether such a discipline is a good idea. He explains he learned from Edmund Santurri that "the vast apparatus of 'ethical inquiry' characteristic of late modern societies may be mostly a device to mask corruption."[2]

Yet that Jenson refuses to "do" ethics is why his work is so important for those such as myself who bear the burden of being identified as "Christian ethicists." I do not particularly enjoy being known as a Christian ethicist, since that description often seems to legitimate for many in the "field" of ethics the leaving behind of a kind of theology represented by Jenson. For example, I cannot remember any session of the annual meeting of the Society of Christian Ethics devoted to a work like Jenson's *Systematic Theology*. Christian ethicists think they should read philosophy, political theory, and/or social science, but theology, it would seem, is not really that important for ethics. Therefore I cannot resist using this essay as an opportunity to argue why theology, and in particular the work of Jenson, is important for ethics. However, before I do so I need, so to speak, to set the stage by suggesting why theology, particularly in America, became ethics and ethics became a form of reflection that could be done whether God exists or not.

Americans are often described as a practical people; thus the presumption that Americans are more like the "practical" Romans than the "theoretical" Greeks. Americans allegedly are not attracted to metaphysical questions but want to know how to "get things done." It is not by accident that pragmatism, which many mistakenly associate with the view that the truth of a proposition is tested by whether it works, is America's most distinctive philosophical contribution. The undeniable metaphysical cast of Jenson's work therefore seems to put him at odds with the American penchant for making practical and ethical questions primary.

Of course the characterization of the "practical American" is overdrawn; but still there is some truth, particularly when considering American church practice and theology, to the generalization that American Christians focus on results. The problem, however, with such a description of American theology is how it occludes the theory that has produced the allegedly practical character of American thought. No matter how the challenge of surviving as well as making a world out of the "American wilderness" may have contributed to American's practical orientation, in fact the emphasis on the practical or the ethical in American theology is the result of European philosophical developments. In short, the experiential and practical character of Christian theology in America but indicates the profound influence of Kant.

If you accept—as Kant taught American liberal theologians to accept—that Christian theology can no longer tell you anything about God or God's relation to God's creation, then all you have left is "ethics." Science, and in particular a science shaped by mechanistic metaphysical assumptions, was assumed to have epistemic privilege. Moreover, the political arrangements necessary to sustain a "pluralist" society were thought to require all strong religious convictions to be relegated to the private realm. As a result it was assumed that theological claims by their very nature cannot be considered to have public status. Theology in America became anthropology in an endeavor to sustain the assumption that our lives can have meaning in a causally determined world and/or to motivate our moral behavior. Protestant liberal theology may have been the brainchild of German theologians, but it was destined to flourish in America.

It is not by accident, therefore, that theology, particularly in America, found it hard to resist becoming ethics. Of course I am not suggesting that theology ceased being a subject in university and seminary curriculums. Theology was and is still taught, particularly in seminaries, but even in seminaries theology is understood as "information" rather than a discipline on which our lives depend. Thus the increasing distinction in seminary curriculums between theoretical and practical/ministerial courses and correlative complaint by seminarians that the former lack relevance. Ironically, one of the results of the division between practical and theoretical courses in seminary curriculums has been unclarity about whether courses in ethics are or should be "practical."

In most mainline Protestant seminaries at the beginning of the twenty-first century, ethics is taught after students have had systematic theology. That order, I suspect, reflects the ongoing assumption that theology at best has become, or is, "theory" necessary to provide the background assumptions for our ethics. Such an assumption not only makes theology irrelevant but frees ethics from any serious theological engagement. Accordingly, theology and ethics have become increasingly understood as separate disciplines, relieving the practitioners of each from any responsibility to read one another's work. That students can now do Ph.D. work in theology *or* ethics (which of course has demanded development of journals and academic associations that serve each discipline) only reinforces the assumption that theology and ethics represent two quite independent spheres of investigation.

Christian ethicists have also thought it important to distance themselves from theology in order to fulfill their assigned task of being agents, or at least theoreticians, of justice in a social order like America. If the moral principles necessary for addressing issues of income distribution, abortion, or war depend on theological claims, then it is assumed that the Christian ethicists would not be able to speak in or to the "public" realm. For many Christians, *ethics* names the attempt to develop natural-law accounts or draw on other nontheological sources of moral wisdom to make it possible for Christians to responsibly participate in, as well as be of service to, the American democratic experiment. Conservative and liberal Christian ethicists, who often disagree about everything else, agree that some "third language" must be developed if Christians are to act in public.

My account of the relation of theology to ethics in America may exaggerate the alienation between these disciplines. There are no doubt individual

119

theologians and ethicists whose work would require me to qualify the generalizations I have made about the relation between theology and ethics. Yet I am more than willing to stand by the general picture I have drawn not only because I think it is accurate but also because it helps us understand better the significance of Jenson's work as a theologian. He has refused to let theology become "theory" by insisting that if we get our speech about God wrong, we cannot help but get our lives wrong. Accordingly he does not understand ethics as something we do after we have done systematic theology; rather Jenson rightly maintains we are already doing "ethics" when we struggle to speak with exactness about God.

WHY JENSON'S THEOLOGY IS ETHICS

Some may find the account I have given of how theology became ethics in America to be self-serving. I, not Jenson, am the one who has waged an undeclared war against those who would do Christian ethics in a theologically minimalist fashion. Am I not simply using Jenson to carry forward my own agenda? The answer is: of course I am using Jenson to advance the way I have tried to do Christian ethics; but I do not think I am "using him" in an illegitimate fashion. After all, at least one of the reasons I have felt I must work to reclaim the theological center of Christian ethics was what I have learned from reading Jenson. What I learned from Jenson is what I think he and I both learned from Barth: God matters.

It may well also be self-serving for me to claim to represent the attempt to reclaim a theological center for Christian ethics. After all, Christian ethics has a theological center: but the theology that is at the center of Christian ethics is liberal Protestant theology. Even more than Jenson, I have aggressively attacked the liberal theological presuppositions that have and continue to shape most of the work done in Christian ethics. To think one can be more aggressive than Jenson is surely, as we say in Texas, "to put on airs." But in this case my critique of Reinhold Niebuhr in itself has been sufficient to give me a much more negative reputation in the field of Christian ethics than Jenson can ever hope to achieve. Jenson, I suspect, has not thought it necessary to criticize representatives of Christian ethics because he felt no need to beat what he considered to be a dead horse. Unfortunately in the world of Christian ethics that horse is anything but dead. Which, of course, is one of the reasons Jenson's theology is not read by those who do Christian ethics. He is simply thought to be too theologically "conservative."

So if I am "using" Jenson to further my own agenda, it is an agenda I hope Jenson will recognize as congruent with his own. He has even suggested that while his understanding of ethics is not to be "fathered" on me, my work has provided a template for his own thinking about ethics.[3] I hope he means by this that the way I do ethics is appropriately theological. Yet if that is the case, then it would be a mistake to begin an account of his ethics by looking at what he explicitly says about ethics—for example, in the second volume of his *Systematic Theology*. Rather, as I suggested above, we must begin with what he says about God.

According to Jenson, "theology is thinking what to say to be saying the gospel."[4] To speak rightly of God requires training by the gospel because the God that is the beginning and end of our existence is "whoever raised Jesus from the dead, having before raised Israel from Egypt."[5] Theology is therefore the ongoing activity of the church to explore the prescriptive grammar required by the presumption that to be known and to know the one God of all requires the acknowledgment that the God Christians worship is the decisive fact about all things. So theology "must be either a universal and founding discipline or a delusion."[6]

"Universal and founding" does not mean for Jenson that theology is not subject to the same contingencies that shape any disciplined mode of inquiry. Theology cannot be timeless, for no other reason (and it is the only reason that matters) than that the God who is the subject of Christian theology is not timeless. The God of Israel and Jesus, the God we find in Scripture, is a storied God. That we learn of God, or more exactly, that we learn who God is through a narrative is not accidental but rather indicative of God's nature. God's storied character expresses, as Aquinas maintained, that "God's act of being is constrained by no form other than itself."[7] Accordingly, the biblical God's eternity is not immunity to time but faithfulness. "God is not eternal in that he secures himself from time, but in that he is faithful to his commitments with time. At the great turning, Israel's God is eternal in that he is faithful to the death, and then yet again faithful."[8]

That the gospel must have a history is but an expression of God's trinitarian nature. The phrase

> "Father, Son, and Holy Spirit" is simultaneously a very compressed telling of the total narrative by which Scripture identifies God and a personal name for the God so specified; in it, name and narrative description not only appear together, as at the beginning of the Ten Commandments, but are identical. By virtue of this logic, the triune phrase offers itself as the unique name for the Christian God, and is then dogmatically mandated for that function by its constitutive place in the rite that establishes Christian identity. The church is the community and a Christian is someone who, when the identity of God is important, names him "Father, Son, and Holy Spirit." Those who do not or will not belong to some other community.[9]

When Christians go to the "public," therefore, they cannot avoid saying what they know to be true: that no public can pretend to the truth that denies that God is Father, Son, and Holy Spirit. Christians will only betray

121

their non-Christian brothers and sisters if, in the name of reason or in the interest of securing societal peace, they act as if it matters not which god or no-god is worshiped.[10] Therefore Christians can never accept the presumption that the gospel bears the burden of proof when confronted by accounts of the "public" or "reason" that pretend theological neutrality. It may happen that God, as a particular culture has understood him, may withdraw from the public realm of that culture, making our communication about God as well as our rational knowledge of him broken and difficult.[11] But such a situation should never tempt Christians to qualify our assumption that reason requires the right worship of God. The loss of that assumption has tempted Christians to save religion by withdrawing it from the demands of reason into the safety of private experience or, in the interest of apologetics, to conflate humanistic gods with the Father, Son, and Holy Spirit. But if Christians have heard the gospel, they have all they need to understand that the very character of reason requires they persist in speaking of God in public.

Christians are a people who have heard a revelation that includes the name of a man called Pontius Pilate, "and of a God who will verify himself by judging the quick and the dead, that is, the entire public history of man. We are therefore called to say our piece about God in the open arena of all nations or not say it at all. And we are promised that the gates of hell will not at last prevail against this attempt."[12]

Ethics but names the theological discipline necessary for Christians "to say our piece about God in the open arena of the nations." So understood, Christian ethical reflection does not belong uniquely to any of the loci of Christian theology. When Jenson does what looks like ethics, however, it is done as an aspect of his ecclesiology. That his ethics is placed in the context of his ecclesiology does not imply that the way Christians must live is peculiar to them, but rather reflects Jenson's conviction that ethical reflection is dependent on the politics through which a community discovers and chooses its future.[13]

Politics names the "process of that mutual moral address by which God speaks to us to initiate and sustain humanity. The polity is nothing less than the public space in which God calls us to be human in that we call each other to come together in justice."[14] Such a politics is not a given, nor can it be assumed. A collective of persons and a state apparatus do not constitute a politics. Absolute rulers may repress deliberation of what ought to be done, but they can sustain the attempt only for a time. An isolated tribal community may live with little awareness that they are reasoning morally until they are confronted by an outer world that presents challenges they cannot master. Indeed, Jenson judges the specifically modern societies that began with the great hope of the expansion of politics called democracy to be driven into a "neo-tribal" existence. "What Americans are likely now to call politics is in fact the functioning of an almost entirely depoliticized collectivity and state: the manipulation of a mass of petitioners and their interests by professional managers of affairs. If there is a functioning American polity, it is the very tight oligarchy of the federal judges."[15]

If we are to understand Jenson's ethics, these remarks cannot be relegated to "his opinion" of the current state of American polity. Rather they reflect what can only be called his theological politics, which is inseparable from his understanding of God's timefulness.[16] Augustine, according to Jenson, rightly maintained that the only polity that could satisfy the earthly polity's own definition of itself, a definition marked by and in time, is "that republic whose founder and governor is Christ." Augustine also rightly argued that in this age the only polity capable of fulfilling that condition was and is the church. Yet the implication is not that Christians are committed to theocracy but Christians should seek to live in a polity that allows us to serve one another through God's law.[17]

But that is exactly what has become impossible in America, since America has become a sexually anarchical society.[18] Many, of course, will think Jenson is being overly moralistic to link questions of political legitimacy to sexual immorality. After all, we have been taught—that is, those of us who are good citizens of a liberal democracy—that sexual behavior is "private," that sex should not be regulated by law or become a political issue. Yet for Jenson any account of justice entails how our bodies are to be formed in order that sex does not become but another way we can terrorize each other. The very interconnections between the commands of the Decalogue are but a reminder that no society

> can subsist in which the generations turn against each other; in which vendetta has not been replaced by public organs of judgment and punishment; in which the forms by which sexuality is socialized, whatever these may be, are flouted; in which property, however defined, is not defended; in which false testimony is allowed to pervert judgment; or in which greed is an accepted motive of action.[19]

According to Jenson, the one instance (and it is not the only example) that makes clear that America is no longer "a people," even by the least rigorous of Augustine's definitions of what constitutes a public, is abortion. A society in which an unborn child can be legally killed on the sole decision of the pregnant person can only be a "horde." "If unborn children are members of the human community, then allowing abortions to be performed on decision of the most interested party is a relapse to pure barbarism."[20] To the extent the American people approve this result—and there is every indication that on the whole they do—they have abdicated the moral coherence necessary to be judged a politics.[21] Jenson does not think abortion is simply an aberration in America but rather an indication of the inevitable result of Enlightenment politics and economics. There was a time, perhaps, when the politics produced by the Enlightenment might have been thought to be a blessing; but it is now plain that if the gospel is true, the politics of liberalism must be false.[22]

That's a bleak enough judgment if we forget the good news that Christians have an alternative to such a politics. The alternative is called church. The church is God's polity whose great character is peace, the "tranquility of order." The church is a government that strives through the practice of the commandments to escape the *libido dominandi*, which requires as well as makes possible that the church forswear all coercion. Yet because the church has this specific mission it must discipline its borders, so when members live in a manner to disprove the church's missionary claim to the Spirit, "the church *must* separate herself from them or be herself unfaithful."[23] Excommunication is the ultimate act of peace.

The commandments therefore work differently in the church from the way they work outside the church. Outside the church the commandments state conditions of a polity's perduring; but in the "specific communal history of Israel and the church they acquire positive meaning as descriptions of virtues. It is the gospel that is the agent of the specific history of God's people and so enables and shapes such meanings."[24] It is the Eucharist above all that shapes the *habitus* of the church's speech, so that, for example, it is not enough that Christian people refrain from perjury. Because Christians are constituted by the fear and love of God, the command not to bear false witness means we are a polity whose "citizens have reason to attribute good to each other, because good is unconditionally and finally promised to the community we make together."[25]

Because Jenson is a Lutheran, some might be tempted to hear echoes of the Lutheran two-kingdoms doctrine in his account of the church and the church's relation to all that is not church. If anything, however, Jenson is closer to the Reformed than to the Lutherans (at least in terms of their past stereotypes) in his understanding of the relation of law and gospel with the correlative assumptions concerning the relation of church to the world. He does not ever assume that the "world" is condemned to live only in accordance with what is prohibited. All are created to live by God's good commands. Yet God has called the church to participate in his life, so that our justification is "a mode of deification."[26] We share with God a history through which we become acquainted. Of course in this age the knowledge that comes from our friendship with God and one another can only be a "beginning and some increase," but even that beginning cannot help but mark us as the people God has made his own.[27]

A Christian, according to Jenson, is someone whose nation and polity is the church, so the "baptized person must be the only available paradigm of human personhood."[28] To know what it means to be human comes from being made part of the church. In other words, we do not know in general what it means to be human and then discover that being a Christian is but a further specification of that more general way of being. Rather, what it means to be human in general is an abstraction from the humanity God has made possible in Christ. This does not mean the church must necessarily be "sectarian," but given the context in which we now find ourselves, the church has been freed

> to be much more decisively and peculiarly Christian, more sectarian even, than it has lately been. Such a church might even be able to preach the gospel again: it might reclaim the omnipotence and universality of God, so long predicates of an inactive state-God, for its Christ. The church might become so specific as again to have a specific thing to say in and to the world, and so become again a messenger-community to the—in this instance, American—ecumene. It might become a messenger-community of God's future that is not bound to America, which if need be will come, both ultimately and penultimately, over America's dead body, and which can be hope also for America just when America can have little hope in itself.[29]

I have not tried to report on everything Jenson has said that might be considered his ethics, but rather to suggest why his ethics is inseparable from his theology. Even that way of putting the matter may be misleading, for "inseparable" may suggest that something like ethical judgments "follow from" his theology. More accurately, Jenson helps us see why the Christian unwillingness to countenance abortion is inseparable from our worship of the Father, Son, and Holy Spirit and why seeing that helps us face the challenge of that world called America. If Jenson is right, and I certainly think he is, Christian ethics and politics are not areas to be developed after we have done theology but rather are constitutive of Christian speech whose form is first and foremost prayer.[30] That is why Jenson, given the account I have provided of how theology became ethics in America, cannot be America's theologian. Rather, he is a church theologian.

A QUESTION FOR JENSON

I noted above Jenson's kind acknowledgment of the influence my work has had on the way he has thought about ethics. The account I have given of his work, moreover, I hope indicates how much I have learned from him. However, in the second volume of his *Systematic Theology* he directs a question to me to which I should respond. He observes rightly that those whom the gospel calls into the church are not without antecedent hopes and fears.

The church shapes and is shaped historically and geographically by the permissions and prohibitions, the morality, it finds among those to whom it witnesses. Therefore "the moral history of the church is not, as it were, pure; it is not simply other than the moral history of the communities around it. The gospel takes its ethical form just as it *interprets* an antecedent morality of those who at a time and place are there to hear and speak it."[31] Professing not to know, Jenson asks if I would agree with these observations.

To disagree with Jenson on these matters would be almost as silly as the young woman who was reported to have told Chesterton she had decided to "accept the world." Chesterton is alleged to have responded, "You had better." So of course I assume that the various ways Christians must learn to live are shaped by "antecedent moralities," not just because we cannot avoid being so shaped but because, given the content of the gospel, that is what we should expect. For example, Christians have debated when a marriage begins because different cultures have quite various markers to indicate when the promise the couple makes to God and one another of lifelong fidelity is "public." There is simply no substitute for the wise exploration of such matters by the wise—which is but another way of indicating the necessity of casuistry for any significant way of life.

If my position on these matters has been misunderstood, I suspect it is partly due to my polemic against those who use abstract notions of nature and grace to justify an account of natural law in the interest of underwriting the presumption that the way things are is the way things ought to be.[32] That, of course, is the Catholic version. The Calvinists, with the same intent and result, appeal to the doctrine of creation abstracted from the Trinity in order to suggest that a "morality" exists that can ensure an a priori agreement between Christians and non-Christians sufficient to sustain joint support for policy formation in democracies. The difficulty is that both these ways of underwriting a "natural ethic" justify an "ethic" that then is alleged to be in principle congruent with the gospel. In contrast, Jenson does not pretend to know how Christians will discover the limits or riches of the "antecedent moralities" they confront without considering their content.

I do not know if Jenson will find my brief response to his question adequate. I hope he will, however, because of the paragraph that follows his question. It reads:

> The gospel turns our antecedent hopes into real possibilities by interpreting them as hopes for a Kingdom that is indeed coming. Just so it also reinterprets them materially. So, to take a central and by now familiar instance, all humans hope for something that may be called peace. But most societies have interpreted peace as the success of violence—in the ideology of Western states, as a "secularity" to be established by "defense." Just so the hope for peace

becomes itself the constant occasion of conflict. The gospel promises the actual advent of peace and invites us to its anticipation in the Eucharist. The gospel makes peace a possibility by telling us that we do not have to defend ourselves, since our lives are hid with God in Christ. Just so, the gospel interprets peace as what Christ brings, as the fruit of his self-surrender.[33]

As a Christian committed to nonviolence, I could not wish for a better account of why Christians are committed to disavow violence. Thus my question to Jenson: "When everything is said and done, at the end of the day, your position would seem to commit you to nonviolence. Why, therefore, have you not made clear that Christians cannot kill, particularly in war, in the name of Christ?"[34] Of course that way of putting the matter may not be sufficiently nuanced. Jenson may well respond that he cannot imagine killing "in the name of Christ" but there may be other modes of killing that are justified. Such justifications no doubt must involve the "antecedent moralities" Christians encounter, but then the question must be asked, on Jenson's own grounds, how such a morality can be given authority if it divides the unity of the church made possible by the celebration of the Eucharist.[35]

In the essay "Violence As a Mode of Language," Jenson suggests that violence is implicated in our most basic relations with one another, that is, in the very way "in which our bodies participate in our communication with each other."[36] Because our language creates a shared life that constitutes the attempts of our bodies to communicate with one another, such attempts often cannot help but be violent. As Jenson puts it, "Violence happens when I want to say something to you that really cannot be said to you, that you are not in a position to hear, and when yet I insist that you are going to hear it. When my words do not move you, and yet I determine that you are going to move, then we have violence."[37] That is why, according to Jenson, we ought to understand Luther's account of the "sword," that is, the recognition that the agents of law are always the agents of violence, as the justified use of violence necessary to say "Let (this) violence cease."[38]

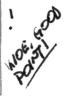

Yet Jenson thinks we now confront a situation that Luther did not foresee. In America we have created a society that has so shaped its language that anything that is said cannot be said without involving violence. In other words, *America* for Jenson names that politics in which the language of our relations with one another cannot help but lie. The words we use cannot honestly face reality as it is and at the same time freely indicate what might and must be. For example, as long as we describe our economy as a "free enterprise" system it is impossible to begin to recognize the powers that possess us, which leads Jenson to the conclusion that "given the language of the world we inhabit, which is a language of violence, the church too will be driven to speaking violently."[39]

127

Yet Jenson asks, "How can the church speak violently when as Christians we are constituted by the liturgical anticipation that celebrates God's peace?" He responds suggesting that the body aspect of our missionary message cannot help but

> be a peculiar sort of violent liturgy. We are called to preach in the language
> of the world; this is now a language of violence. We are called to speak to a
> society that understands only violence, and to speak of the utter overthrowing
> of all that is. But we are called to be nonviolent. I suggest that the body-side
> of such a word will be *violent* action in contradiction of injustice and hate,
> that is, transformed into liturgy by being done uselessly, as *play*.[40]

As an example of how such a liturgy might look Jenson calls attention (surprising, he acknowledges, even himself) to the destruction of draft files by the Berrigan brothers and their friends.

If Jenson refrains from clearly declaring himself to be among those who must disavow war because he believes even the witness of nonviolence is implicated in violence, I can only say to him that we who are committed to nonviolence welcome just that challenge. We may want to explore with him whether and how the violence of language can be distinguished from other forms of violence such as war.[41] But that is exactly the kind of work we have been taught by Jenson to expect as required by any theology that speaks truthfully about and to the world. Such work turns out, interestingly enough, to be the same kind of activity Jenson's question above asked if I were willing to undertake. I only hope this reveals why I think his theology is an ethic that no one who wants to be a Christian ethicist in our time can or should ignore.

8

■WHY *THE POLITICS OF JESUS* IS NOT A CLASSIC

John Howard Yoder's *The Politics of Jesus* surely would be an odd choice for a classic. As a fairly recent book (1972), it has not had a chance to prove its staying power.[1] For that matter, it does not now command great attention in contemporary discussions of theology or ethics. To be sure, most mark it as an important work, but not as one that has decisively changed the way we think. Indeed, Yoder does not pretend that the book is anything more than a report on the mainstream scholarly consensus concerning the political character of Jesus' proclamation of the kingdom of God as found in the Book of Luke. Yet I am convinced that when Christians look back on theology in twentieth-century America *The Politics of Jesus* will be seen as a new beginning.

Prior to Yoder the subject of Christian ethics in America was always America. The more America became the democratic society that the social gospelers so desired, the more difficult it became to do ethics in a theologically candid manner. Chastened by the Niebuhrs, those trained in ethics no longer sought to "Christianize" the social order. Instead they pursued, in the name of love, a more nearly just political arrangement.

The social gospel spawned ethicists who became social scientists, or at least read social science, in the interest of social transformation. The "realists" spawned ethicists who became moral philosophers, clarifying moral questions in medicine and business and, in their spare time, keeping alive the "God question." In this mode Christian ethics continues, but it becomes increasingly difficult to say what makes it Christian. Indeed, the effort to discover the relationship between policy questions or basic moral principles and theological warrants now preoccupies many ethicists.

Yoder comes into this territory from the sectarian badlands. He is the lone hero standing up to the mob that is willing to secure justice through the anguished acceptance of violence. He insists that the christologically disciplined account of nonviolence displayed in *The Politics of Jesus* cannot be dismissed the way Reinhold Niebuhr, for example, rejected liberal Protestant pacifism. Also, Yoder's account of nonviolence requires theologians to acknowledge that their work makes no sense abstracted from the church. In short, for Yoder both the subject and the audience of Christian ethics are Christians—the people who are constituted by that polity called church.

The image of the lone gunman facing down the bad guys does not really fit Yoder, however, because his work is meant to defeat the myth of the hero. His work is based on the life of a community. Nonviolence is a way of life for Christians. If that community produces people whose stories it remembers, it calls them martyrs, not heroes.

Good! Point!

It is odd, then, to regard *The Politics of Jesus* as a classic. The very idea of "classic" suggests heroic narratives. The classic is the category of dominant and dominating traditions. Yoder does not want *The Politics of Jesus* to be a classic but rather to serve those who are living better than he writes. The very character of the book defies the effort to categorize it as a classic, since it does not articulate an elegant position but rather provides a close reading of Luke. Indeed, one of the problems with the book is our inability to locate it in a recognizable genre. It is not a commentary, though it consists primarily of comments on Scripture; it is not theology, though Yoder makes extraordinary theological asides of a systematic nature; it is not ethics, though it challenges and perhaps changes our very idea of what ethics might be.

For many people, the classics are works that are ends in themselves because they embody essential truths about the human condition. It is assumed that if you have never read Shakespeare your life is less rich, since you may fail to appreciate the truths about life that his plays present. But what is important is not that certain books be read as an end in themselves but that they be read because of their relationship to other books in a tradition and community that make such a conversation significant. Thus we should read Thomas Aquinas not only because the *Summa Theologica* is a classic but because reading Aquinas teaches us how better to read Augustine and the Scriptures.

In like manner I want to promote the reading of *The Politics of Jesus* because it helps us locate our lives as Christians in the catholic faith. Yoder needs to be read in the tradition of liberal Protestantism not only because he helps us recognize the strengths of that tradition but also because he helps us see why that tradition has come to an end (which accounts for why he remains something of an outcast in mainstream Protestant theology). Yoder cannot be made to fit into the presuppositions we have learned from the Niebuhrs and their successors. Such theologians keep saying, "We have seen this Christ-against-culture type before." In mainstream hands, such typologies become power plays to keep in their place those who might challenge the reigning explanatory categories.

Yoder challenges the philosophical moves we have learned so thoroughly from Troeltsch through the Niebuhrs, and so we are desperate to make him but another example of what it means to be a sectarian. What gives *The Politics of Jesus* its power is that Yoder knows us better than we know him. Yoder sees the peculiar way that Troeltsch and the Niebuhrs dehistoricized the Christian faith in the name of "history," and he sets himself against the dichotomy of faith and history.

In fairness it should be said that it is easy to miss Yoder's challenge because he is so free of theory. For example, he notes in *The Priestly Kingdom* that while he is not disrespectful of self-critical conceptual analysis, he is skeptical that such exercises can come logically, chronologically, or developmentally first. You cannot start trying to formulate the conditions of meaningful discourse if such discourse is not already established. There is simply no place to start thinking prior to being engaged in a tradition. As Yoder says, "What must replace the prolegomenal search for 'scratch' is the confession of rootedness in historical community. Then one directs one's critical acuity toward making clear the distance between that community's charter or covenant and its present faithfulness."[2]

Yoder does not talk about how he might do theology if he ever got around to doing any. Rather, like Barth, he simply begins to train us to read Luke with eyes unclouded by the presumption that Jesus is irrelevant for matters of social and political ethics. By doing so he challenges all pietistic readings of salvation, whether of the left or of the right.

Reinhold Niebuhr's understanding of salvation was fundamentally individualistic, if not gnostic. Indeed this has been a characteristic of most Protestant liberals, excepting Rauschenbusch. Yoder helps us see that Niebuhr's understanding of salvation had to be depoliticized exactly because he assumed the normative status of a politics based on violence. Correlatively, the cross for Niebuhr becomes a symbol of the tragic character of the human condition. Niebuhr's fatal concession to a very narrow understanding of the political made his Christology deficient.

131

Yet Yoder also challenges those evangelicals who describe salvation in terms of personal fulfillment. "The cross of Calvary was not a difficult family situation, not a frustration of visions of personal fulfillment, a crushing debt or a nagging in-law; it was the political, legally to be expected result of a moral clash with the powers ruling his society."[3] Yoder does not invite us to become concerned with our personal salvation, since that cannot help but depoliticize the salvation wrought in Christ.

Yoder does not think he is offering a radical new account of Jesus. "We do not here advocate an unheard-of modern understanding of Jesus; we ask rather that the implications of what the church has always said about Jesus as Word of the Father, as true God and true Man, be taken more seriously, as relevant to our social problems, than ever before."[4] Commenting on *The Politics of Jesus* in *The Priestly Kingdom*, he notes:

> There my point was that the book's emphasis on the concrete historical-political humanity of the Jesus of the Gospel accounts was compatible with the classic confession of the true humanity of Christ (i.e., the core meaning of "incarnation"); whereas those who deny that humanity (or its normative exemplarity) in favor of "some more spiritual" message are implicitly Docetic. Secondly, I argue that the New Testament's seeing Jesus as example is a necessary correlate of what later theology calls his divine sonship (the other side of the "incarnation"), in such a way that those who downgrade the weight of Jesus' example, on the grounds that his particular social location or example cannot be a norm, renew a counterpart of the old "Ebionite" heresy. This is a small sample of a wider claim; the convictions argued here do not admit to being categorized as a sectarian oddity or a prophetic exception. Their appeal is to classical catholic Christian convictions properly understood.[5]

This quote should make clear that Yoder does not understand himself as a Mennonite thinker. Indeed, if anything makes him testy it is being so pigeonholed. Those who so designate him often mean to honor him as representing a position that is necessary for reminding us of our sinfulness. But Yoder is not trying to be a reminder. He is trying to force us to recognize that in spite of what appear to be orthodox christological affirmations, we are embedded in social practices that deny that Jesus' life, death, and resurrection make any difference. Thus incarnation does not mean that God approves of all of human nature:

> The point is just the opposite; that God broke through the borders of our definition of what is human, and gave a new, formative definition in Jesus. "Trinity" did not originally mean, as it does for some later, that there are three kinds of revelation, the Father speaking through creation and the Spirit through experience, by which the words and example of the Son must be corrected; it meant rather that language must be found and definitions cre-

ated so that Christians, who believe in only one God, can affirm that he is most adequately and bindingly known in Jesus.[6]

In a manner that can only be described as catholic, Yoder returns Jesus to the center of Christian ethics by freeing us from the political presuppositions sponsored by liberal social orders. The directness of his style belies the complex nature of his thought. His clarity makes the power of his arguments deceptive. He shows us that our sense of the alternatives—that we must choose between the Jesus of history and the Christ of faith, between prophet and institution, between catastrophic kingdom and inner kingdom, between being political and being sectarian, between the individual and the social—derives not from categories intrinsic to the human condition but from a depoliticization of salvation that has made Christianity a faithful servant of the status quo.

That Yoder's significance has not been widely acknowledged is no doubt due to his unwillingness to put himself forward. Yoder is not good at self-promotion. He does not try to find us; he lets us find him. He neither tries to hide nor calls attention to himself. The way of nonviolence cannot seek easy victories, and Yoder does not want to make it easy for us to agree with him. His purpose is to commit us to Jesus' nonviolent mode of discipleship, making that way of life our own. He is interested not in promoting himself but in inviting others to live in a way that acknowledges Jesus as the new possibility of human, social, and therefore political relationships. His baptism inaugurates and his cross culminates a new regime in which his disciples are called to share.

My introduction to Yoder came in the bookstore at Yale Divinity School. Since Barth was playing a large part in my dissertation, I bought a mimeographed forty-seven-page pamphlet called "Karl Barth and Christian Pacifism" written by someone named J. H. Yoder. It noted that it was "work paper number four," prepared as a study document for the peace section of the Mennonite Central Committee.[7] In short, this was not an impressive-looking document. But I took it back to my carrel and began to read, and was absolutely stunned by Yoder's powerful analysis and critique of Barth. I thought, of course, that the criticisms were based on an ecclesiology that you would have to be crazy to accept.[8]

I more or less forgot about Yoder until I began to teach at Notre Dame in 1970. I assumed that Yoder must teach at Goshen College, which is not far from South Bend. In the process of learning the lay of the land around South Bend I found myself in Goshen. I discovered that Yoder taught not at Goshen College but rather in Elkhart at the Associated Mennonite Biblical Seminary. But in my exploration of Goshen, I discovered that Yoder had written numerous pamphlets that could be bought off a rack in College Church for a dime apiece. Always ready for the unusual and bizarre, I bought among others his pamphlets on Reinhold Niebuhr and on capital punishment, and another treatment of Barth. In reading these pamphlets, I began to understand that this was not just "another" theologian. I was sure he had to be wrong, though I was increasingly having trouble saying how.

Thinking I needed to know more about him, I called him in Elkhart and asked if I could meet him. He invited me over, though I am sure he must have thought he was going to be besieged by another mainstream Protestant collecting data on the odd ideas of the Mennonites. When we met, he did nothing to try to ingratiate himself. He answered questions that I put to him but seldom went beyond the answer itself. If Yoder was trying to make disciples, he certainly was not doing it through flattery.

I told him of my enthusiasm for his work and asked if he had written anything else. Little did I know how much Yoder had written, but he did not use that as an opportunity to expose my ignorance. He simply gave me copies of the Yoder mimeograph library. I left Elkhart with a stack of papers a foot high, thinking that this guy did not know how to make it as an academic. He thought mimeograph papers written to specific people in response to concrete requests were appropriate.

Within those papers lay the basic material we now know as *The Politics of Jesus*. The more I read it and the other material, the more I was frightened. Here was a position I was sure implied withdrawal from the world, but that certainly did not seem to be what Yoder was about. Indeed, his *Christian Witness to the State* was an extraordinary attempt to convince Mennonites not to accept Niebuhrian characterizations of them as morally necessary but politically irrelevant.[9] Yoder simply challenged all the neat intellectual and theological classifications with which I had been so carefully educated.

At that time the yearly ecumenical effort of Notre Dame's theology department was to have a colloquium with the theology department at Valparaiso University. That year I was asked to prepare the paper for the colloquium. Since I had spent a good deal of the year reading Yoder, I decided that I would write on him. I introduced my remarks by saying that here I was, a Methodist of doubtful theological background (Methodists by definition have a doubtful theological background), representing a Catholic department of theology speaking to a bunch of Lutherans to say that the Mennonites had been right all along. I suggested that this would be an ecumenical effort, since I thought by presenting the work of John Howard Yoder to Catholics and Lutherans I would help them see they had much in common—namely, Catholics and Lutherans had always assumed it was a good thing to kill the Anabaptists. Of course that was what happened. In response to my paper the Catholics and Lutherans competed to show why they shared the view that it is not always a bad thing to kill. At the time I tried not to take it personally.

■ 134

I called the paper "The Non-resistant Church: The Theological Ethics of John Howard Yoder." I sent it to at least six journals, all of which rejected it, not because editors thought the paper badly done but because they disliked what the paper was about.[10] One of the objections was that Yoder's position reflected a pre-Bultmannian view of biblical exegesis. I was beginning to learn that Yoder was perceived by many as deeply problematic because he is such a decisive threat to our accepted ways of thinking. (The characterization of Yoder as pre-Bultmannian now almost strikes one as humorous given recent developments in biblical criticism. Even on historical grounds, at least the historical grounds of E. P. Sanders,[11] Yoder's Jesus in *The Politics of Jesus* appears more historically defensible than Bultmann's Jesus.)

Yoder rightly understood that the real Jesus is not to be discovered in discontinuity from Judaism but in his continuity with the extraordinarily diverse modes of life we now call Jewish. Indeed, one of the aspects of Yoder's work that has been unfairly overlooked is his way of reconceiving the relationship between Christianity and Judaism.

The liberal dismissal of Yoder appears quite odd in light of the celebration of him as a "postmodern theologian" by Frederic Jameson in his *Postmodernism: Or, The Cultural Logic of Late Capitalism*. Jameson notes that the central hermeneutic of theological modernism was posed by the anthropomorphism of the narrative character of a historical Jesus. Modern theologians assumed that

> only intense philosophical effort is capable of turning this character into this or that christological abstraction. As for the commandments and the ethical doctrine, casuistry has long since settled the matter; they also need no longer be taken literally, and confronted with properly modern forms of injustice, bureaucratic warfare, systemic or economic inequality, and so forth, modern theologians and churchmen can work up persuasive accommodations to the constraints of complex modern societies, and provide excellent reasons for bombing civilian populations or executing criminals which do not disqualify the executors from Christian status.[12]

Yoder challenges that accommodation by his account of "the politics of Jesus." That is why a secular intellectual like Jameson admires him—even though the mainstream maintains that such people should not be able to appreciate Yoder.

Of course Yoder would not be impressed to know that people like Jameson admire his work. His task was not to represent a position interesting to other intellectuals. Rather, he worked as a theologian in subordination to a church pledged to witness to the nonviolent politics of the gospel. (The fact that he submitted to his church's discipline process regarding sexual misconduct was but a testimony to his commitment to nonviolence as the community's form of behavior.)

Nor would Yoder be impressed with my reading of the significance of *The Politics of Jesus*. In many ways my reading remains still far too laden with theory, which always threatens to become a substitute for the church rather than an enhancement of ecclesial practice. Nor would I want to imply that Yoder will help us reconceive the tradition of liberal Protestantism simply because of the mainstream churches' loss of institutional and social power. On the contrary, Yoder's work may well help us to use the remaining resources of that tradition to help Christians rediscover ways to serve our non-Christian brothers and sisters by being unwavering in our commitment to the politics of Jesus.

PART 3

CHURCH
TIME

9

■WHY TIME CANNOT AND SHOULD NOT HEAL THE WOUNDS OF HISTORY, BUT TIME HAS BEEN AND CAN BE REDEEMED

ON NOT FORGETTING

I am honored to be asked to address this conference, but I am also frightened to be here.[1] I am not frightened for myself but for you. Like most people who have followed your history from afar, I am aware you are living in a fragile time. It may be, as the conference title suggests, "a time to heal," but I do not presuppose that such a time is without its tensions. I assume you stand somewhere between not-quite peace and the hope of peace. Moreover, what concrete reality that hope might take remains vague, which is as frightening as it is hopeful. This is salutary, for I do not want to say anything to make matters worse; but as a result I might not say anything worth saying.

Moreover, given the arrogance of most Americans—particularly Christian Americans—I fear that it is quite easy for us to make a terrible mess by trying to tell other people how to get along. Part of the problem, of course, is that being American hides the arrogance of being an American from Americans because we assume, exactly because we are American, we can speak from the position of anyone. America is, after all, the embodiment of an alleged universal culture—that is, Americans believe that given the opportunity to think about it, anyone would want to be like us. To be already what everyone is trying to be is but another way to say that what it means to be an American is to be a people without a history. We think that gives us the place, which is no place, to tell everyone else how to be what we already are. All you have to do is forget who you are and become like us. Accordingly, Americans giving advice are right up there with the Christian who observed that the Jews and Palestinians could get along better if they acted like Christians.

All of which is to say that I am well aware of just how much of an outsider I am. We share the faith made possible by the resurrection of Jesus, but that faith does not mean our different histories are irrelevant. Since the time I was invited to speak to you, I have tried to read everything I could about "the troubles,"[2] yet I well understand that no amount of reading can give the kind of understanding that comes from having suffered your history. So I will make no attempt to address the Irish situation.

Making no attempt to address the Irish situation, however, can result in a kind of fatal abstractness. Such abstractness is a particular problem if you are a theologian. In our time, what many call modern times, unbelievers and believers (and even some theologians who actually may be believers!) do not believe that theological claims do any work. I assume that helps explain that no matter how sincerely many believe what it is they believe about God, they in fact live lives of practical atheism. Accordingly, quite profound and sophisticated theological systems can be developed, but the theological discourse seems to "float," making no difference for how we live.

The most sophisticated theological speech has difficulty being heard, even by those sympathetic to that speech, as anything other than pious platitudes. What good is a God that does no more than stand as some kind of ultimate warrant for appeals that when all is said and done we ought to try harder, even in places like Northern Ireland, to get along? I do not know if I can avoid being platitudinous, but I am not going to argue that God's peace means that Catholics and Protestants should forget their history and love one another. Rather I am going to argue why you cannot have peace in Ireland if you forget the wrongs Protestants have done to Catholics or Catholics to Protestants. There can be no healing of the wounds of history if you forget the murders perpetrated by Catholics and Protestants alike. Moreover, the reasons you cannot forget the terror Catholics and Protestants have perpetrated on one another is that you are Christians. Christians are required to confess and remember their sins, but they are also required to remember the sins of those who have sinned against us. Any reconciliation that does not require such a remembering cannot be the reconciliation made possible by the cross of Christ.

"The wrongs Protestants have done to Catholics and Catholics have done to Protestants" is, of course, already to oversimplify your history. *Protestant* and *Catholic* are referents that fail to do justice to the complexity of the differences that constitute the conflict called the "troubles." Part of the difficulty, I suspect, is that *Protestant* and *Catholic* become overdetermined names for differences hiding the fact that Protestants and Catholics are more alike than different. Michael Ignatieff reports that a Serbian soldier told him the Serbs and the Croat were really all the same, which makes it all the more necessary to emphasize the difference. As Ignatieff observes, "It is not a sense of radical difference that leads to conflict with others, but the refusal to admit a moment of recognition. Violence must be done to the self before it can be done to others. Living tissue of connection and recognition must be cauterized before a neighbor is reinvented as an enemy."[3]

The irony, moreover, is that once such difference is in place, people need one another's difference in order to know who they are. Such need, however, can become but further fuel for our hatred of the other, as we fear the knowledge that we need our enemy because without our enemy we will not know who we are. Wendell Berry, one of America's great contemporary writers, notes that it may be the most significant irony in the history of racism in America that racism,

> by dividing the two races, has made them not separate but in a fundamental way inseparable, not independent but dependent on each other, incomplete without each other, each needing desperately to understand and make use of the experience of the other. After so much time together we are one body, and the division between us is the disease of one body, not of two. Even the white man and the black man who hate each other are, by that very token, each other's emotional dependents.[4]

I am aware that what I have just said is not exactly an upbeat message. Indeed it almost seems perverse to tell people in Northern Ireland that any peace worth having will require that they remember one another's sins. Surely the way forward is to "forgive and forget"; or, if unable to forgive, at least to try to get along well enough to gain time to develop a perspective— which is just another name for loss of memory, in which the wrongs done by both sides seem less important. After all, what do you do when what has been done is so wrong there is nothing you can do to make it right?[5] The way forward, and there has to be a way forward, seems rightly to require some kind of forgetting.

The United States exemplifies the attempt to have time blot out past wrongs through forgetfulness. There can be no question that slavery was

141

an institution so wrong there is nothing that can be done to make it right. Slavery and its continuing effects are a wound so deep in the American soul that we prefer, both black and white, to ignore its continuing presence in our lives. Yet our very denial of our history haunts us, frightening us with the reality so that we feel helpless before this ghost of our past. Berry, reflecting on the fact that his forebears owned slaves, observes:

> There is a peculiar tension in the casualness of this hereditary knowledge of hereditary evil; once it begins to be released, once you begin to awaken to the realities of what you know, you are subject to staggering recognitions of your complicity in history and in the events of your own life. The truth keeps leaping on you from behind. For me, that my people had owned slaves once seemed merely a curious fact. Later, I think, I took it to prove that I was somehow special, being associated with a historical scandal. It took me a long time, and in fact a good deal of effort, to finally realize that in owning slaves my ancestors assumed limitations and implicated themselves in troubles that have lived on to afflict me—and I still bear that knowledge with a sort of astonishment.[6]

"I was somehow special, being associated with a historical scandal" but exemplifies the power of past wrongs over our present lives. Such burdens, of course, are but continuing forms of deception necessary to claim some decency in a more encompassing indecent system. The continuing effects of slavery Berry describes as a wound—"a historical wound, prepared centuries ago to come alive in me at my birth like a hereditary disease, and to be augmented and deepened by my life."[7] Moreover, to the extent the wound is unacknowledged, white people lack the means to name how the wound of racism they have inflicted on black people—who have certainly suffered more than whites—wounds also their own lives. Yet the master, or later the member of the dominant race—failing to know how to speak of our wound—knows it only grows more painful the more deeply it is hidden within ourselves.

For example, Berry tells the story of his great-grandfather's selling of a slave who was so defiant and rebellious he could not be made to do anything worthwhile. Berry observes such a selling but exposes the inherent violence of the slave system: any kindness in slavery was dependent on the docility of the slave. A slave who was rebellious had to be dealt with by answering the slave's violence with greater violence or using the institutional violence of slavery by selling the slave to someone more willing to enact the necessary cruelty. Berry's great-grandfather, a mild and gentle man by nature, who was unwilling to commit personal violence against the slave, sold the slave to a local slave buyer who had a reputation for knowing how to deal with "mean niggers." The selling resulted in the slave's being horribly beaten and led away with a rope.

Berry observes that it is impossible to believe his great-grandfather was oblivious to the pain in this. He had a reputation for being kind to his slaves. He could not have wanted the slave beaten. Yet they, and we, became burdened "with a malignant history and a malignant inheritance, and they endeavored to protect themselves by a carefully contrived myth, preserving them against any acknowledgment, spoken or unspoken, of their involvement."[8] Such silence envelops us, making it impossible for the wound to be lanced or cauterized. As a result, we literally lack the language to recognize ourselves across the divisions our history names. We are left in silence, playing out endless games of guilt and recrimination benefiting no one.

As a result, blacks and whites can find no common story that will enable them to heal the wound. Such a situation ironically means blacks are better able to negotiate the everyday racism that constitutes our lives than whites. As Berry observes,

> Blacks know harsher truth about the whites than the whites have ever admitted to themselves—and the whites know it. No matter how friendly a given white may *seem*, the black man, of course, fears that he is being stereotyped and misjudged. Whites fear what they feel, secretly or otherwise, to be the righteousness of the anger of blacks; as the oppressors they feel, secretly or otherwise, morally inferior to those they have oppressed. In their struggle to advance themselves, the blacks fear to be disarmed by the proffered friendliness of whites. It is even possible for whites to hesitate to offer friendliness to blacks for fear that they will seem to condescend or patronize.[9]

So we stare at one another and in the staring become less known to one another—and thus to ourselves. Allegedly having broken down the past walls of racism and slavery, we become even more divided from one another.[10] That blacks and whites increasingly know one another only as abstractions, Berry observes, is not the intensification of the crisis, it *is* the crisis. A crisis, I might add, that feels like being caught in a ditch with walls so high you cannot climb out, nor can you see the end—in short, it feels like being in a grave with the end kicked out.

C. Eric Lincoln, one of our most thoughtful commentators on race in America, thinks our only way forward is through forgetting. Lincoln observes that we suffer from a national malaise, a "melancholia," that derives from an "acute sense of moral wretchedness over the silent recognition of an ethic that failed in a historic surrender to expediency and avarice."[11] In spite of our protestations of personal innocence—"my family never owned slaves" or "I am not a racist"—Lincoln notes this brings us no relief because we have not distinguished the fact of history from the sense of obligation to justify it after the fact. He argues that we can do nothing about the reality of the past. History cannot be recalled and made right. With his usual eloquence, Lincoln argues:

> What *was* remains in fact what it was. But we can and we must separate ourselves from the psychological trauma of a history we did not commit, *and which does not require our endorsement* for its justification. The justifications for the dehumanization and enslavement of the Africans were invented *before* the fact. They were institutionalized in the fact, and they died *with* the fact. Let them rest where they are. They belong to another time, another order, another civilization. They do not belong to us, or to our children. We are beyond the past. It is irrevocable, and our chief loyalties must be to the future, to a new beginning.[12]

Lincoln calls for "no-fault reconciliation" as our only way forward in America. We must, he suggests, learn to accept each other with appreciation for what we are but even more for what we can become. He knows this will not be easily accomplished, because, as he puts it, too much "history" keeps getting in the way. Yet he thinks such reconciliation necessary. And it is not impossible. As he puts it, it "is the least we can do for our country; that is the most we can do for each other; that is the best we can do for ourselves and for our posterity. That is the ultimate meaning of survival, and the only strategy that will work."[13]

Yet I do not believe such a strategy will work in America or Northern Ireland. As Berry makes clear, and as I think Lincoln knows, the wound that silences our speech will continue to haunt us. The blood of the past has drenched our land and will continue to make it impossible to "forget" in the name of easy reconciliation. In his wonderful book *The Warrior's Honor: Ethnic War and the Modern Conscience*, Michael Ignatieff observes the process of healing the wounds of the past is the most mysterious process of all. Yugoslavia, Rwanda, South Africa are names that remind us that the past continues to torment us because it is not the past. "These places are not living in a serial order of time but in a simultaneous one, in which the past and the present are continuous, an agglutinated mass of fantasies, distortions, myths, and lies."[14]

Ignatieff notes that reporters in the Balkan war often discovered when they were told about atrocities that they were uncertain whether the stories they were hearing had occurred yesterday or in 1941 or 1841 or 1441. For those who told the tales, yesterday and today were the same. Ignatieff observes that simultaneity "is the dream time of vengeance. Crimes can never be safely fixed in the historical past; they remain locked in the eternal present, crying out for blood. Joyce understood that in Ireland the bodies of the past were never safely dead and buried; they were always roaming through the sleep of the living in search of retribution."[15]

Modern people believe that the unwillingness to forgive past wrongs is wrong. We need to simply forget our past, recognizing that when all is said and done we really share more than we differ. Ignatieff rightly, I think, challenges our modern sensibilities not only because they are unrealistic but, even more important, because they are morally superficial. The price we pay to make such strategies work is to become superficial people. There can be no "no-fault reconciliation." Good people, morally substantive people, rightly want revenge. In Ignatieff's words:

> The chief moral obstacle in the path of reconciliation is the desire for revenge. Now, revenge is commonly regarded as a low and unworthy emotion, and because it is regarded as such, its deep moral hold on people is rarely understood. But revenge—morally considered—is a desire to keep faith with the dead, to honor their memory by taking up their cause where they left off. Revenge keeps faith between generations; the violence it engenders is a ritual form of respect for the community's dead—therein lies its legitimacy. Reconciliation is difficult precisely because it must compete with the powerful alternative morality of violence. Political terror is tenacious because it is an ethical practice. It is a cult of the dead, a dire and absolute expression of respect.[16]

From this perspective the conflicts in Bosnia, South Africa, and Northern Ireland are not, as is often implicitly implied, the work of morally inferior people. Indeed the exact opposite may well be the case. For at least in these societies you still have people willing to be killed as well as to kill in honor of their forebears. Such societies are probably the only kind in modernity that deserve to be called "historical," to the extent they live by memory. I am not, of course, suggesting that all fighters in such societies fight in the name of preserving such memory. Warriors, as well as peacemakers, will have their share of cruel and sociopathological people. Rather my point is that irrespective of how the conflict may be misused by some, the conflict itself is morally worthy.

I am acutely aware that by now some of you may begin to become distinctly uncomfortable. I am sure that I must have been invited to speak to you partly because some of you knew I am an advocate of Christian nonviolence. But so far what I have had to say sounds anything but nonviolent. Indeed if I follow out the implications of my last remarks in relation to the race problem in America, it seems I should argue that what we need is a good old race war. I am, of course, not advocating such a war—though it is by no means clear to me that in fact that is not what we have been going through in America since the so-called Civil War.

But if I am not advocating war, then what alternative do I have, given the analysis I have provided to this point? My alternative, like yours, I am sure, is the name and confession: Jesus is the Christ of God. Jesus Christ is the language that ends the silences that threaten to destroy us. Christ is the memory that makes possible the memory of the wrongs we have done as well as that have been done to us. All this I believe. All this I know to be true. But such believing and knowing, as I suggested above, cannot help but be simplistic preachments without the material display of the costs required.

Ignatieff suggests that only reconciliation can break the spiral of inter-generational vengeance. Such reconciliation means, he says, substituting the vicious downward spiral of violence with the virtuous upward spiral of mutually reinforcing respect. Yet he observes further that such

> reconciliation has no chance against vengeance unless it respects the emo-tions that sustain vengeance, unless it can replace the respect entailed in vengeance with the rituals in which communities once at war learn to mourn their dead together. Reconciliation must reach into the shared inheritance of the democracy of death to teach the drastic nullity of all struggles that end in killing, the unending futility of all attempts to avenge those who are no more.[17]

Wise words, but they are not Christian words; for the reconciliation for which Ignatieff appeals is not the reconciliation of Christ. The cult of the dead is no doubt profound, but it is not the Christian cult. Our cult is called the communion of saints, and we believe that communion makes possible a reconciliation of memory otherwise impossible. But Ignatieff's account of reconciliation rightly insists that any account of such a healing of mem-ories is a politics. The challenge of articulating that politics is what remains before us. It is a fearful task requiring nothing less than making explicit what we really think the difference God makes in our world.

A BRIEF INTERLUDE FOR A WORD FROM THE OPPOSITION

Before I take up that task, I need to let the opposition to the position I am taking have a word. The position of the opposition was nicely articu-lated by a column by one of the most respected journalists in America, George Will. The column concerned the report written by President Clin-ton's Advisory Committee on Race. Will's column was entitled "Race Advi-sory Report Immune to Time's Passage."[18] Will's criticism of the Advisory Committee Report is quite simple—the report did not understand that the Civil War is over. His evidence for the Advisory Committee's failure is that the committee still thinks America should be seen in black and white. Will thinks this is perverse because Hispanics are close to becoming America's largest minority, with Asian-Americans not far behind.

According to Will, the principal impediment to upward mobility is not "institutionalized repression" but certain behaviors (principally illegitimacy) best understood in terms of class rather than race. The Advisory Committee stayed with the old racial paradigm by encouraging minorities to continue to believe their progress depends on minting ever-new rights to be secured by governmental interventions. Yet Will notes that happily old habits of mind do die. He tells the story of Douglas MacArthur, who in 1925, when he was newly stationed in Atlanta, entered the Episcopal cathedral with his staff. The result was that three-quarters of the congregation walked out. Why? They remembered his father's role in the Union capture of Atlanta.

But according to Will, sensibilities have changed. Memories of that war have long ago lost their power. Will thinks that is what is now happening to the idea of "civil rights," though many, and in particular many associated with government, fail to notice that is the case. From Will's perspective, the wonders of capitalism combined with liberal democracy mean that the battles of the past are just that, battles of the past that we are foolish to continue to fight. In a society that promises to make us all rich, all free, what is a little slavery between friends!

You may well think the last comment to be an unfair characterization. But if you do, you do not understand why the very character of democracy (at least the kind of democracy that characterizes the American political system) is an attempt to substitute freedom—which turns out to be primarily the freedom to make money—for memory. This can be nicely confirmed by an earlier column by the same George Will concerning a church-state decision made by the Supreme Court concerning Native Americans' use of peyote in religious ceremonies. Approving of the Court's decision to deny the use of peyote, Will observed,

> A central purpose of America's political arrangements is the subordination of religion to the political order, meaning the primacy of democracy. The founders, like Locke before them, wished to take and domesticate religious passions of the sort that convulsed Europe. They aimed to do so not by establishing religion, but by establishing a commercial republic—capitalism. They aimed to submerge people's turbulent energies in self-interested pursuit of material comforts.[19]

Will obviously assumes that what worked for domesticating religion— and there can certainly be no argument that it did work just as Will's characterization of the founders' intent said it would—will also work for ending the conflicts between the races in America.

I could not help but think of Will's formula for peace when I read an article called "Peace in Northern Ireland?" that appeared in *PeaceWatch*.[20] *PeaceWatch* is a magazine sponsored by the United States Institute of Peace, which is an agency of the United States Department of State. The article was a report of presentations by Professors Paul Arthur and John Darby of the University of Ulster. They are reported to believe that though the movement toward peace is still vulnerable to disruption after May 22, the peace process probably cannot be stopped.

Arthur is quoted to the effect that "the peace agreement received genuine communal support. Instead of focusing on the wounds of the past, it allows us to be visionary for the first time since Northern Ireland was created in 1921." The report goes on to characterize Arthur's views as believing that the Irish can now begin to think about building a new society in which they, like all modern peoples, can have many identities, not simply one—Catholic or Protestant. In summary, Arthur is reported to have said, "We can follow a global phenomenon in which the great stress is on diversity and the richness of diversity."[21]

I am aware that I should not make more of these brief comments by Professors Arthur and Darby than is warranted, but I fear what they say may be Ireland's future. Namely, that you will learn to resolve your differences by becoming Irish/Americans, which is but another way of saying you will leave your violence behind in the interest of becoming rich. Money is but another name for loss of memory in modernity.[22] To be sure, conflicts take place around money; but they are the conflicts of interest, not memory. Government will be necessary for seeing that such conflicts do not get out of control; but such governments will no longer be about the goods held in common, one good of which is the memory that makes you who you are. Until now Ireland's great resource for community and the conflict between communities has been your poverty. You may well believe that is too high a price to pay for being a people of memory. But if memory must be lost, I for one will be saddened.

Of course I have no standing to judge if you go the way of forgetfulness promised by capitalism and liberal democracy. I have no idea whether you have any idea how you might produce that strange entity of modernity called the "individual." I need to make clear, however, that my regret at the prospect of your finding your way to that result is a moral regret. I am, like many, charmed by your "Irishness," even the Irishness of the Protestant variety. But what you should fear is that Irishness become charming for yourselves. When that happens you will no longer be a people capable of remembering your dead. When that happens we will have all lost another moral resource, a moral example, necessary for us to have an account of how moral traditions work.[23]

GOD REMEMBERS

In a profound set of reflections on memory and its role in reconciliation, Miroslav Volf argues that a certain kind of forgetting—a forgetting quite different from that exemplified by liberalism and capitalism—is nonetheless required. Such a forgetting requires that matters of "truth" and "justice" have been taken care of, that those who have committed crimes have been named, judged, and (hopefully) transformed, that victims are safe and healed. When all this has happened, Volf argues, then we must hope for a forgetting.

> Since no final redemption is possible without the redemption of the past, and since every attempt to redeem the past through reflection must fail because no theodicy can succeed, the final redemption is unthinkable without a certain kind of forgetting.
>
> Put starkly, the alternative is: either heaven *or* the memory of horror.[24]

Volf argues that to appreciate his argument appropriately we must give up our prejudice against nonremembering. He observes that in complex relations between friends complete remembering of the past is not only impossible: it is terrifying. Memory is not simple retention but rather a complex process in which every remembering entails a forgetting. That is why the memory of a wound can be the source of our unwillingness to be redeemed. According to Volf, we must learn that we cannot make "sense" or "non-sense" as noetic responses to "solve" the problem of evil, but rather we must come to understand that the problem of *past* suffering can only be overcome by a *"nontheoretical act of non-remembering."*[25]

Such a "non-remembering" is what God makes possible. As Volf puts it,

> What will happen after God has narrated the history of the offender's sin in the context of grace and has given the offender a new identity? The answer is so simple and we are so used to hearing it that we miss its profundity: God, to whom all things are present, will *forget* the forgiven sin. The God of Israel, who is about "to do a new thing" and who calls people "not to remember the former things," promises to blot their transgression out of God's own memory (Isaiah 43:18–19, 25; cf. 65:17). "I will forgive their iniquity, and remember their sin no more" (Jeremiah 31:34).[26]

God's "forgetfulness" is nothing less than our final redemption:

149

Enveloped in God's glory we will redeem ourselves and our enemies by one final act of the most difficult grace made easy by the experience of salvation that cannot be undone—the grace of non-remembering. When not born out of resentment, the memory of inhumanity is a shield against inhumanity. But where there are no swords, no shields will be necessary. Freed by the loss of memory of all unredeemed past that un-redeems every present and separated only by the boundaries of their identities, the former enemies will embrace each other within the embrace of the triune God.[27]

Volf quickly cautions that this *last act* of nonremembering does not mean that we can forget that the Messiah has not come in glory, which means for the sake of the victims we must keep alive the memory of their suffering. But that indispensable remembering must be guided by the hope that one day we will lose the memory of hurts and offenses. We remember in the hope we may forget.

Yet I am not convinced Volf is right about the consummation as a nonremembering or about how a hope in such a consummation ought to guide our lives between the times. As Gregory Jones has put it, what protects us from our sin becoming the justification for sinning all the more is not the hope that God will forget but rather that we are able to remember forgiven sin.[28] God remembers, because if God does not remember then God is not the timeful God we find in Israel and the cross and resurrection of Christ. That God, the God of Israel, the God that raised Jesus from the dead, is the God who makes time, makes memory, possible.

The problem with Volf's nonremembering is not only the implications it seems to have for our current practices but what it implies about God's life. Consummation comes too close to a false eternity. God's eternity, as Robert Jenson maintains, is not the simple contradiction of time.

> The biblical God's eternity is his temporal infinity. What he transcends is not having of beginnings and goals and reconciliations, but any personal limitations in having them. What he transcends is any limit imposed on what can be by what he has been, except the limit of his personal self-identity, and any limit imposed on his action by the availability of time. The true God is not eternal because he lacks time, but because he takes time. The eternity of Israel's God is his faithfulness. He is not eternal in that he secures himself from time, but in that he is faithful to his commitments within time. At the great turning, Israel's God is eternal in that he is faithful to the death, and then yet again faithful. God's eternity is temporal infinity.[29]

This is but a way to say that God makes possible all the time in the world to make our time, our memories, redeemed. Our time can be redeemed because time has been redeemed by Christ. That is why we do not need to deny our memories, shaped as they are by sin, but why we can trust memories to be transformed by forgiveness and reconciliation. Christian forgiveness is not that our sins no longer matter but that our sins are now made part of an economy of salvation for the constitution of a new community otherwise impossible. As Jones puts it:

> Our forgiveness is not a gift that we receive as isolated individuals; it is a gift from the Spirit that is irreducibly particular in terms of the narratives of our pasts, yet that gift calls us into communion. In such communion, we are invited and required to learn to tell the story of each of our pasts, not ultimately in terms of diminutions, of betrayals and being betrayed, of violence committed or suffered, but in terms of the new life that induces us to repent and invites us to become holy in the future.[30]

Christian Duquoc, in an extraordinary article titled "The Forgiveness of God," suggests that what God has done through Jesus' cross is to break the link between offense and death and, in so doing, bring to an end history as a history of violence.[31] The God of Jesus interrupts the logic of violence by forgiving those who crucified his Son. It is exactly, however, because the crime is not forgotten that forgiveness is possible. "Forgiveness is not forgetfulness, it maintains the offending past in all its concreteness; nor is it lax, it calls for conversion."[32] Through the resurrection God takes up the forgiveness of his envoy and confesses his Son. Pentecost becomes the confirmation of that new beginning by which this forgiveness is offered to everyone through the church. The church is quite simply those converted, those made vulnerable, to God's history of forgiveness. They are those who have been given a new history, a new story rather than the world's story.

That is why we quite literally receive at baptism a new self and name. Baptism is but a reminder that we need the whole church to help us understand the ongoing task of unlearning the old self and learning to appropriate our new life.[33] Such an "unlearning," rather than a forgetting, turns out to be a restoration of memory by our being given a new story that makes truthful memory possible. We thereby learn as Christians that we become whom we have been made not first by learning how to forgive but by learning to be forgiven. We receive our lives individually and communally as gifts. Our lives are constituted by discovering we are part of a history we have not created, a history without which we cannot make sense of what we think we have done as well as what we think has happened to us. Baptism is thereby completed in Eucharist, through which we discover that our lives are constituted by the lifelong project of forgiveness and repentance.[34] God does not forget our sins but rather redeems our sins through eucharistic transformation.

God does not only make possible the church as a community of memory: the church is God's memory for the world. That is why it is such a scandal when the church fails to confess its sins. Too often such confessions occur when they seem no longer to matter. Yet I am not convinced confessions for past wrongs are pointless. It was a good thing for the Southern Baptists to confess that they had sinned against their black brothers and sisters. It is a good thing for Roman Catholics to confess the sin of the Protestant Reformation. It is a good thing for the French bishops to confess their complicity in the destruction of the Jews.

Indeed I think the French bishops were particularly candid as well as eloquent, insofar as they acknowledged that it is not so much what the bishops did when the Jews were put into concentration camps as what the bishops did not do. The current French bishops pass no judgments on those who acquiesced by their silence, nor do they attempt to claim that the current bishops are guilty of what took place in the past. Rather, they say they must be aware of the cost such behavior has had. "It is our church, and we are obliged to acknowledge objectively today that ecclesiastical interests, understood in an overly restrictive sense, took priority over the demands of conscience—and we must ask ourselves why."[35]

What I find remarkable about the confession of the French bishops is, first, that they were able to make such a confession. To be able to confess the sin of silence, to ask the Jewish people to hear their words of repentance, I think was possible because the Catholic Church in France is no longer politically powerful. It has nothing to lose by making such a confession. But that makes the confession no less significant. That the bishops made such a confession, moreover, suggests that the Catholic Church in France is sufficiently coherent to know that someone needs to make that confession. One of our difficulties in Protestantism is that even if we felt the need to confess our sin for the disunion of the church, who would confess it? In like manner, one of our difficulties in coming to any resolution of the problem of race in America is that we have no idea who has the status to forgive and whom to be forgiven.[36]

The French confession I also find remarkable because it surely involves the most troubled history Christians share—that is, our relationship with the Jews. Can we hope in eucharistic transformation of our memories of Christian hatred and murder of our Jewish brothers and sisters? To even speak of eucharistic transformation in such a context seems to reproduce the very practice that has justified Christian disdain for the Jew. But speak of it we must, for otherwise we lose the very resource God has given us that makes possible our belief that someday the Jewish and Christian stories, the Jewish and Christian bodies, will be one storied body. We will delight together in the lawful celebration of God's great banquet in which our sins, great though they are, do not determine our identity as God's peoples.

That, I believe, is the way forward: not forgetting but having our memories transformed through the discovery that our sins cannot determine God's will for our lives. I know of no "solution" to the relations between blacks and whites in America that is not finally the solution of a people who have learned they can pray together. To so pray is not to pretend unity by playing at being pious; rather it is to discover we are God's people.

I marvel at the miracle that African Americans do not each day have to refrain from killing a white person. That they do not I take to be not just acquiescence to the social and legal power of whites but a testimony of the depth of God's love that has and continues to sustain them. That love, I believe, moreover, to be the hope that in the future the children of slaves and the children of slaveholders will discover they worship the same God and in so doing can honor their dead without the necessity of vengeance. For do we not believe that the God we worship makes possible even the reconciliation of the dead?

ARE TRUTH AND RECONCILIATION POSSIBLE IN AND BETWEEN NATIONS?

My argument has been unapologetically theological. The possibility of reconciled memory between peoples who have wronged and been wronged by one another is but another name for church. To be such a church takes time and in the taking becomes time in God's very life.[37] God knows such a reconciled history is difficult enough for church. How could we ever think it possible for relations between people who are not church? Would we not be better off in so-called secular contexts to try to secure no more than tolerance? Forgiveness and reconciliation are far too demanding.

Timothy Garton Ash wonderfully makes this point in an article in *The New York Review of Books* about the Truth and Reconciliation Commission in South Africa.[38] Ash notes that one of the criticisms of the commission is the emphasis placed on forgiveness by Archbishop Tutu. For example, Ash tells the story of Marius Schoon, who came home to find his wife and daughter murdered by a South African security service bomb. Schoon objected bitterly to what he calls "the imposition of a Christian morality of forgiveness" that the commission represented. Or there is the story of a black African woman whose husband was abducted and killed; she now sat listening to his killer. After hearing for the first time how her husband had died, she was asked if she could forgive the man who did it. "Speaking slowly, in one of the native languages, her message came back through the interpreters: 'No government can forgive.' Pause. 'No commission can forgive.' Pause. 'Only I can forgive.' Pause. 'And I am not ready to forgive.'"[39]

Ash notes that there are no rules for handling these emotional encounters. Tutu, whom Ash describes as a fervent Anglican (even though, as Ash

153 ∎

observes, to English ears "fervent Anglican" sounds like a contradiction in terms!), strongly believes in forgiveness. In contrast, the white liberals on the commission go for sober brevity and understated sympathy. Ash confesses he prefers the understated sympathy of the white liberals, but, as he candidly acknowledges, that is what we should expect because he is a white liberal. Which accounts for the following remarks by him:

> The call for forgiveness reflects the overall priority given to "reconciliation." "Truth. The Road to Reconciliation," says a commission leaflet. Thanking de Klerk for his testimony, the Archbishop said it had contributed to finding the truth but "much more importantly to reconciliation and the healing of our nation." Later I asked him: Why "much more importantly"? For the simple reason, he said, that exposing this painful truth could so easily lead in another direction. Revelations about how the bombs were implanted could tear the nation apart almost as badly as bombs themselves. That's why he keeps harping on the need for reconciliation and *ubuntu*. Yet taken to the extreme, the reconciliation of all with all is a deeply illiberal idea. As Isaiah Berlin has taught us, liberalism means living with unresolvable conflicts of values and goals and South Africa has those in plenty. Furthermore, the history of past "reconciliations"—between Germans and Poles, for example, or Poles and Jews—reminds us that their reconciliation time is measured not in months but in generations. Here there are more than three hundred years of racial conflict to be worked through. Would it not be more realistic to define a more modest goal: peaceful coexistence, cooperation, tolerance?[40]

Ash is right. Reconciliation is a deeply illiberal idea. It is, moreover, an "idea" that is fundamentally at odds with liberal political arrangements. Reconciliation does take time—slow and painful time. All of which is a reminder, as I suggested above, that reconciliation, the refusal to forget, is a counterpolitics to the world's politics. But that does not mean that reconciliation is impossible for the politics of nations.[41] Indeed I take the Truth and Reconciliation Commission in South Africa to be a sign that such a process is possible. Of course that possibility was created by Dutch Calvinism, which in spite of being a church deeply compromised by racism remained a sufficient witness to the gospel to make just such a process possible.[42] Whether Ireland has such resources I have no basis to judge.[43]

But I do know that the church is in Ireland. I know that if the church is in Ireland then God is here. So I believe that truth and reconciliation are possible here. Indeed I believe, even in a society as secular as the United States, truth and reconciliation are even possible between blacks and whites. God never tires of miracles.

10

◼ WORSHIP, EVANGELISM, ETHICS

ON ELIMINATING THE "AND"

THE BACKGROUND OF THE "AND"

Tents—I think the problem began with tents. At least I know that tents created the problem for me. When I was a kid growing up in Texas, it never occurred to me that a revival could be had in the church building. You could only have a revival in a tent. You "went to church" in the church. You "got saved" in the tent. Worship was what you did in the church. Evangelism was what you did in the tent. Thus was created "the problem" of how to understand the relationship between worship, evangelism, and ethics.

I do not know if Don Saliers was a product of, or even participated in, tent evangelism, but I do know that, like me, he has benefited from but also suffered at the hands of an American form of Christianity that tents produced. That form of American Christianity is called Methodism. Moreover, like me, he has become "Catholic"—or at least our fellow Methodists often think the importance that Saliers and I attribute to "liturgy" has made us Catholic.[1] Saliers was trained to be a philosophical theologian, and I am supposed to be an ethicist. How and why did we ever become so fascinated

155 ◼

with liturgy, not only as something the church does but as crucial for helping us better understand how theology should be done?

It would be presumptuous for me to speak for Saliers, but I suspect that he is as concerned about liturgy, and for the same reason, as I am—he is a Methodist. This may seem a strange confession, given the separation between worship and theology so often legitimated by current Methodist practice. Yet Saliers represents personally and intellectually the Methodist refusal to separate theology and piety. Indeed, Saliers's focus on worship becomes a way to explore how the *and* might be eliminated between theology and evangelism or theology and ethics. Our difficulty, of course, is that we are members of a church whose history, particularly in America, was shaped by the tent-sanctuary divide. Currently some Methodists are even suggesting, in the interest of church growth (which has become synonymous in some circles with evangelism), that worship must be made more "user friendly." They thus assume a tension exists between worship and evangelism.

I am not suggesting that the tensions some currently feel between worship and evangelism is due to "the tents," but I think there are analogies between then and now. Certain pictures of worship and/or evangelism hold some Christians captive, leading them to think there must be a deep difference between the church at worship and the church in its evangelistic mode. At least some seem to think that the only kind of worship consistent with effective evangelism cannot be identified, let alone associated, with what the church understands as "traditional" Sunday morning worship.[2]

I would venture that those who have never experienced a tent revival, which includes many Methodists as well as Protestant evangelicals, associate evangelism with a Billy Graham crusade. Of course Billy Graham just moved the venue to football stadiums, combined that move with media savvy and organizational sophistication, and got the same tent-revival results albeit on a larger scale. What some Methodists now want and have tried to do is to move the football stadium back into the church in an effort to attract the "unchurched." The tents have become the church, which makes some worry that "traditional" Methodist worship is being watered down.

That is the context within which Saliers has tried to help us recover liturgy as the locus of the theologian's work. Of course, for him the very assumption that there may be a tension between worship and evangelism (or ethics) is indicative that something has gone terribly wrong. He rightly assumes that Christian worship has always been the way the church has both evangelized and gone about its moral formation. "Go therefore and make disciples of all nations" is a command of Jesus, not a suggestion about which we might make up our minds. Making disciples is the legitimating activity that makes the church the church. As Julian Hartt, another good Methodist, noted in his *Toward a Theology of Evangelism*, "Whenever the church is authentically Christian the conviction yet lives that its sole reason for existence is to preach the gospel of the kingdom in Christ."[3] There can be no such preaching without the church at worship. The way the church "wins converts," therefore, is by making us faithful worshipers of the God who alone is worthy of worship.

TRUTHFUL WORSHIP

Saliers has tried to help Methodists recover the way worship is evangelism and ethics by reminding us how worship is about the shaping of the affections. In what I hope has been a supportive move, I have tried to help Methodists recover the social and political significance of worship by claiming that the first task of the church is not to make the world more just but to make the world the world. Such a claim is not, as is often alleged, designed to legitimate a withdrawal of the church from the world, but just the opposite. If the church's first task is to be the church, it is so because without the church the world would have no way to understand what justice entails. For as Augustine observed, "justice is found where God, the one supreme God, rules an obedient City according to his grace, forbidding sacrifice to any being save himself alone."[4] That the "cities" in which we now exist do not worship the one true God only indicates how important it is that the church be truthful in its worship.

The church's worship, therefore, is evangelism. That we Methodists thought we had to erect tents to evangelize should have suggested to us that something had gone wrong with our worship. The tents, to be sure, assumed a generalized Christian culture in which everyone, at least everyone in the South, assumed that sometime in their life they ought to be "saved."[5] This resulted in the further problem that many who "got saved" in the tent did not show up on Sunday morning with a regularity that might testify to the lasting effects of their being saved. Nonetheless, the same people got to claim the name Christian, since they had been saved. That the saved did not act like those who had been saved, moreover, was one of the reasons "ethics" became such a concern. Some hoped if we just thought harder about something called ethics we might find a way to make people live better lives. This was a deep mistake, as it turned out.

These problems are simply reproduced by those who are currently trying to make the church the tent in order that they might reach the "seekers." They assume that what is important is that new people should come to church. As a result, they fail to see that the more important question should be, does the church to which they are coming worship God truthfully? As Saliers has insisted, in worship "form matters" for the truthful

157 ∎

shaping of our emotions. The words we use matter.[6] That the Word should be followed by table matters if we are to be rightly formed as Christians. It matters what kind of music shapes our response to the Psalms, since what the psalm declares is not separable from how we as the church sing that declaration.[7]

In this respect there is an interesting parallel between liturgy and ethics as disciplines. To think liturgically and ethically is to try to help the church discover connections by developing historical analogies, exploring philosophical and theological implications, and in the process make normative recommendations. That is why, hopefully, it is hard to distinguish the work done in liturgy from that done in ethics.[8] After all, when all is said and done liturgy and ethics are just ways to do theology, and theology, so understood, might again be construed as worship.

The liturgist's concern to have the different parts of the liturgy "make sense" is quite similar to the ethicist's concern to help the church understand the relation between certain kinds of behavior and moral judgment. Adultery means having sex with someone who is not your spouse, no matter how "loving" the extramarital encounter is or may have been. "I come to the garden alone" are not appropriate words to be sung in corporate worship, no matter how meaningful some people may find the hymn.[9] Part of the difficulty is that Protestant Christians, evangelical and mainstream alike, have lost their ability to make such judgments. They have done so, moreover, because they debased their worship in the name of evangelism and moral uplift.

As Marva Dawn reminds us in her *Reaching Out without Dumbing Down*, worship is "for" God, which is not the same thing as "meaningful for us."[10] Worship that is for God is, she argues, character forming. That truthful worship of God requires that we proceed in "good order" is a reminder of the very God who alone is deserving of worship. For, as the quote from Augustine reminds us, it is not any God that Christians worship, but the God whose justice is to be found in Jesus' cross and resurrection. To learn to worship that God truthfully requires that our bodies be formed by truthful habits of speech and gesture. To be so habituated is to acquire a character befitting lives capable of worshiping God.

One of the ironies of our times is that many "conservative" Christians fail to understand the relation between truthful worship and truthful living. For example, many "conservatives" became upset at women and men allegedly worshiping Sophia in the name of making liturgy "meaningful for women." Yet too often the same people who criticize the worship of God as Sophia are more than ready to distort the proper order of Christian worship in the name of evangelism. They, of course, say they use the name of Jesus, but they fail to see that *how* Jesus' name is used makes all the difference.

Without the Eucharist, for example, we lack the means to know the kind of presence made possible by Jesus' resurrection.

The Eucharist is usually not considered an essential aspect of Christian worship by those concerned with church growth. Evangelism means getting people to church, because unless we goes to church, it is assumed, our lives are without moral compass. Thus the assumption that lack of attendance at church and our society's "moral decay" go hand and hand. What such people fail to see is that such decay begins with the assumption that worship is about "my" finding meaning for my life rather than the glorification of God. Such evangelism is but another name for narcissism. Christian worship requires that our bodies submit to a training otherwise unavailable so that we can become capable of discerning those who use the name of Jesus to tempt us to worship foreign gods. Without the Eucharist we lose the resource to discover how those gods rule our lives.

It is important to note the problem is not whether our worship is "contemporary" or "traditional." Too often such an alternative is an attempt to make us choose hymns that were contemporary in the seventeenth century but sound "traditional" today because we no longer remember what seventeenth-century music sounded like. Nor is it a question of whether worship can be changed. Worship is always being "changed." To remain "the same" when everything around you is changing, whether you like it or not, *is* to be changed. That is why those who sometimes insist on the actual use of tents may think they are doing the same thing that was done in the past, but in fact the very consciousness required to use tents when tents are no longer necessary makes the use of these tents different.

The question, then, is not choosing between "contemporary" or "traditional," to change or not to change, but rather the faithful character of our worship, insofar as such worship shapes the truthful witness of the church to the world. The problem with churches that make "evangelism" (that is, the continuing acquisition of new members) the purpose of their worship is not whether the worship is contemporary. The question is whether they are worshiping the God of Jesus Christ. Moreover, it is not just the "church growth" churches, the Willow Creeks, that have that problem, but "normal" mainstream churches.[11]

Consider, for example, this statement on the back of the bulletin of a very "successful" Methodist church (name changed to protect the guilty): "You are welcome, just as you are, at 'Pleasant City'! Everyone is welcome here. We particularly welcome those who have been away from church for a while, and those who are not members of any church. Whether you're married, single, divorced or in transition, you truly matter to us because you matter to God. We would be honored to have you become a member of Pleasant City Church. Check the box on the friendship pad if you wish to discuss church membership."[12]

Is that evangelism? What would worship in such a church look like? How would anyone in that church know which god it is that seems allegedly so concerned about them? It is easy to criticize Willow Creeks, but Willow Creeks merely exemplify the loss of the Christian worship of God in the name of "more members." The difficulty with worship intentionally shaped to entertain those who are "new" is not that it is entertaining but that the god that is entertained in such worship cannot be the Trinity. For example, to worship the Trinity requires at the very least that we learn to say together the Apostles' Creed. That such a discipline has, in the name of evangelism, become odd, even for Methodists, is but an indication of how distorted our worship has become.

The heart of Saliers's work has been to try to remind his church, the Methodist Church, that faithful and truthful worship of the crucified God is evangelism. That he has done so has not won him universal acclaim among Methodists. That he insists that worship be done "right" is rightly seen by some as a threat to church growth. I suspect that Saliers does not make that erroneous assumption. The fact that large numbers of people are attracted to a church is not in itself a sign of false worship, but like me he probably thinks that if such is the case it is an indication that a close examination of how that church worships is a good idea.[13] That we, moreover, feel the need for such an examination is because we are Methodists who believe that the shaping of our lives in worship is inseparable from the moral shaping of our lives—a shaping that cannot help make us appear quite odd given the assumptions about what it means to be "morally normal" in American society.

HOLINESS

The name we Methodists have used to indicate the inseparability of worship, evangelism, and ethics is *holiness*. We believe that God's salvation is nothing less than participation in God's very life through word and sacrament. Worship is what we do for God, but in that doing we believe our lives are made part of God's care of creation. To be made holy is to have our lives rendered unintelligible if the God who has claimed us in Jesus Christ is not the true God. To be made holy is to have our lives "exposed" to one another in the hope that we will become what we have been made.

From Wesley's perspective, Christian worship is evangelism because worship is converting work.[14] Though this may sound Pelagian, the work that worship does is not something we do apart from God. Worship requires that our sins be named, confessed, forgiven.[15] In worship we discover that sin is not something we do, but rather it is a power that holds us captive.[16]

The good news of the gospel, the message proclaimed to the nations, is that we are freed from sin by the God who would be honored, who would be worshiped, before all else.

From a Wesleyan perspective, to be made holy, to be made capable of accepting forgiveness for our sins so that we might worthily worship God, does not involve just "personal holiness." As Augustine suggested above, nothing is more important for a society than to worship God justly. Without such worship terrible sacrifices will be made to false gods. Contrary to the modern presumption that as enlightened people we are beyond sacrifice, few societies are more intent on sacrifice than those we call modern.[17] Societies that think they have left sacrifice behind end up basing their existence on the sacrifice of the poor in the name of human progress. Christians believe that we are the alternative to such sacrificial systems because we have been given the gift of offering our "sacrifice of thanksgiving" to the One who alone is worthy to receive such praise. That is what makes us a holy people, a people set apart, so that the world might know there is an alternative to murder.

That I teach "ethics" through the liturgy and Saliers refuses to do theology as if prayer does not matter is, I hope, testimony to the fact that we are Methodist "perfectionists."[18] We have staked our work and our lives on the assumption that if in some small way we can help our church recover liturgical integrity, we will not have to deal with a question about the relation between worship, evangelism, and ethics. Of course it may still be useful to distinguish between worship, evangelism, and ethics as subjects of study, but hopefully such distinctions will be seen as part of the church's ministry reflected in a diversity of gifts. Such gifts, however, cannot become separate disciplines or realms if they are to be of service.

Yet neither of us can deny that if we do in fact worship God truthfully, we may well find the church again worshiping in tents. For such worship creates a people who by necessity are on the move, forced to wander among the nations, home nowhere yet everywhere. Such a people are bound to attract followers, because the God who has called them from the nations is so beautifully compelling. That is, after all, why we believe that there is nothing more important in a world that does not believe it has the time to worship God than to take time to worship God truthfully.[19]

161

11

■ENDURING

OR, HOW ROWAN GREER TAUGHT ME HOW TO READ

BEGINNING WITH FRIENDSHIP

I must begin with friendship. That Rowan claimed me as a friend has everything to do with how he taught me how to read. Such a claim seems odd today, but then it was Rowan who taught me the oddness of our now thinking it odd to think that friendship and reading are separate activities. In the ancient world it was assumed that reading and friendship were interrelated. Thus the importance of our friendship for how Rowan taught me to read and, in particular, to read the Scripture.

Some might think us unlikely friends. We are very different. Rowan is urbane; I am not. He went to Yale. I went to Southwestern University in Georgetown, Texas. He is a scholar's scholar; I am not. He actually knows what he is talking about. I am never sure I "know" anything, yet I must go on talking. I suppose that is the difference between historians and theologians in our time, but then one of the lessons Rowan taught me was to distrust the very distinction between history and theology. Nevertheless, in our time the distinction between historians and theologians is undeniable—

thus the "oddness" of my presumption that I can say anything interesting about Rowan Greer's work. I have to talk about "methodological" questions because I do not know, for example, Paulinus of Pella the way Rowan knows Paulinus of Pella. Indeed, I know Paulinus only because Rowan taught me to understand the importance of the life of Paulinus.

That Rowan has taught me the importance of lives such as that of Paulinus is inseparable from our friendship. I was never formally Rowan's student, but I have always been his student. It was Rowan who taught me to be suspicious of the "historical-critical" method as *the* way to get at the meaning of the biblical text. It was Rowan who taught me that there is something quite curious about the curricular division between New Testament and patristics. And it was from Rowan that I began to understand that the study of Scripture makes sense only as a theological task of the church. I suspect that Rowan never knew he was my teacher, but like most good teachers Rowan never notices how he teaches those lessons that animate his life.

Friendship between a teacher and a student is not, of course, always possible. A teacher-student relationship is not a relationship between equals. Yet equality is a slippery notion. Thus Aristotle, with his usual insight about things human, notes that friendship does not so much require a strict equality between friends as create equality through common judgments.[1] Such judgments require time; indeed, such judgments make time possible. Rowan and I have now been friends for over thirty years, which means the character of our friendship has changed; what has not changed is that we remain friends bonded not only by the history of our friendship but by common loves.

Over the years, of course, we have discovered not only common judgments but differences. He loves dogs; I love cats. I am angry about the church's accommodation to the world; he is bemused. I am at war with the current intellectual formations that produce and reproduce the knowledges that legitimate liberal Protestantism; Rowan goes his own way willing to ignore them if they will ignore him. I am angry he is ignored. He would be aghast if the significance of his work were discovered. It never occurs to him to think of his work as "having significance." What a "silly" thought. All of which is to say that the very character of this essay, where I show the significance of his work, or at least the difference it has made for the way I "do" theology, would not be altogether welcomed by him. But as he would say, "There you have it."

In short, what I want to show is that Rowan Greer must bear at least some of the blame that I am labeled a "sectarian, fideistic tribalist." The way he taught me to "read" the Bible through the Fathers forced me to challenge the very notion of "history" as a given. The notion that "history" is just "there," moreover, is part of the legitimating structure of modernity necessary for schooling us to believe the way things are is the way things have to be. By teaching me to read differently, Rowan taught me that being a Christian could not help but make one odd.

In truth, I suspect that such "oddness" is one of the "likenesses" that Rowan and I have always seen in each other. Indeed some may think, not without cause, that our willingness to be "out of step" with the world around us is pathological. There are, of course, differences in the way we have gone about being odd. For Rowan it is a way of living. I have turned it into a career. Rowan is less likely to make the mistake of confusing our oddness with being Christian, but I should like to think our willingness to live against the stream might in some ways be of use to God.

Broken Lights and Mended Lives: Helping Christians Live Historically

In the preface to *Broken Lights and Mended Lives*, Rowan observes that his approach in the book is peculiar for two reasons: (1) he attempts to enter the world of early Christianity on its own terms and (2) he is sympathetic to the early church, since he finds himself to be "a convinced Christian, at least as convinced as an Anglican can be."[2] Rowan notes that some may find these "peculiarities" to be an indication that he has abandoned any attempt at objectivity, which would be tantamount to repudiating the conventions of modern scholarship. He denies such to be the case, noting that we must aim for disinterested and impartial assessment of the historical while never forgetting that we will never be able to remove our prejudices altogether.

I confess I am not convinced that he can have it both ways. Of course everything hangs on what you mean by "objectivity," "disinterestedness," and "impartial." I am not opposed to attempts to be objective, but I assume "objectivity" but names one's willingness to locate one's work in some context or other, so that others equally committed to similar endeavors can help us know the limits and possibilities of what we are trying to do. To be sure, the wonderful thing about Rowan is that he has never been preoccupied with devising a theory about history; rather he simply got on with it. For if anyone has exemplified what might be called theology in a historical mode, it has been Rowan.

Let me try to explain these last remarks by contrasting Rowan's way of doing history with recent proposals of George Marsden. The argument Marsden makes in *The Outrageous Idea of Christian Scholarship* might appear quite congenial to the way Rowan works as a Christian historian.[3] Marsden's defense of Christian scholarship certainly seems to support Rowan's attempt to provide sympathetic accounts of the Fathers. Yet I believe Rowan's way of working to be much more radical than Marsden's proposal allows.

For example, Marsden draws on William James in conceiving of the modern university as the embodiment of pragmatic liberal discourse. An apt metaphor for the university is a corridor in a hotel. In one room off the corridor, a man writes an atheistic volume; in another, a person prays for strength; and in yet another, a chemist investigates the properties of a substance. James concludes that these diverse scholars jointly own the corridor "and they must pass through it if they want a practicable way of getting into or out of their respective rooms."[4] Marsden notes that he finds this image quite congenial, because if it is the modus operandi of the contemporary university, then there is no justification for marginalizing all religious viewpoints.

Those who work as Christian historians are therefore identified by their subject matter more than by any peculiar method. Marsden concedes that Christians and non-Christians will likely use precisely the same methods for determining certain matters of historical fact—for example, the date Washington crossed the Delaware. Putting the matter more forcefully, Marsden claims that as a matter of fact "explicitly Christian convictions do not very often have substantial impact on the techniques used in academic detective work, which make up the bulk of the technical, scientific side of academic inquiry."[5] Marsden calls this "methodological secularization." According to this perspective, most historical work centers on a body of natural phenomena equally accessible to all. The Christian historian can accept this common ground, while not ignoring history's "spiritual dimensions as created and ordered by God."[6]

There is no question that Marsden's heart is in the right place, but unfortunately his account of history nicely confirms Nietzsche's suggestion that such an understanding of history can only be an attempt by the living to bury the past. As Nietzsche puts it:

> A historical phenomenon clearly and completely understood and reduced to an intellectual phenomenon, is for him who has understood it dead: for in it he has understood the mania, the injustice, the blind passion, and in general the whole earthly darkened horizon of that phenomenon, and just in this he has understood its historical power. So far as he is a knower this power has now become powerless for him: not yet perhaps so fast as he is a living being. History, conceived as pure science and become sovereign, would constitute a kind of final closing out of the accounts of life for mankind. Historical education is wholesome and promising for the future only in the service of a powerful new life-giving influence, of a rising culture for example; that is, only when it is ruled and guided by a higher power and does not itself rule and guide.[7]

It may seem quite unfair to attribute to Marsden Nietzsche's view that objective history is the way the living exact revenge on the dead. Marsden would surely object that he has no wish to make history a "pure science." But it is not a question of intention but of execution. If Christian historians are to be Christians in their writing of history, it is not enough for them to differ only in what they choose to study. The truth is that Christians and non-Christians alike may use quite different methods and ways to date when Washington crossed the Delaware. Nothing is more controversial than the calendar. After all, few matters are more normative than dating, if you remember that 1776 is not a fact but a story. The expression "Washington crossed the Delaware" is not a brute fact, free-standing, intelligible in isolation from one narrative or another.[8]

The extraordinary thing about the way Rowan has done history—the way he has taught us to be readers of Irenaeus, Theodore, Origen, Gregory of Nyssa, Augustine, and so many more—is his learned innocence about the matters that exercise Marsden. Rowan never needed James's permission to do history from a Christian standpoint. He just did it, and in the doing he helped us understand not only Theodore but what Theodore's work was about—namely, God. Theology, to be sure, is a broken light; but if such a light does not make a difference for how the historian works, then the very way history is done, the way we are taught to read "the past," cannot help but reproduce a world in which God does not matter. Accordingly, Rowan has not written in an attempt to make the story he tells "intelligible to anyone," whoever that may be; rather his history has been done at the service of those who desire to live lives appropriate to the view that God matters.[9]

Rowan, without calling attention to how he works, makes no hard-and-fast distinction between history and theology. He does not because he could not, given the texts he was helping us read. He therefore takes as his task in *Broken Lights and Mended Lives* to help us see the relationship between theological developments and Christian behavior. As he puts it,

> The broken lights are meant to mend lives; vision ought to be translated into virtue. How may the Christian destiny, the vision of Christ's victory, be related to the Christian life? To what degree does that life participate in the destiny, and to what degree does it merely anticipate it? Moreover, is the translation one meant to include all people and capable of doing so? These issues could be addressed in a number of ways. For example, we might examine what were supposed Christian virtues with a view to discovering their relation to theological themes. But what seems remarkable to me about the Christian vision of Christ's victory is the consensus of the Fathers that this victory is mediated to us through the common life of the Church.[10]

Broken Lights and Mended Lives is written to help us understand that Christian theology is not just more thought. For the church fathers, knowing the good and doing the good could not be separated. "The Christian life was for them a growth toward perfection, and as the Christian's knowledge grew, so did his virtue. Similarly, progress in virtue meant progress in knowledge; and the dialectic pressed the Christian forward toward his destiny."[11] Thus questions of the humanity of Christ took the form of metaphysical issues of substance but—like all important theological and metaphysical questions—could not and cannot be abstracted from inquiry about how we are to live.[12] Consider, for example, this illuminating paragraph from *Broken Lights and Mended Lives*:

> The place we have seen given to the individual in Cappadocian monasticism correlates with Nyssa's understanding of the individual. By thinking of individuality in terms of relationship, Nyssa suggest that the more fully Christians are related to one another in Christ, the more they realize their true identity. As relations of the one human nature of Christ, which is the image of God, all human beings are meant to find their perfection in the completed and perfected image of God. This destiny is in some measure a present possibility when the members of the monastic community bring their gifts to the service of one another. The balance Basil attempts to strike between the cenobite and the hermit is one that is defined by the image theology we find in Nyssa's thought. If we ask how we are to imagine or to understand Nyssa's corporate understanding of human nature, we must think of the monastery where all hold everything in common, using and possessing one another's gifts.[13]

In short, *Broken Lights and Mended Lives* helps us see why "theology in the early Church was always directly and indirectly concerned with the common life of Christians. From one point of view, theologians attempted to put into words the corporate experience of the Church. The Christian story, continuously repeated in the reading of Scripture and in the liturgy, found its focus for the Fathers of the Church in the victorious Christ, the new humanity. And even more the technical aspects of early Christian theology were designed to explain this Christ and his significance."[14] Rowan knew how to do "postmodern" historiography before there was a postmodern historiography. He did not need "theory" to help him know how to "do history." He had something much more important than theory—he had, and has, the confidence that comes only through many readings that the Fathers meant what they said about God.[15] Moreover, if what they said about God is to be presented "objectively," then what they said about God must make a difference for how, as well as to whom, we tell their stories.

LIVING BETWEEN THE TWO CITIES

That history is written to and for a specific community is but a reminder, as Marsden suggested above, that the historian's work both reflects and serves a politics. Some may object to the account I have given of how Rowan taught me to read as an attempt at self-justification, to the extent that I read him in support of my peculiar theological politics. It is one thing to read Rowan's account in *Broken Lights and Mended Lives* as underwriting my contention that the very distinction between theology and ethics (and history) can distort the character of Christian speech; but it is quite another matter to suggest that his account of the church is congruent with my "sectarianism." He is, after all, an Episcopalian—which is not exactly like being a Mennonite.

But then I am not a Mennonite. I have always insisted that I am a *High-Church* Mennonite. That means I am a Methodist, or perhaps, more candidly, I am trying to live and write and think according to what I think Methodism should be. Methodism, moreover, has at least some claim to be within the Episcopal tradition. By saying I am a High-Church Mennonite, I am trying to suggest the Mennonite understanding of the church's position toward the world is possible only if such a church is sustained by the kind of theology found in the church fathers, and in particular in that confession we call the Nicene Creed.[16]

Even if Will Willimon and I stole the title *Resident Aliens* from Rowan's depiction of "alien citizens" in *Broken Lights and Mended Lives*, the verbal similarities may hide deep differences.[17] Rowan, after all, does describe the Christian caught between church and world as "a marvelous paradox."[18] In order to explain the paradoxical character of Christian existence, Rowan provides wonderful accounts of Tertullian and Clement, noting how the latter saw Christian release from bondage to custom and idolatry as a freeing not only *from* the world but also *for* the world.[19]

Rowan, moreover, provides a quite sympathetic account of Constantine's effect on Christian thinkers such as Chrysostom, Eusebius, and Lactantius. These theologians and churchmen, while no doubt wanting to put the church to the cause of *Romanitas*, never lost the tension between the transforming character of Christianity and the establishment of the church as the religion of Rome. Yet, Rowan observes, there is little evidence that the lives of ordinary citizens were transformed in any obvious or far-reaching way by Christianity, which may indicate that the ideal itself had become corrupted insofar as it lost touch with the paradox of alien citizenship. Which leads Rowan to observe that he is "tempted" to the view "that, however viable as an ideal, alien citizenship cannot be put into practice, at least on a social scale".[20]

By "social scale" I think Rowan means the gospel cannot run an empire. The gospel, however, did create monasticism, which Rowan characterizes as "a protest against a Church gone public and an attempt to retain the spirit of the martyrs."[21] Indeed, in his wonderful chapter on monasticism in *Broken Lights and Mended Lives*, "The City on a Hill," Rowan

169

observes that monasticism, even in its most radical forms as protest against the church, remained tied to essential practices such as the celebration of the Eucharist.[22] Thus Basil, like Chrysostom, thought monasticism to be "a light shining into the surrounding world, persuading people towards the ideal of the Christian life. The monastic ideal is meant to be a leaven in the Church and in all society."[23] Here we have no Troeltsch-like claims that monasticism is a forerunner of a sectarian withdrawal from the world. Instead Rowan helps us see the complexity of the "alien" character of the Christian witness in a world falling apart.

Yet in truth I suspect Rowan does not think monasticism is *the* way, or at least the only way, that the alien character of our existence as Christians finds expression. In the last chapter of *Broken Lights and Mended Lives*, "The Collapse of the West," Rowan observes,

> As I have pointed out, the monasteries in the early Middle Ages served the double function of refuges and of foundations for the reordering of society. There is something to be said for the view that the Church began by providing deliverance from the disasters that attended the collapse of Roman rule in the West, but ended by becoming the basis for a new order of society. A pattern that can be discerned in the first centuries of the Church's existence, leading to the new order of the Christian Empire, seems to repeat itself when we examine the end of late antiquity and the birth of the new order of the Middle Ages. Is this a way of looking at our own times? And are we living in the midst of the death of an old culture in which Christ brings us not so much an ordering of our society as a deliverance from it?[24]

Broken Lights and Mended Lives can be read as a meditation on how we are to live as Christians, assuming a positive answer to these questions.

Accordingly, Paulinus of Pella becomes for Rowan a central character for instructing us how to endure when we live in a world coming apart. For the story of Paulinus, the story of how a fairly worldly young man lost possessions and power in the changing empire, is, as Rowan tells, a story of endurance. Paulinus regards his life as God's gift; for, as he says, God has reasonably chastened him "with continual misfortunes, he [God] has clearly taught me that I ought neither to love too earnestly present prosperity which I knew I might lose, nor to be greatly dismayed by adversities wherein I had found that his mercies could succor me." To which Rowan adds the following observation: "His Christian faith did not empower Paulinus to take an active and constructive part in the events of his time, nor did it lead him to withdraw from society to the security of the monastery. But it did enable him to endure, and in that enduring there is testimony to the victory of Christ."[25]

Paulinus thus becomes for Rowan the exemplification of Augustine's account of the fall of Rome in *The City of God*. Augustine, according to

Rowan, rightly refuses to interpret the fall of Rome as apocalyptic, since Augustine does not accept the theory that the Christian empire was sacred. Yet he also denies that the disaster can be anything less than tragic.

> The paradox of the Christian life is that the evils we suffer in our earthly pilgrimage must be taken with absolute seriousness, but so must the destiny that awaits us in the City of God. There are no victories or defeats in the present that really matter. All that counts is the final victory for the saints in the age to come. The practical implications of Augustine's view is that what matters is to endure. The Christian can be neither fully involved in society nor fully withdrawn from it. . . . I am persuaded by Faulkner's view that we cannot alter the tragic character of human life, but that we can endure and so prevail.[26]

I cannot deny, in contrast to Rowan, that the position I have been developing regarding the church's position vis-à-vis liberal social orders may seem to entail more active stances than that captured by the phrase "mere endurance." For one thing, I would never qualify endurance by "mere." Nor would Rowan, I think, if I have rightly understood his account of endurance. Indeed, Christian endurance may take quite aggressive stances (monasticism being one example) toward the world. I am, moreover, quite sympathetic with figures such as Paulinus to the extent that they teach us how to go on in a world where we have no means of locating ourselves or of determining if we might even be lost.[27]

Yet finally—and I suppose many would take this to be the nub of the matter—it must surely be the case that Rowan remains at best indifferent to, if not supportive of, a Constantinian social strategy by the church. Or perhaps, put more accurately, Rowan simply assumes that the accusation of Constantinianism does not do justice to the complexity of lives like that of Paulinus.[28] Yet my attack on Constantinianism has never denied the importance of witnesses like Paulinus. Rather the question has always been what kind of church disciplines, disciplines such as knowing how to read our Christian past in the way Rowan has taught us in *Broken Lights and Mended Lives*, are necessary to make lives like Paulinus's possible even today.[29]

ENDING WITH FRIENDSHIP

Which brings me back to friendship. For if, as Rowan suggests, Christians are to live "both in this world and in light of the next," as well as "preserve both the holiness and the catholicity of the Church," we will do so only to the extent God has made us his friends and, thus, friends with one another.[30] Such friendship but names the possibility that God's victory in Christ made possible. In an extraordinary "summing up" of Christian doctrine, Rowan observes:

> As Irenaeus says, it was necessary that the victory be human; and yet only God could win it, and only the union of God and humanity could make it effective. The development of the doctrine of the Trinity serves to enable the Church to define the Victor as God without compromising Christian commitment to the heritage of Jewish monotheism; the christological debates revolved around how to maintain that the divine Victor was also the human Victor and the human being given victory. Christ is the Mediator. Both divine and human, he is the saved Savior and the sanctified Sanctifier. Thus, the Christian can see in him not only the power of God to save, but the ways in which that power works: It conquers death, whereby the Resurrection of Christ becomes the principle for the general resurrection in which all shall partake, and it conquers the sin and blindness that separate human beings from God. And so redemption carries with it the idea of God's triumph over sin and his self-disclosure as perfect Truth, Goodness, and Beauty. The physical, moral, and spiritual dimensions of Redemption are all rooted in the classical accounts of Christ as divine and human, as the Victor who also supplies the paradigm of what victory means.[31]

That Rowan taught me how to read, how to be friends with those who make up that great tradition called Catholic, by claiming me as friend is not simply a biographical point. Such is the way God has chosen to befriend us: by becoming one of us. Another name of "the way" is *church*. I am forever grateful that Rowan helped me discover that way.

12

■Captured in Time

Friendship and Aging

Stanley Hauerwas and Laura Yordy

GROWING OLD IN AMERICA

In our society the single most striking portrayal of old people is their loneliness. Friendship with the elderly is almost unimaginable, as our very conception of what it means to be old is isolation. This isolation compounds with frailty, lack of usefulness to the world, dislocation from home and possessions, forced dependency, and nostalgia to construct a pitiable picture of a person who is unloved and, in many ways, unlovable.

We think, therefore, an exploration of the relation of friendship and aging long overdue. Obviously, any account of the relationship between aging and friendship involves questions of how one conceives of aging and growing old in itself. Though we all grow old, how we grow old and how we understand its significance obviously vary from one historical context and community to another. We cannot pretend to speak for all communities concerning the relation between friendship and aging. Rather, we intend to draw on Christian resources to illumine how Christians should understand how friendship is possible not only between the elderly but across generations.

We need to be as candid as we can, however, about our own perspective. Our account is shaped by our own experiences in middle-class white Protestant America and consciously directed toward mainstream middle-class churches (which are too often "white"). African-American, Asian-American, and Hispanic experiences of aging and friendship seem substantially different from those of whites. Nonetheless, we hope that the stories and practices we share in the Christian tradition can illustrate both the issues and resources for addressing those issues. We want to understand how friendship is not only possible but necessary for that community through time we call the church. Of course there are and have been many ways of being old even within the Christian community, just as there are many ways of being young. We are not suggesting that all elderly people will be the same, but rather that the very diversity of gifts present in the young and the old is a resource for the building up of a community in time that has time enough for friendship.

Our account is at once descriptive and normative, but it will not be easy to distinguish one from the other clearly. We begin descriptively, by providing an account of aging and loneliness particularly as it occurs in American society. We do not pretend, however, that our account is free of normative presumptions, in that we make generalizations about the relation of growing old and death which we assume should not be avoided. The middle section of the essay is more explicitly normative. We draw, perhaps somewhat surprisingly, on monastic accounts of friendship in order to develop an account of Christian friendship. We think this account is important for teaching us the nature of friendship in a community determined not to let time alienate us from one another. In conclusion, we make some suggestions about what churches might do to make friendship within and between generations a reality.

We realize that our writing from an explicitly theological perspective may be a bit surprising for readers who do not share our theological conviction. Yet we hope that our willingness to speak from our own tradition will illumine other perspectives. We need to make clear, however, that assumed in the "method" of this article is what some would characterize as a "postmodern" theological point of view. That is, we assume no universal perspective on aging (or anything else) is possible. Accordingly, we can do nothing else but speak from the traditions in which we live. We make no apology for the tack we take in this article but hope it will encourage others to write from other traditions.

To grow old is to lose our acquaintances and lifelong friends to distance, illness, and death. As our friends move away or die, we lose the confirmation of our own life stories and identities. We are not even sure, as we grow old, that we are still the same people we were. We are unable to recognize in our flesh and bones the image of who we thought we were. The body that stares back at us from the mirror just does not seem to be "our body." So we are alienated not only from others but from ourselves.

Of course the old have memories, but memory itself may fail, thus contributing to our alienation from our own lives. Alternatively memory may remind us, in excruciating detail, of the person we used to be but are no longer. The stories that make up our lives, that constitute who we are, are in many ways too rich to be told. Our telling them can increase our loneliness, because the telling is always less than the life lived or shared. In short, growing old cannot help but be a continuing alienation from who we once were.

In his wonderful book *Old Friends*, which describes life in a retirement home, Tracy Kidder reports that one elderly man had, since his wife died, "suffered from memories."[1] That describes our situation perfectly—we suffer from our memories since we cannot live without our memories. For example, Kidder notes, the same elderly gentleman recalled the time early in his marriage when his wife dropped a frying pan and he yelled at her. "If she could come back to life now, she could drop a hundred of them and I wouldn't give a darn," he now says. Kidder observes that such a remembrance is an indication that we do not control our memories so much as they control us. This man remembered his marriage as a happy one overall, yet the stories he now recalled and most wanted to tell were about a dropped frying pan and his sixty-year-long disagreement with his wife about demonstrativeness.

> His wife would say she wished he'd tell her that he loved her, and he would protest that he preferred to do the sorts of things that proved it. She would say she understood, but that any woman wants to hear the words, and Art would answer, "It doesn't run in my family to be like that." He started telling his wife he loved her several times each day, in their room in Sunrise, during the weeks before she died. "But she never said a word. Not 'Yes, dear, I forgive you.' I would've liked that. It seemed it hurt her all her life."[2]

Later in his book Kidder notes that a basic principle of neurology holds that failures in memory tend to proceed inversely with time. "As memory fades, the past comes nearer."[3] This process, Kidder observes, no doubt has a biological origin, but the psychological result has a logic of its own. In old age many people seem to remember best what has mattered most to them. Such memory cannot help but create a kind of sadness to the extent it is a reminder that what we so cared about is no longer "us."

Another way to put the matter is that as we grow old, our attempts to live in the past, which should be one of the benefits of growing old, can also be alienating to the extent that nostalgia distorts the story of our lives. This is particularly the case given the artificial life created by retirement and nursing homes. There the elderly discover they are not only strangers to one another but to themselves. They try to create commonalities through the telling of stories as a way to discover friendships, but too often such tellings make the story foreign for both the narrator and the listener. What seems lacking is any shared tradition through which such tellings contribute to the building of a wider community.

The obituaries common at retirement homes are poignant indications of the loneliness that seems unavoidable in such circumstances. Kidder describes the obituaries often posted on the ubiquitous obituary board. The activities director or her aide usually writes the brief encomiums, which consist of a standard line or two—"'a loving woman,' 'will be missed by family, friends, and staff.'" Some attempt is usually made to say something of the person's individuality, but not much can be said—"'a lover of plants,' 'an avid bingo player,' 'enjoyed children.'"[4] Anonymous deaths testifying to the sad fact that if you live too long in this society you will, by necessity, die alone.

Such anonymity is not just the fate of the elderly but the intensification of our society's emphasis on autonomy. We believe that our first task is to create our own stories, to make our lives ours, without the help of others. We can never accomplish that task without the help of others, of course, but our very attempt to be autonomous prevents the acknowledgment that we are dependent. And, unfortunately, we bring these habits with us to our aging.

For example, one of the ways we try to fend off the anonymity that is the inextricable byproduct of the quest for autonomy is to try to become "successful." This effort is closely tied to our cultural habits of consumption. Many expensive "luxury" products are advertised as markers of the buyer's "arrival" at a status of wealth, financial security, worldly achievement. You, the buyer, have worked hard, made a contribution to society, hoarded your money ("invested wisely"), and now in retirement you "deserve" to drive an expensive car. You are someone; you have arrived. You stand on the peak of success.

Contrast this advertisement image with the far more common reality: a person (usually male in this scenario, but more and more often female) works hard for many years, acquires a house and possessions over time, and reaches the age of voluntary or forced retirement. He no longer makes a tangible contribution. He receives a smaller income and gradually has to give up the possessions he worked so hard to acquire: the house is too hard to maintain, the driver's license must be relinquished, the furniture given away. You are nobody; you have arrived. Instead of standing on the peak of success, however, you have tumbled into the abyss of old age in working-class or middle-class America. Because achievement is so often defined as "having it all," having less *means* failure. And who wants to be friends with a failure?

To grow old, therefore, means to learn to live without friends. This unfortunately means in our society that we are put completely at the mercy of the family. Many old people, especially widows and widowers, are directly cared for by the family—most often spouses, daughters, daughters-in-law, or nieces. The old person depends on family for anything ranging from financial advice to championship to transportation to daily feeding, toileting, and bathing. This dependency violates our sense of autonomy; we cannot manage by ourselves. But it also violates the autonomy of the family caregivers. Contrary to the common cultural image of adults as people who make choices about their lives, we do not choose our aging family members, and we may not feel we chose to care for them—even as we engage in that care for long periods. Moreover, because we often view friendship as a chosen relationship between equals, this dependency seems to erode or even prohibit any friendship between adults and aging parents.

Of course, as we have already indicated, retired people can escape the family by moving away from their homes and their communities into retirement homes. Such "homes" can be and often are quite wonderful and may provide the additional care needed. Or the move may be prompted by social mandates to seek a more comfortable climate or a city with cultural resources and activities directed toward the elderly. Such moves may be quite appropriate, but they have the effect of making the elderly displaced people—without clear membership in community and its attendant responsibilities, without close neighbors, without friends to remind us who (and whose) we are.

In fact, one of the ways the elderly are isolated in our society is the assumption that to be old is to be free. The elderly are assumed no longer to bear "normal" responsibilities. They can return to "childhood," seeking nothing but their own immediate gratification. Too often such "freedom," however, turns out to be a form of abandonment by family and community. Such an abandonment is what we should expect in a society that assumes it can survive without memory; on the other hand, surely the most important obligation the elderly have toward the young is not to just remember but to be our memory.

That the elderly are freed from such obligations in our society correlates with the view that human development ends in early adulthood, or at least middle age. Many dominant images in American culture portray old people as set in their ways, that is, not capable of learning anything significant, much less growing in virtue. The elderly are thus thought capable of engaging in superficial friendships with other old people through time-filling "activities" rather than profound friendships of character. Old people are

177 ■

portrayed as simpler creatures than younger adults; an old person typically is either "sweet" or "irascible," neither of which evokes the interesting and complicated character of close friends. It is as though there is little reason to get to know old people, because they are not very compelling as persons. Yet what could be more important than friendship between the old and the not so old? For otherwise how will the young ever know how to die?

It is not unimportant that this essay is being written by an older (Hauerwas) and a younger person (Yordy). Youth still has energy and enthusiasm (or so say the old). The older one of us says that while he has known death is always a theoretical possibility, it is only recently that he has begun to think it might happen to him. Though the possibility of death still remains largely an abstraction, he cannot help but begin to think that it changes one's perspective on one's life. It is the kind of perspective that aging inextricably brings.

To become old means, for example, we are forced to be reintroduced to the fact that whatever else we are, or think we may be, we are our bodies. To be old, to be subject to the small and not-so-small pains and illnesses, makes us aware that we do not just have bodies; we *are* bodies. We can become obsessed by our bodies as every little ache and pain frightens us, intimating our death. Indeed it is interesting how often the elderly forge common judgments, if not friendships, through the ongoing comparison of illnesses and what can and cannot be done for and, far too often, *to* them in the name of "cure."

We believe the awareness of death that growing old brings is a gift, but it can often appear as just another impediment to friendship. Why even begin the difficult struggle toward intimacy when one of us is going to die soon? Surely this is one of the most poignant aspects of life in a nursing home. For as desperately as those in such homes desire to overcome loneliness through friendship, such friendships seem fruitless because they are threatened by a not-too-distant death. Most of us can rightly stand only so much death. Grief is hard, and friendship requires mourning. The isolation of the elderly from the young is surely one of the cruelest aspects of our need to house the elderly in "one place." Young people often lack the experience to be good friends with the old, for they do not really believe they will ever die. However, the only way to overcome the superficiality of cross-generational friendships is through more opportunities for these friendships to arise and develop over time.

CHRISTIAN FRIENDSHIP

We think these obstacles to friendship for old people are real, but we also think that Christianity has rich resources to make possible friendship between the elderly and, perhaps most important, becoming and remaining friends with ourselves as we age. Actually, friendship across generations as well as friendship among the elderly becomes crucial if we are to be the kinds of communities in which aging can be seen as an opportunity for a rich life of service. We need, however, to be clear: we do not regard the church as another social-service agency simply to provide the benefits of "support structures" as do other associations. Instead, the Christian story as embodied in the practices of the church offers a different understanding of both aging and friendship from the one we have just described.

We can only gesture toward the complex relation between Christian ways of growing old and how Christians have understood the nature and importance of friendship. To this end we will draw on the work of Aelred of Rievaulx (1109–1167) because he left us rich accounts of friendships we believe embody Christian wisdom. It may seem odd to enlist a medieval monk to illumine Christian friendship among twentieth-century people. Not only does his account of friendship among brothers in a religious community provide a prismatic account of Christian friendship, however, but we think it also highlights by contrast the problematic status and concept of friendship in our culture.[5]

Of course we are not claiming that Christians have some corner on friendship. Plato, Aristotle, and Cicero wrote profoundly about friendship, and what they wrote certainly influenced Christian practice and thought. Aristotle, for example, distinguished between three kinds of friendships—friendship of use, pleasure, and character. He thought the first two forms of friendship deficient because the friend is loved not because he is a friend but because he is useful or pleasant. The problem with such friendships is that they are easily dissolved when the partners "do not remain unchanged: the affection ceases as soon as one partner is no longer pleasant or useful to the other."[6]

In contrast, Aristotle describes the perfect form of friendship, that is, character friendship, as that between good people who are alike in excellence or virtue. "For these friends wish alike for one another's good because they are good men [sic], and they are good per se (that is, their goodness is something intrinsic, not incidental)."[7] Such friendships are lasting because such people are constituted by virtues that are perduring. On the other hand, according to Aristotle, such friendships are rare because such people are few. Moreover, time and familiarity are required for these friendships to develop. Aristotle notes that nothing characterizes friends as much as the pleasure they derive from living in each other's company.[8]

Christian accounts of friendship agree with Aristotle that any intelligible account of friendship must consider the pleasure intrinsic to friendship. Nonetheless, the Christian account of friendship assumes a quite different context, one that reshapes Aristotle's understanding of friendship.

179 ∎

Christians do not begin by trying to develop an account of friendship in the abstract, for friendship among Christians is intelligible only in the context of corporate, timeful discipleship which they call the body of Christ.[9] Aelred put it this way: "Friendship excels everything . . . for friendship is a path that leads very close to the perfection which consists of the enjoyment and knowledge of God, such that [one] who is a friend of man is made into a friend of God, according to what the Savior said in the Gospel: 'Now I will not call you servants, but my friends' [John 15:15]."[10]

Christian friendship, therefore, seems to have three closely related aspects: (1) to enable and assist each friend in the acquisition and practice of Christian virtues, (2) to build up the Christian community as the body of Christ, and (3) to make possible, under God's gracious favor through the Holy Spirit, friendship with God. The fact that Christian friendship has functions does not, of course, mean that its value is "merely" instrumental rather than intrinsic; for the nature of these functions should make clear that Christian friendship is itself a goal worth seeking and a gift from God. We should note, however, that these functions have little to do with spending time together in diverting activities. Christian friendship as described here is much tougher than a diversion *from* the preoccupations of aging; rather, it is a redirection *to* the gift of aging in a Christian community.

The first purpose of friendship is to encourage the good character of the friends. As Aelred explains, "Friendship bears fruit in this life as well as in the life to come [1 Tim. 4:8]. Friendship establishes all the virtues by means of its own charm, and it strikes down vices by its own excellence."[11] This assumes that friends, regardless of age, can be moved to the good by God's grace acting through the influence of their friends.

> The Lord says in the gospel of John, "I have chosen you, so that you may go and bear fruit," that is, so that you might love one another. For in this true friendship one makes progress by bettering oneself, and one bears fruit by experiencing the enjoyment of this increasing degree of perfection. And so spiritual friendship is born among good people through the similarity of their characters, goals, and habits in life.[12]

Old people therefore are not necessarily "set in their ways," incapable of conversion, transformation, or even minute, imperceptible steps in virtue. Think, for instance, of the many biblical examples of God calling quite elderly people to greater faithfulness, to surprising acts of discipleship: Abraham and Sarah, Jesse, David, Zechariah and Elizabeth, Anna. These stories tell us that our common cultural images are not truthful depictions of Christian life: old people are still called to discipleship in the community, and that discipleship may involve radical change in their way of life.

How do friends enable this sort of vigorous, difficult discipleship? They do so first by understanding that friendship itself is a gift of God. Like all such gifts, it is inherently christological. Friendship "is both formed in Christ and preserved according to Christ, and . . . friendship's goal and usefulness are ultimately referred to Christ."[13] To say that friendship is christological means that the fundamental shared good between friends is the love of Christ, that friendship occurs in Christ and is sustained in Christ, and that friendship will ultimately be perfected only in Christ's kingdom. This christological basis of friendship calls friends to be Christlike to one another in particular ways: to give and receive service to each other, to offer correction when appropriate, to be patient, and so forth. Friends help us live into our own stories through enacting the story of a Christian life.

Aelred's assumption that we must live into our own stories stands in stark contrast to the modern desire for autonomy. He says, "These are not so much humans as beasts who say that one ought to live so as to be a consolation to no one, to be a burden or a grief to no one; who derive no enjoyment from another person's good, who would cause through their own misfortune no bitterness at all to another person."[14] Christians understand that our lives are gifts, not achievements. By that we mean that we are completely vulnerable, dependent creatures of a gracious God who has "storied" us prior to any choices we might make. We call rebellion against our giftedness "sin." Sin is part of the story we must tell about our lives if we are to be truthful. Therefore we need friends in order to learn to tell the truth about our lives; otherwise we are tempted toward delusional stories about our righteousness.

Consequently, friendship for Christians is both a necessary activity for the discovery that we are less than we were meant to be and the resource to start us on the journey through which we become what we were created to be. So "practicing" friendship, both in the sense of rehearsal and of habit, makes us disciples. As Aelred observes, "Friends are concerned for each other, pray for each other, one blushes for the other, another rejoices for the other, one mourns the fall of the other as his own. A friend uses whatever means he can to encourage the timid, strengthen the weak, console the sad, and check the enraged."[15]

Cross-generational friendships manifest this mutual upbuilding in particularly important ways. The older person can teach, by example, how to age and die well; the young learn to honor the elderly as those with such an obligation. The young, too, can remind the old that aging is not an excuse to slip into irresponsibility, indifference, or despair. Most people never think of how we must live when we're younger in order to be able to live well when we're older; it is through friendship with an older person that a young person can both appreciate the lifelong value of friendship and acquire friendship's virtues.

181

It is important, in the context of a discussion of aging, to note that the limit of friendship is not death but sin. Aelred says,

> We can see the certain and true goal of spiritual friendship: that is, nothing should be denied to a friend, and anything should be undertaken for a friend, even to the point at which we must lay down our life for our friend—a sacrifice ordained by divine authority. Therefore, since the life of the soul is far more important than the life of the body, I believe that only this one thing should be denied to a friend: that which causes the death of the soul, which is nothing other than sin—that which separates God from the soul and the soul from life.[16]

Aelred's observation about what should be denied to a friend startles those of us who have been trained to believe that death, not sin, is our deepest enemy. Yet we believe Aelred is right to remind us that when our lives are constituted by the fear or the denial of death, our friendships cannot help but be fragile. Friendship cannot be a hedge against death, because there is no hedge against death. Instead friendship must be constituted as part of a narrative that makes our lives good. Put dramatically, what makes Christian friendship possible is the Christian assumption that we are bound together in a story that gives us something worth dying for.

This brings us to the second aspect of the Christian understanding of friendship, that is, that friendship among Christians is understood to build up the community of faith—the body of Christ. For Christians, friendship between individuals is not and cannot be opposed to the community, but rather serves the community good. Such a good is called common because we do not understand it as a good constituting the sum of our individual interests but as a good unknowable without the discovery through friendships that "friendship has its source in God; the happiness of individuals is the happiness of all."[17] Moreover, for us such friendship is not only with those now present but with those who have gone before; we call this the communion of saints.

That is why Christian communities live by memory. Our central feast is a feast of memory by which we are made part of God's very life in memory for the world. It therefore becomes crucial for Christianity to be about the formation of communities in which memory is not only a possibility but a necessity. Christianity can only be Christianity if we remember those who have gone before and made our faith possible. The very language of faith implies faithfulness to those who have gone before. They live on through our memories, and we live on in the memories of those who follow. The church therefore cannot be the church without the elderly. They are the embodied memories of the church's story. Of course we do not expect that all the elderly of the church should express the "wisdom of their years." But there can be no substitute for some old people in the church being wise. Someone must know how to tell the stories well.

Because the church's story is our story, the church offers an alternative to family because through our baptisms we understand that we have been made part of one another in a more determinative way than biology could ever do. By being so made, we also discover the possibility of friendships we had not otherwise imagined. So old people are not stranded in their families; instead they are members of Christ's body along with all the children and other adults of all backgrounds, talents, sexualities, races, and classes. We become who we are, we become truly ourselves, only through Christ. Christian worship enables our lives to be enmeshed in practices and narratives through which we can discover ourselves in our growing old as well as others in their growing old. This requires, of course, that old people not merely be "Sunday acquaintances" but that they be entangled and succored in close friendships.

Moreover, the fact that old people are often stripped of worldly power becomes a resource for the church. For through such "stripping" we are left with what matters—presence to one another. We are reminded that Christian life is less about doing than about being, and that being happens only by way of our bodies. Bodies that cannot "do" very much any more—bear children, drive cars, read small print, climb steps—can still "be," can offer through their very presence the knowledge of God's Spirit present with us.

The third aspect of friendship is actually its culmination, its *telos*: friendship with God. Perhaps no image is more powerful than Aquinas's suggestion that beatitude—blessedness—is ultimately friendship with God. Aelred, anticipating Aquinas, notes that Christ has made such friendship possible in a manner that defeats the loneliness of aging and death.

> Is it not a certain share of blessedness so to love and be loved, so to help and be helped, and thus to fly higher, from the sweetness of brotherly charity to that more sublime splendor of divine love, and now to ascend the ladder of charity to the embrace of Christ himself, and then to descend by the same ladder to the love of one's neighbor, where one may sweetly rest?[18]

For Aelred, then, friendship with God happens through human friendships, and only for those who are friends with themselves and others.

The possibility of friendship with God does not mean we are, or may become, God's equals.[19] On the contrary, friendship with God requires first of all a profound acknowledgment of our inequality. Acknowledgment of difference is important in any friendship, lest we merely project our self-image onto the other in a way that friendship disintegrates into narcissism. Christians believe that difference need not impede friendship because we share the same body in Christ. In our relationship with God, of course, the

183 ∎

difference is infinite. God is Creator, eternal Lord of all, and we are God's flawed, finite creatures. Here is another reason friendships among and with old people, and participation of elderly people at worship, becomes crucial. To be elderly means to be vulnerable. The elderly, like the sick, need help. But their very need of help creates the conditions for them to help community members come to enjoyment of one another as *fellow creatures* of God. We are all vulnerable; we all need help. For a few years as young adults we may pretend (egged on by social and cultural forces) that we can live forever as autonomous, self-reliant, self-fulfilling beings. The pretense, however, collapses soon enough. So the presence of the visibly vulnerable elderly is a reminder that we are not our own creators. Consequently, Christians must ask the elderly to be among us so we will not take our lives for granted.

The acknowledgment of our creatureliness, that we will die, is a necessary condition for our ability to be our own best friend. Aristotle maintained that in order to be friends with others we must be our own best friends. As he observes, we count as friends those who (1) wish for and do what is good for their friend's sake, (2) wish for the existence and life of their friend for their friend's sake, (3) spend their time in our company, (4) desire the same things we do, (5) share our sorrows and joys. A good person has, Aristotle maintains, all these feelings in relation to himself and therefore must be his own best friend. In particular, a good person wishes to spend "time with himself, for he does so with pleasure. The memory of his achievements gives him delight, and his hopes for the future are good; and such memories and hopes are pleasant."[20] All this is true if we remember that Christians should not be anxious, for we believe we can "rest easy" in the face of death.

We are creatures "caught in time"; the span from birth to death is short and inexorable. Christians believe, though, that our being made part of God's life transforms time from threat to gift. We have the time, in time, to be friends with one another, destined as we are for death. We were created and are destined for friendship with God; this creation and destiny make us friends with ourselves and thus with one another. Christians mourn no less our own deaths or the deaths of our friends, but such mourning does not make us doubt that we should be lesser friends to one another. Rather, we discover in and through friendship that we have been made part of a common memory; and that common memory makes growing old a pleasure, a discipleship, and a blessing.

THE CHURCH AND THE ELDERLY

We are acutely aware that this account of friendship and aging may seem unrealistic given the reality of the contemporary church. Churches are more likely to be shaped by the American way of growing old than by the kinds of responsibilities we think are incumbent on the elderly in the Christian community. We do not believe, however, that the church is without resources for response. Indeed, we hope Christians might see themselves enough in our account of aging and friendship to begin to act differently. We have no ready-made "solutions." We do, however, offer some suggestions about small—but we believe significant—practices that may help Christians recover the art of friendship between generations.

First and foremost, we believe the church must be the kind of community that insists that those who have grown in years are not relieved of moral responsibilities. They cannot leave the church to survive on its own and move to Florida. For Christians there is no "Florida," even if they happen to live in Florida. That is, we must continue to be present to those who have made us what we are, so that we can make future generations what they are called to be. So aging among Christians is not and cannot be a lost opportunity, but rather a transformation of what the world understands to be a loss of power into service for the good of the Christian community.

The problem, however, is that when we are old it is too late to learn how to grow old. We must be taught how to live well when we are young if we are to know how to live well when we are old. (In fact, one of the great problems of our time is the assumption that we can and should live as if we will never grow old.) This will require the church to find ways to avoid isolating the young, the not so young, and the elderly from one another. If, as we maintained above, the church is a community of memory, such isolation certainly makes the church's work impossible. What it means for the church to be a community of memory is the gospel; it is not some truth that can be known without memory. The gospel is a story with myriad subplots, intricacies, colors, and textures. Stories live through memory, through being told over and over again, and in the telling new aspects of the story are discovered. That is why the church is so dependent on those who can help us remember the complexity of the story that constitutes who we are.

So the church names a community that depends on those who have gone before to remember the skills necessary for the telling and retelling of the story. We do not mean to suggest that the full responsibility of this task falls particularly on the elderly, but we do think they have work to do if the church is to survive as church. In short, we rightly expect Christians to grow old wisely, for the church is a community constituted by wisdom. And wisdom is acquired not through means-end principles but through corporate experience, by living the church's stories. We do not presume that all Christians as they grow old should be wise, but we do expect the church to live as a community that requires the wise, particularly the elderly among us, to exist.

185

In this respect it is quite interesting to contrast the church as a community of wisdom with the generalized acceptance of the "expert" as the assumed legitimate authority in modernity.[21] The expert is not expected to be wise but to know the best ways to achieve results through the use of technical rationality. The whole point of a society constituted by the authority of the expert is to be a community that can live without stories. The elderly, similarly, simply are not required. Obviously we do not think the church is this type of community, living as it does through memory. As a community dependent on the wisdom of the elders, therefore, the church inevitably stands in tension with the culture of modernity.

Of course, to say that the church is a community that lives by wisdom means that it must also be a community in which friendship is possible between generations. For wisdom is not learned easily but requires the ongoing transformation provided by friendships over time. As Aelred says on the relation between friendship and wisdom, "Friendship cannot even exist without grace. Therefore, since eternity thrives in friendship, and truth shines forth in it, and grace likewise becomes pleasant through friendship, you be the judge whether you should separate the name of wisdom from these three."[22] So the church must find ways to have children and those we currently call "the youth" sit at the feet of their elders, where they learn the wisdom of the past. This "sitting" requires that the church not be a people in a hurry but rather a people who have learned to wait. That is, Christians should be oriented toward witnessing God's work in God's time rather than achieving our goals in our own time.[23]

Perhaps the hardest thing the church must ask of the elderly is to teach us how to die. Such teaching requires a vulnerability none find easy, particularly in a society based on autonomy. Yet none of us know how to die "by nature." Rather, we must be taught how to die through friendship. For, contrary to the oft-made claim, we do not need to die alone; we can die knowing that we will not be abandoned by our friends simply because we are dying. If the church could be such a community, then we might discover that we are again able to attract young and old alike, if only because they see that these people are happy.

We conclude with Aelred's idyllic description of this happiness, which he wrote as a relatively old man:

When I was walking around the monastery cloister three days ago, as the beloved crowd of brothers was sitting together . . . I marveled as though walking among the pleasures of paradise, enjoying the leaves, flowers, and fruits of each single tree. I found not one brother in that whole multitude whom I did not love, and by whom I did not think I was loved in turn; and so I was filled with joy so great that it surpassed all the delights of this world. Indeed, I felt as though my spirit had been poured into all of them, and their affection

186

had been transplanted into me, so that I could say with the Prophet, "Behold, how good and pleasant it is, when brothers dwell together in unity" [Psalm 133].[24]

Rather than dismissing this passage as an unrealistic portrait, we believe that Christians should read it as a prescription for friendship with and among the elderly. In such friendships do we become church; in church are such friendships possible.

■Sinsick

People are religious to the extent that they believe themselves to be not so much imperfect, as ill. Any man who is halfway decent will think himself extremely imperfect, but a religious man thinks himself wretched.

LUDWIG WITTGENSTEIN, *CULTURE AND VALUE*

SICKNESS AS SIN

Given the choice, most people in America would rather be sick than a sinner. "Sin" sounds too judgmental for a "compassionate culture." Sickness has become our way to indicate deviancy without blame. Karl Menninger lamented this development in his book *Whatever Became of Sin?* He acknowledged, however, that his attempt to rehabilitate the language of sin is not for the sake of the word itself "but for the reintroduction of the concepts of guilt and moral responsibility."[1] It is ironic that many conservative Christians were sympathetic with Menninger's effort to reclaim sin, not only because his account of sin drew on conceptions derived from Protestant liberalism, that is, Tillich and Reinhold Niebuhr, but because his conception was hopelessly moralistic.[2] What could be more sinful than

189 ■

the assumption that our guilt might tell us something interesting about our sin? Guilt is, after all, just an invitation to self-righteousness.

Sin and sickness are not easily distinguished, but distinguish them we must. I believe sickness is a manifestation of sin, but how to say that without inviting false theodical speculations is difficult. Indeed in our time the discovery that we are sick is often the nearest analogy we have for understanding what it means to discover and confess we are sinners. Alcoholics discover they are possessed by a power they do not remembering choosing but for which they must take responsibility if they are to stand any chance of being free from that possession. In like manner Christians confess that we are sinners. Sin, like sickness, seems like something that happens to us more than what we do. Yet Christians believe we are rightly held accountable for our sins.

Before exploring how sickness manifests our sin I need to make clear why for most people the language of being sick seems more intelligible than the language of being a sinner. I think the answer is very simple—we are atheists. Even if we say we believe in God, most of our lives are constituted by practices that assume that God does not exist. The most effective means I have discovered to illustrate this is to ask people how they want to die. We all want to die quickly, painlessly, in our sleep, and without being a burden. We do not want to be a burden because we can no longer trust our children. We want to die quickly, painlessly, and in our sleep because when we die we do not want to know we are dying.

It is quite interesting to contrast this way of dying with the past, when the death Christians feared was a sudden death. Such a death meant they might die unreconciled with their neighbors, their church, and, of course, God. We no longer fear the judgment of God, but we do fear death. So our lives are lived in an attempt to avoid death (or at least the knowledge that we are to die) as long as we can. As any doctor can tell you, sickness—even hangnails—is the intimation of death. Accordingly we order our lives to be free of sickness. But so ordered, sickness becomes overdetermined as a description that indicates any aspect of our lives that threatens death. Growing old turns out therefore to be an illness.

This set of assumptions, of course, has resulted in giving extraordinary power to the medical profession. The hospitals at Duke, Duke North and Duke South, are like the cathedrals of the past—our Chartres and Notre Dames that testify not as those cathedrals did to what we love but rather to what we fear. As I often point out to seminarians, if you want some idea of what medieval Christianity felt like, hang around any modern research medical center. The term *byzantine* fails to do justice to the complex forms of power exercised in such a context. Nowhere is such power more manifest than in the ability of those in medicine to redescribe our lives through the language of illness. Thus we are now being taught that "baldness" is a condition that we can "cure."

That medicine has such power is one of the reasons medical schools are more morally impressive than, for example, divinity schools. When challenged about where schools of virtue may exist, I often say Paris Island and/or medical schools. For example, a person can come to divinity school today saying, "I am not really into Christology this year. I am really into relating. I would like to take more courses in CPE." They are likely to be confirmed in that option by being told, "Right, take CPE; after all that is what ministry is—relating. Learn to be a wounded healer."

Contrast that with a medical student who might say, "I am not really into anatomy this year. I am really into people. I would like to take another course in psychiatry." He or she would be told, "We do not care what you are 'into.' Take anatomy or ship out." That is real moral education, if not formation. Why is medical education so morally superior to ministerial education? I think the answer is very simple. No one believes that an inadequately trained priest might damage their salvation; but people do believe that an inadequately trained doctor might hurt them.

It is a mistake, moreover, to blame physicians for having such power over our lives. They simply reflect who we are. In many ways those in medicine suffer from our determination to redescribe our lives in the language of sickness. For example, we now expect doctors to keep us alive to the point that when we die we do not have to know we are dying. We then get to blame doctors for keeping us alive to no point. Physicians are sued for doing too much or too little to "cure us," because they now serve patients who have no sense of the limits of medicine. Patients have forgotten what every doctor knows, namely, that the final description for every patient for whom a physician cares is "dead."[3]

I think it would be a mistake to think the overdetermination of the language of sickness in our culture to be a conspiracy by those in medicine to acquire power. On the contrary, I believe patient and physician alike to manifest the fundamental presumption of liberal social orders that assume freedom to be not only the ideal but the necessary condition for moral and political life. As I am fond of putting the matter, the project of modernity has been to produce people who believe they should have no story other than the story they choose when they have no story. Of course what such a story cannot explain is how that story became our story. In short, modernity names those social orders in which freedom became our fate.

As a result we suffer from those forms of life we believe necessary to make us free. We desire to be free from illness, and illness is now understood as any condition that limits my choices. Sickness names those aspects of my life I have not chosen. This creates the desire of modern people to find the "cause" of their illness in some "lifestyle" choice: such a "cause" at least

191 ▪

makes their suffering intelligible. That is why the illness and death of children, which is a challenge for any time and people, is a particular challenge for us.[4] Medicine too often becomes the institutionalized practice we use to free us from our fear of sickness and death which, because we can only view death and our fear of it as surds, now threaten to tyrannize our lives. That we have now become subject to the power of medicine is not the fault of doctors and others in healthcare professions but the reflection of our inability to make sense that we are creatures destined to die. Put bluntly, we are unable to make sense of our being sick because we no longer understand what it means for our lives to be captured by sin.

SINSICK

In fact we are sinsick. I learned to use the word sinsick by singing (God knows how many times) "There is a balm in Gilead."[5] That balm, it turns out, can "cleanse the sinsick soul." *Sinsick* was one of those "Southern" expressions we used "down home" to describe someone who was on his or her last leg. To describe someone as "sinsick" meant his or her life was in shambles involving both physical and spiritual conditions. We presumed that sickness and sin could not be separated, though we did not assume an exact causality. Rather sickness itself was regarded as part of our natural condition, given our natural condition was one of sin. We knew we had not been created to be sinners, but we knew that's what we were—namely, a people quite literally made sick by sin.

I think the assumption that we are made sick by sin is theologically right no matter how much it may offend our sensibilities. Moreover, I think that is also what the church has taught, or at least it is what Aquinas taught. Aquinas simply assumed that sickness, and the death sickness intimates, was the result of sin. Of course Aquinas thought his account of sin and sickness was but commentary on Paul's claim in Romans (5:12) that "by one man sin entered into this world, and by sin death." Responding to the objection that death and other bodily defects are not the result of sin, Aquinas observes:

> As death and such like defects are beside the intention of the sinner, it is evident that sin is not, of itself, the cause of these defects. Accidentally one thing is the cause of another if it causes it by removing an obstacle: thus it is stated in *Phys.* viii, 32, that "by displacing a pillar a man moves accidentally the stone resting thereon." In this way the sin of our first parent is the cause of death and all such like defects in human nature, in so far as by the sin of our first parent original justice was taken away, whereby not only were the lower powers of the soul held together under the control of reason, without any disorder whatever, but also the whole body was held together in subjection to the soul,

without any defect. Wherefore, original justice being forfeited through the sin of our first parent; just as human nature was stricken in the soul by the disorder among the powers, so also it became subject to corruption, by reason of disorder in the body. Now the withdrawal of original justice has the character of punishment, even as the withdrawal of grace has. Consequently, death and all consequent bodily defects are punishments of original sin, and although the defects are not intended by the sinner, nevertheless they are ordered to the justice of God who inflicts them as punishments.[6]

In an earlier article on whether original sin infects the will before the other powers, Aquinas observed that original sin is like an infection. In fact he compares it to leprosy. It spreads from the flesh to the soul and then from the essence of the soul to the powers. The infection is most apparent in those aspects of our lives that are not subject to reason, such as the "members of generation" that serve for the "mingling of sexes." The concupiscible and the sense of touch are also among our faculties most subject to original sin, since they are subject to transmission from one subject to another.[7]

Aquinas's understanding of the effect of sin can be understood only against the background of his view that we were not created to die. He quotes Wisdom 1:13, "Now God made not death," and concludes that death is not natural to humankind.[8] The position of Aquinas about the naturalness of our deaths is, however, quite complex. As regards our form—that is, our rational soul—death is not, according to Aquinas, natural to man. But the matter of man, which is our body, is composed of contraries, "of which corruptibility is a necessary consequence, and in this respect death is natural to man." Aquinas illustrates this claim by providing an example of a craftsman, who, if he could, would make a saw that at once would be hard enough to cut but would not rust. So God, who is the all-powerful author of man, when "He first made man, He conferred on him the favor of being exempt from the necessity resulting from such matter: which favor, however, was withdrawn through the sin of our first parents. Accordingly death is both natural on account of a condition attaching to matter and penal on account of the loss of the Divine favor preserving man from death."[9]

Interestingly enough, Aquinas does not think that the first sin was in the flesh, because "man was so appointed in the state of innocence, that there was no rebellion of the flesh against the spirit." Rather the first sin was our prideful and inordinate desiring of a spiritual good, which Aquinas identifies as the desire to be like God. Of course our first parents could not have desired absolute equality with God, since such a likeness is not conceivable to the mind. Rather, the first man desired knowledge of good and evil; that is, he desired by his own natural power to determine what was good and what was evil for him to do.[10] Such a desire had the effect of disordering our lives so that we became subject to death and disease.

193 ■

In our primitive state God had bestowed his favor on human beings so that their minds were subject to God, the lower powers of the soul were subject to the rational mind, and the body to the soul. But through sin the human mind was no longer subject to God, with the result that human lower powers were no longer subject to reason.

> Whence there followed so great a rebellion of the carnal appetite against the reason; nor was the body wholly subject to the soul; whence arose death and other bodily defects. For life and soundness of body depend on the body being subject to the soul, as the perfectible is subject to its perfection. Consequently, on the other hand, death, sickness, and all defects of the body are due to the lack of the body's subjection to the soul.[11]

The punishment of death and sickness was proportionate to the first sin insofar as they are the result of the withdrawal of divine favor necessary for the rectitude and integrity of human nature. These punishments need not be equal in those to whom the first sin appertains. But since God foreknows all future events, God, according to Aquinas, providentially apportioned these penalties in different ways to different people. Aquinas argues that this is not, as Origen held, on account of merits or demerits of a previous life, for such a view would be contrary to the words of Romans 9:11, "when they . . . had not done any good or evil." Moreover, Origen's view falsely assumes the soul was created before the body. Rather, such punishments are for parents' sins, since the child belongs to the parents, and parents are thus often punished in their children. Or penalty is as a "remedy intended for the spiritual welfare of the person who suffers these penalties, to wit that he may thus be turned away from his sins, or lest he take pride in his virtues, and that he may be crowned for his patience."[12]

Aquinas does not presume that everything we might regard as unpleasant is the result of the fall. He observes, for example, that even prior to the first sin man was the head and governor of the woman. Sin transforms that relation into punishment, as now the woman must obey her husband against her will. In like manner thorns and thistles would have existed to provide food for animals prior to the fall. Only after the fall do they become punishment, making our labor more difficult.[13] I think it is not hard to see that Aquinas thinks the body, which was destined to die, analogous to thorns and thistles.

How Aquinas thinks about these matters is wonderfully illustrated in his discussion in the third part of the *Summa*, where he speculates on the integrity of the body in the resurrection. For example, he answers the question whether all the parts of the human body will rise again by noting that since the resurrection is the work of God, and since the works of God are perfect, in the resurrection human beings will be made perfect in all their members. Just as a work of art would not be perfect if its product lacked any of the things that are contained in the art, so "at the resurrection it behooves man's body to correspond entirely to the soul, for it will not rise again except according to the relation it bears to the rational soul, it follows that man also must rise again perfect, seeing that he is thereby repaired in order that he may obtain his ultimate perfection. Consequently all the members that are now in man's body must needs be restored at the resurrection."[14]

If we have lost a hand or a leg during our life—even if the member was cut off before we repented and therefore did not cooperate with us in the state whereby we merit glory—yet, according to Aquinas, we will be restored whole, since it is the whole being that serves God. Moreover, we will be raised at the height of our powers: Christ rose at a youthful age, that is, around thirty, and so we will also be raised. It is appropriate for us to be raised at the most perfect stage of nature, and human nature is most perfect in the age of youth, so we will be raised at that age.[15] I regret to report that the only slip Aquinas made in his discussion of our resurrected state involved a misreading of Luke 21:18, where we are told not a hair of our head shall perish. Aquinas comments: "Hair and nails were given to man as an ornament. Now the bodies of men, especially of the elect, ought to rise again with all their adornment. Therefore they ought to rise again with the hair."[16]

That we—that is, people schooled on the presumption that sickness and sin are not related—find Aquinas's discussion of these matters somewhat bizarre I take to be an indication of the pathology of the modern soul. "Sickness" for us, as I noted above, is pointless. To "be sick" names a condition that should not exist, thereby justifying unlimited interventions to eliminate whatever we regard as an arbitrary inconvenience. For Aquinas, sickness was not "pointless" but rather an indication of the distorting effect sin has in our lives. We were not created to be sick or to die, but the fact that our lives are unavoidably constituted by death and sickness serves as an indication that something terrible has gone wrong. We are sinsick.

Aquinas says no more than what Christians are bound to say about sickness and death. The problem, of course, is that saying these things sounds like such bad news to modern ears. Death and sickness so narrated appears to make God a divine sadist arbitrarily punishing his creatures in an effort to get minimal respect. Yet I believe Aquinas's account to be the exact opposite of such a reading: the discovery of sin and death is part of the good news that we were not created to die. Moreover, I believe Aquinas's way of framing our understanding of sin, sickness, and death offers exactly the kinds of discriminations necessary to sustain the practice of medicine that will not be driven mad by its inability to cure. In order to show how this might be the case, I need to develop why the discovery we are sinners is part of the good news of the gospel.

195

THE JOY OF BEING SICK[17]

> As he walked along, he saw a man blind from birth. His disciples asked him, "Rabbi, who sinned, this man or his parents, that he was born blind?" Jesus answered, "Neither this man nor his parents sinned; he was born blind so that God's works might be revealed in him."

This passage from the ninth chapter of John is the appropriate place for Christians to reflect on sin, sickness, and death. As James Alison points out, in the encounter between Jesus and this blind man we have a meditation on how Jesus' life and resurrection transforms our understanding of sin as well as the relation of sin and sickness.[18] Moreover, Jesus' treatment of the man born blind is a wonderful indication that while sickness is the result of our sin, it is usually a mistake to correlate a person's sickness with a particular sin.

Alison observes that the story of Jesus' healing of the man born blind is one of inclusion and exclusion. The blind man is excluded not only from the good of seeing but also from full participation in the cultic life of Israel, since his blindness was considered a moral impediment. Jesus uses the resources of the original creation, that is, clay mixed with his own spittle, to cure the man's blindness even though it is on the Sabbath. The man is sent to wash in a pool, a place of purification, making possible his reintegration, intimating for us the baptism to be ours through resurrection.

Yet the man is not accepted back into Israel, since the Pharisees rightly realize that the cure unavoidably requires acknowledgment of the messianic nature of Jesus' ministry. So they throw the blind man out. During the process, however, the former blind man, who had never seen Jesus because he only received his sight at the pool of Siloam, becomes increasingly aware of who Jesus is: first just another man, then a prophet, and finally someone from God who is superior even to Moses. Like the disciples, who also must be trained to see through discipleship, so the man born blind comes to see who Jesus is by being rejected.

"I came into the world for judgment so that those who do not see may see, and those who do see may become blind" is Jesus' final judgment on this proceeding (John 9:38). Yet Alison rightly comments that this is ironic, since Jesus makes no active judgment in the narrative. Rather it is the Pharisees who judge by casting out the man born blind. Alison suggests this is the Johannine recasting of judgment—by being crucified, Jesus is the real judge of his judges. Jesus does not abolish the notion of judgment; rather, Jesus is a judge who subverts from within the notion of those who would judge. That is, the judgment that excludes the blind man is revealed as the judgment that those who would expel are blind.

196

Alison's reading of John 9 substantiates the argument he makes throughout *The Joy of Being Wrong* that "the doctrine of original sin is not prior to,
but follows from and is utterly dependent on, Jesus' resurrection from the
dead and thus cannot be understood at all except in the light of that event."[19]
This revolution in the concept of sin is worked on in the life of the man
born blind, Alison argues, because John quite rightly applies to what is
without doubt one of Jesus' historical healings the understanding of sin
made possible by the resurrection. The sin of the world is understood, following from John 8:44, as the work of "your father the devil," who "was a
murderer from the beginning." That reign of sin has now been overturned,
making possible a new creation embodied in a community that is at once
as old and new as creation. As Alison puts it:

> When Jesus speaks, at the end, about judgment it is clear that he is not con-
> cerned with a particular local incident, but about a discernment relating to
> the whole world *(kosmos)*. Here we have a highly subtle teaching about the
> whole world being blind from birth, from the beginning, and about Jesus, in
> the light of the world coming to bring sight to the world, being rejected pre-
> cisely by those who, though blind, claimed to be able to see. All humans are
> blind, but where this blindness is compounded by active participation in the
> mechanisms of exclusion pretending to sight, this blindness is culpable.[20]

The doctrine of original sin, according to Alison, is good news made possible only by Christ's resurrection.[21] "The doctrine of original sin is not an
accusation against humanity, and by keeping the doctrine alive the Church
is not engaged in a generalized condemnation of humanity." Rather what
is at stake in the doctrine of original sin is the possibility "that even those
who bear the tremendous burden of being 'right' may recognize their complicity with those who are not, and so construct a sociality that is not cru-
ciform."[22] So understood, what the doctrine of original sin or any account
of sin cannot be is an explanation for evil or suffering. Original sin does
not "explain" death and sickness because, as Alison puts it, the Catholic
faith is not an explanation for anything. Rather than an explanation the
church has a salvific revelation:

> What is revealed as something now operative is the mystery of God's plan
> of salvation for us. This plan of salvation enables us to know the Father and
> share in his life by sharing in the life and death of his Son. Any Catholic
> understanding of evil cannot be part of a general human understanding of
> evil, and this for two reasons. In the first place there is no such thing as a
> general human understanding of evil any more than there is a general human
> understanding of good. It is contingent and competing human traditions
> that give shape and form to differing notions of good and evil, and such tra-
> ditions all carry with them, either explicitly or implicitly, a theology that

197

undergirds them. Secondly, the Catholic faith considers itself radically sub-versive of all forms of human knowledge (1 Cor. 1:18–25) because of a very peculiar epistemological starting point: the resurrection with historical cir-cumstances of a murdered man as the beginnings of a new creation.[23]

Accordingly the church's approach to sin (and sickness) is not to pro-vide an explanation but to be a contingent human transformation whereby our condition as sinners is bounded by the more determinative reality of our salvation. Sin and sickness from the church's perspective just "are." In Alison's terms, sin for Christians is "that which we are on our way out of."[24] We must not, like Lot's wife, turn around to see what we have left. To do so is to let sin become the primary character in the story. Moreover, when original sin becomes an explanation it too easily becomes an excuse for not overcoming evil, "a way of justifying the present state of affairs rather than being the understanding of what it is that is being overcome on our way out of it."[25]

Alison argues, rightly I think, that the account he has given of original sin as the good news made possible by the resurrection is not only consis-tent with Aquinas's account of these matters but in fact is Aquinas's account of original sin. That Aquinas understands original sin to result in a priva-tion of original justice makes clear that the doctrine of original sin is an ancillary concept rather than a basic one. Put differently: the story of the "fall" Christians believe to be the appropriate reading of the account of Adam and Eve in Genesis is a reading made possible only because we now understand that Jesus is the new Adam.[26]

Such a view makes the effects of sin no less serious. We suffer from sin and the sickness that is a result of sin. It may be true that we were not cre-ated to die, but we know we continue to die deadly deaths. Yet if Aquinas and Alison are right, the great good news is that our lives do not need to be determined by sin or death. Rather through baptism our lives have been reconstituted, making possible freedom from death and the threat of death so often intimated by sickness. Accordingly, sin and sickness have lost their power to dominate our lives as Christians. As a result we do not fear sick-ness but can now imagine our bodies in sickness and in health to be an invi-tation for the care of one another. That I take to be the joy of sickness.

Accordingly those called to care for us when we are sick do so not as if our illnesses have no purpose. Rather, through baptism our lives have been reborn so that neither death nor sickness can have the last word about our care for one another. Suffering sickness can even be an opportunity to share in Christ's suffering so that the world might know that death has been defeated. Therefore the practice of medicine by Christians is not an attempt to deny death but a way to be of service to one another as people who under-stand that the death we die in this life is not our destiny.

In an extraordinary chapter entitled "Original Sin Known in Its Ecclesial Overcoming," Alison observes that the tragedy of original sin is not that it is universal but that by it the incapacity for universality

> is revealed by the coming into being of the ecclesial hypothesis in which alone particularity is made capable of bearing universality. Original sin, the an-ecclesial hypostasis, is simultaneously incapable of real particularity (and capable of only ersatz particularity grasped at defensively over against others) and of real universality (and capable of only abstract universality as the rhetoric of rights or denunciations). The doctrine of original sin, rather than being the abstract declaration of the universal equality in sin of all human beings, is the doctrine of the incapacity for equality outside the ecclesial hypothesis. This can be seen even in the most basic existential terms. It is life in the ecclesial communion that enables persons to discover, to their relief, and relax into their similarity with others.[27]

I take the implications of this to be quite simple. The reason that Christian and non-Christian find ourselves dominated by our "concern for health" is that in the absence of the church, medicine cannot help but dominate our lives. For medicine has become a powerful practice without end, without context, without any wider community to give it purpose. Accordingly nothing could be more important today than for Christians to recover a Christian practice of medicine shaped by the practices of the church, and in particular baptism. For as Alison observes, it is through baptism that we are introduced to undistorting desire through the pacific imitation of Christ. That this is not a voluntaristic exercise is clear from the fact that exorcisms, which free us from Satan's kingdom, are celebrated as intrinsic to baptism. Thus through baptism simultaneously we are incorporated into the church and our sins are forgiven. As Alison observes, incorporation into the church and the forgiveness of sins become the same reality: induction into eternal life.[28] For lives determined by that reality—that is, the reality of life with God—how sickness is understood and cared for cannot help but look quite different from how the world understands what it means to be sick.[29]

14

■McInerny Did It

Or, Should a Pacifist Read Murder Mysteries?

READING MYSTERIES

I am not supposed to begin this way. At least I am not supposed to begin this way if Ronald Knox is right about the first law of detective stories in his "A Detective Story Decalogue." Knox decrees that the first commandment for writing detective stories is "The criminal must be someone mentioned in the early part of the story, but must not be anyone whose thoughts the reader has been allowed to follow."[1] Yet as my title indicates, I want you to know the perpetrator from the beginning. Ralph McInerny did it. He made me hopelessly addicted to murder mysteries.

It happened this way. I was just another member of the Notre Dame faculty that inhabited the basement of the library. The one advantage of the basement of the library was that faculty from diverse disciplines actually had to talk to one another. Usually such conversations were about the latest game or comparing notes about our families, but after we grew tired of those subjects we might even say something like this: "What are you working on now? I see, very interesting. Have you read X's or Y's recent book on that subject? I think you would find it very interesting." And so on and so on. I never expected that in one of these exchanges I would be blindsided by Ralph McInerny.

I had always had some problem putting McInerny together. As a Texas Protestant I had no idea that someone like Ralph McInerny existed or could exist. Possible world metaphysics did not prepare me to believe it was possible to combine in one person philosophical astuteness, conservative Catholicism, and cultural urbanity. But McInerny was all of that and more. Indeed for me he was Notre Dame: he signaled that this was an intellectually serious place. So I was completely unprepared when Ralph, without embarrassment, told me he was writing a murder mystery. I had never heard an academic admit to reading a murder mystery, much less writing one. Yet Ralph McInerny, the representative of all that was good at Notre Dame, acknowledged that he not only reads mysteries but writes them. What could I possibly make of this counterfactual?

I did what any self-respecting academic would do. I started reading murder mysteries, some of them written by Ralph, to try to understand Ralph's fascination with mysteries. I soon lost interest in understanding Ralph's interest in mysteries: I became such an avid reader of mysteries that the problem was now understanding *my* fascination with them. So it is McInerny's fault that I now use this occasion to try to understand why I love to read about murders and murderers. If the reader of this essay feels compelled to discover the dark figure behind this exercise, please remember: McInerny did it!

JUSTIFYING MYSTERIES: OR, WHY READING ABOUT MURDER IS GOOD FOR YOU

One of the problems for people who like to think they are "serious thinkers" is they are inclined to provide more reasons than necessary to justify *anything* they do, but in particular for reading work that is not by definition serious. Mysteries are not considered serious by most academics. No one knows why mysteries are not considered to be literature, but at least one of the reasons is their popularity. It is assumed by many intellectuals that if a book or genre is popular then it cannot deal with the eternal verities of the human condition. Chesterton observed this has led some "modern critics" falsely to infer that not only may a masterpiece be unpopular, but unless it is unpopular it cannot be a masterpiece.[2]

Of course writers of detective fiction are aware of these putdowns. They realize there is no way to defeat those who dismiss murder mysteries as "entertainment" other than to write well about matters that matter. For example,

Arthur Upfield in his mystery *An Author Bites the Dust* makes the discovery of the murderer of a "modern critic" (of the kind Chesterton described above) turn on whether the distinction between commercial fiction and literature could be maintained. Upfield's detective, Napoleon Bonaparte, half aboriginal and half white, usually solves murders in the Australian outback by combining aboriginal and modern police skills. Confronted by the murder of Mervyn Blake, a critic intent on the development of an Australian literature, Bony went to his friend, popular author Clarence Bagshott, to help him understand the difference between literature and popular fiction. In response to Bony's question whether Blake ever criticized Bagshott's work, he was told:

> "Mine! Lord, no! I don't produce literature."
>   "Then what do you produce?"
>   "Commercial fiction."
>   "There is a distinction?"
>   "Terrific."
>   "Will you define it, please."
>   "I'll try to," Bagshott said slowly. "In this country literature is a piece of writing executed in schoolmasterly fashion and yet so lacking in entertainment values that the general public won't buy it. Commercial fiction—and this is a term employed by the highbrows—is imaginative writing that easily satisfies publishers and editors because the public will buy it."[3]

I do not want to keep the reader in suspense—it turns out that Blake was killed by his wife, who, in order to make a living for them, had written popular fiction under a pseudonym. Her husband's novels sold only when she helped him with them; when he tried to write on his own, he could not get his work published. This led him to treat her so badly that she finally killed him—I might add, in a quite ingenious way. Bony was able to discover she had been the killer, learning that (at least in this case) the only difference between literature and popular fiction was between what was written poorly and what was written well. Which is but a reminder, as Chesterton remarks, that there is as much difference between a good detective story and a bad detective story as between a good epic and a bad one.[4]

That murder mysteries can be not only entertaining but good literature does not, however, explain how the crime novel became only recently such a distinctive as well as such a popular genre. I have no great insight about the rise of the mystery novel from a historical and cultural standpoint (though I will make some suggestions about that below), but I confess I cannot resist speculating about their moral significance. I am after all, like McInerny, something of a "moralist." Accordingly I cannot help but think that there is something morally important about murder mysteries.

203

Chesterton thought the essential value of the detective story consists in its ability as a form of popular literature to express what he called "the poetry of modern life." According to Chesterton the detective story helps us see at once the chaos and beauty of the city, so that "even under the fantastic form of the minutiae of Sherlock Holmes, to assert this romance of detail in civilization, to emphasize this unfathomably human character in flints and tiles, is a good thing. It is good that the average man should fall into the habit of looking imaginatively at ten men in the street even if it is only on the chance that the eleventh might be a notorious thief."[5]

Chesterton's observation does not entail that murder mysteries are a peculiarly urban phenomenon. The English village is obviously one of the prime sites for murder, as is the Australian outback or the American south.[6] Chesterton's point, I believe, is rather that murder mysteries depend on the development of rich detail of place and character, which turns out to be a training in practical reasoning. Practical reason deals, at least according to Aristotle, with matters that can be other. But the "other" is constituted by the rich detail displayed through storied description. Murder mysteries are about the testing and retesting of stories by which the subtle interrelation of character and circumstance is discovered and displayed.[7] What better training in practical reason could one wish? To learn the complexities involved in distinguishing good from bad writing in order to discover "who did it" is at least analogous to learning to distinguish between honesty and bluntness.

Of course such skills are not peculiar to murder mysteries. Novels, plays, poetry, conversations are equally good schools for developing practical reason and, in particular, how such reasoning involves narrative display. Chesterton, however, argues that detective stories involve another good work that is peculiar to the genre. He identifies that work as nothing less than resistance to the tendency of the old Adam to rebel against so "universal and automatic thing" as civilization. In Chesterton's words:

> The romance of police activity keeps in some sense before the mind the fact that civilization itself is the most sensational of departures and the most romantic of rebellions. By dealing with the unsleeping sentinels who guard the outposts of society, it tends to remind us that we live in an armed camp, making war with a chaotic world, and that the criminals, the children of chaos, are nothing but the traitors within our gates. The romance of the police force is thus the whole romance of man. It is based on the fact that morality is the most dark and daring of conspiracies. It reminds us that the whole of noiseless and unnoticeable police management by which we are ruled and protected is only a successful knight-errantry.[8]

If Chesterton is right—that morality is this "dark and daring conspiracy"—then it can be asked why it took so long to develop the peculiar genre we currently identify as murder mysteries. For surely morality so understood has always been present confronting the chaos of immorality and crime.[9] Dorothy Sayers argues the reason detective fiction is a rather recent development is that the detective cannot flourish until the public has some idea of what constitutes proof, which requires that there be in place common criminal procedures such as arrest, confession, and punishment. In short, the detective story could not flourish until "public sympathy had veered round to the side of law and order."[10]

Somewhat more speculatively, Sayers also suggests that the development of detective fiction is the result of the end of the age of exploration. In place of the adventurer and the knight errant

> popular imagination hailed the doctor, the scientist, and the policeman as saviours and protectors. But if one could no longer hunt the manticore, one could still hunt the murderer; if the armed escort had grown less necessary, yet one still needed the analyst to frustrate the wiles of the poisoner; from this point of view, the detective steps into his right place as the protector of the weak—the latest of the popular heroes, the true successor of Roland and Lancelot.[11]

Sayers's most eloquent account of the moral significance of detective fiction occurs in the last Peter Wimsey/Harriet Vane mystery, *Thrones, Dominations*, left unpublished at her death.[12] Newly married Peter asks Harriet if she thinks his detective work a frivolous pose—a rich man's game:

> "No; I think it is very serious. A matter of life and death, after all. What I haven't got clear is how this connects with the war. I think it does, in some subterranean fashion."

> "When you have seen people die," he said, "when you have seen at what abominable and appalling cost the peace and safety of England was secured, and then you see the peace squalidly broken, you see killing that has been perpetrated for vile and selfish motives . . ."

> "Oh, yes, I can see that," she said. "Beloved, I do see."

> "Justice is a terrible thing," he said, "but injustice is worse."

> He came suddenly towards her, and knelt in front of her chair, putting his arms around her knees, and laying his head in her lap. When he spoke again his voice was muffled in the folds of her dress. "Dearest, do you want me to discuss this case with you? Or would you rather not?"

> "I'd rather you did, if you can bear to."

"It's what you can bear that I was thinking of. I would spare you distressing topics, if I could."

"Nothing you could tell me would be as bad as the thought that there was some subject we couldn't talk over together. That would be really hateful."

"It is to be the marriage of true minds we try for," he said, looking up at her.

"I thought it was; yes."

"Then so it shall be. We'll bear it out even to the edge of doom—Yes, Meredith, what is it?"

"Dinner is served, my lord."

"Later," said Peter, getting up and extending her his hand. "I will tell you all later."[13]

"Telling all later" is what the mystery writer does, and in particular what Sayers did. Later in the novel Peter and Harriet have an exchange that is impossible not to read as Sayers's justification for her work. Harriet observes that she knows writing detective stories is not great art. "You read them and write them for fun." Peter objects to this description of her work, noting that she takes great pride in her craft. Harriet acknowledges the point but notes that a craft may be admirable yet nonetheless frivolous. She observes, for example, that it is simply a given that detective stories are not of the same quality as *Paradise Lost* or *Crime and Punishment* or real detection that deals with real crimes. Peter responds:

"You seem not to appreciate the importance of your special form. Detective stories contain a dream of justice. They project a vision of a world in which wrongs are righted, and villains are betrayed by clues that they did not know they were leaving. A world in which murderers are caught and hanged, and innocent victims are avenged, and future murder is deterred."

"But it is just a vision, Peter. The world we live in is not like that."

"It sometimes is," he said. "Besides, hasn't it occurred to you that to be beneficent, a vision does not have to be true?"

"What benefits could be conferred by falsehood?" she asked.

"Not falsehood, Harriet; idealism. Detective stories keep alive a view of the world which ought to be true. Of course people read them for fun, for diversion, as they do crossword puzzles. But underneath they feed a hunger for justice, and heaven help us if ordinary people cease to feel that."

"You have rather an exalted view of it, Peter."

"I suppose very clever people can get their visions of justice from Dostoyevski," he said. "But there aren't enough of them to make a climate of opinion. Ordinary people in great numbers read what you write."

"But not for enlightenment. They are the slackest. They only want a good story with a few thrills and reversals along the way."

"You get under their guard," he said. "If they thought they were being preached at they would stop their ears. If they thought you were bent on improving their minds, they would probably never pick up the book. But you offer to divert them, and you show them by stealth the orderly world in which we should all try to be living."

"But are you serious?" she asked.

"Never more so, Domina. Your vocation seems no more frivolous to me than mine does to you. We are each, it seems, more weighty in each other's eyes than in our own. It's probably rather a good formula: self-respect without vanity."

"Frivolity for ever?"

"For as long as possible," he said, suddenly sombre. "I rather wish the Germans were addicted to your kind of light reading."[14]

As I suggested at the beginning of this section, the reader may suspect that all this is a very elaborate and largely unnecessary justification for the pleasure we get from reading murder mysteries. Yet I think Chesterton and Sayers are right to think that detective fiction involves an extraordinary metaphysical draft on the way things are. That draft is nothing less than the presumption that justice is deeper than injustice. Accordingly detective fiction can be profoundly Christian, in that evil is bounded by a greater good. Such a presumption does not entail that justice will always be done, that the murderer will always be caught, or even that we will not be sometimes more sympathetic with the murderer than the victim. Rather it means that we are not irrational to hope that justice will be done.

P. D. James observes that the crime novel reassures us that we live in a morally comprehensible universe and accordingly we have an obligation to try to put things right.[15] But she notes that though it may appear you get justice at the end of the modern detective story, all you in fact get is the fallible justice of human beings:

You don't get divine justice, you can't achieve that. It is very reassuring to have a form of fiction which says that every form of human life is sacred, and if it is taken away, then the law, society, will address itself to finding out who did it. The attitude is not, "Well, one more chap's got murdered—hard luck." Infinite pains and money are spent trying to find out who did it because we still have the belief that the individual human life is sacred; we all have a right to live out our lives to the last moment.[16]

Moreover, if this account of the moral presuppositions of the murder mystery is right, and I think it is, it makes it particularly important for those of us who think about as well as teach ethics to be students as well as readers of novels about crime. For one of the temptations for those of us who "do ethics" is to assume that ethics is about the more subtle aspects of our lives. As a result we forget that few things are more important for the sustaining of our lives than the conviction that murder is wrong. As Chesterton suggested above, to lose our hold on that fundamental conviction would mean to lose our hold on the very possibility of living humane, to say nothing of godly, lives. To the extent that the reading of murder mysteries reminds us that we were not created to kill one another we are made better.

BUT CAN A PACIFIST READ MURDER MYSTERIES WITH PLEASURE?

So runs my justification for reading murder mysteries. But have I "justified" myself into a contradiction? I am, after all, a declared proponent of Christian nonviolence. McInerny is a well-known proponent of just war. Was tempting me to read murder mysteries a clever way to undermine my nonviolence?[17] If I believe murderers should be caught and punished, have I not in effect accepted the fundamental practice that justifies the restrained use of violence by public authorities?[18] To answer this challenge would require an extended discussion of how Christian nonviolence should be understood as well as the complexities of just war thinking.[19] I have no intention of imposing either on readers who have read this essay because they thought it was about murder mysteries.

Besides, I have a witness in defense of not only why pacifists do not contradict themselves when they read murder mysteries but why reading murder mysteries may be further training in a nonviolent way of life.[20] That witness is Ralph McInerny. McInerny observes that most readers are content to use rather superficial criteria to distinguish Catholic mysteries from those that are not Catholic—for example, Catholic mysteries require the presence of a priest or a nun. Yet commenting on his own work, which obviously accepts the convention of having a priest or nun as the detective, McInerny notes, "I wanted a priest to represent the contrast of sin and forgiveness and a cop, Captain Keegan, to represent that between crime and punishment."[21]

I may well be overreading McInerny's comment, but "sin and forgiveness" names the realities that make the Christian commitment to peace intelligible. Crime is ontologically a subset of sin, which means, for Christians, forgiveness is a more determinative reality than punishment. Christians rightly believe that sin is punishment healed through reconciliation with God, ourselves, and our wronged neighbor. Such reconciliation creates the space that allows the narration of our lives, individually and collectively, through which our sins can be acknowledged without deception. The "realism" of the crime novel is but the realism required by the acknowledgment of sin and made possible through reconciliation.

Such realism is at the heart of the Christian commitment to nonviolence. Christians are not committed to nonviolence because we believe nonviolence is an effective strategy to free the world of war. Rather, we are nonviolent because we know we live in a world at war yet believe that the forgiveness wrought on the cross of Christ makes it possible for us to live nonviolently in a world at war. In like manner we know we do not live in a world free of murder. Indeed, like advocates of just war, we know how important it is to distinguish between murder and other ways life is taken. Yet we also know that God's forgiveness is not only for those who are the victims of murder but for murderers.[22] Indeed we know part of the process such forgiveness names is the discovery of those who have unjustly killed. For without discovery, they have no way to be made part of the process of judgment, penance, and reconciliation.

To be a murderer is to be condemned to absolute aloneness. To kill another human being is to be enveloped in secrecy, even if others know of it, that makes our lives incapable of being shared. To be discovered is therefore a kind of redemption. Indeed one of the remarkable aspects of most murder mysteries is they end with discovery. What happens after discovery is anticlimactic, because what matters is that the murderer is known not just by us but by themselves. Such knowing is the beginning of the process that redemption names. The name Christians have been taught to call that process is *peace*.

I should like to end with these enigmatic remarks pretending I have given adequate justification for pacifists to read murder mysteries. Yet there is a challenge I cannot avoid. It is wonderfully put by Sayers and Walsh at the end of *Thrones, Dominations*. Harriet tells Peter she is pregnant and asks if he is "pleased."

"Pleased?" he responds. "*Pleased? That's no sort of word for it—my blood rejoices in my veins! I can feel the eternal stage-hands shift the scenery around us as we stand.*" Continuing, he turns somber, observing that "the future opens up before us real and urgent."

Which elicits from Harriet, knowing the threat of war, the question "Do we do right to bring a child into the present time?" Peter responds,

"There's what we can do for any child of ours," he said, "and there's what no one can do for any child at all."

"They make their own way, you mean?"

"They claim or renounce their inheritance in their own time, and make or break the time accordingly. We shall lavish every gift we can on ours, but we cannot give it safety."

"You know, until this happened I would have said that I no longer cared a fig for the fate of the world as long as you and I were together."

"Let Rome in Tiber melt, and the wide arc of the ranged empire fall? No, Domina, that's not our style. If there's another war we shall have to face it, and we shall have to win it," said Peter.[23]

This I take to be Sayers's final answer to the earlier question of the relation between detective work and war.[24] Her answer is profound but, I believe for Christians, a wrong answer. It is wrong just to the extent we know we cannot make our children safe. At least we cannot make them safe if it means we must use violence to ensure their safety. Rather we believe we have been given better work to do in a world at war. We have been made part of a company of people who would not have our lives or our children's lives protected through further killing. It is a dangerous way to live, but then the alternative, as we learn from murder mysteries, is that lives lived safely are not worth living.

■Appendix: The Ekklesia Project

A Declaration and an Invitation to All Christians

THROUGH THE CHURCH, the Wisdom of God is being made known to the world (see Ephesians 3:10). This may come as a surprise to many, both inside and outside the church. The economic, political, and social structures of the contemporary era are so powerful that they frequently seem to eclipse God's Wisdom, substituting for it the "wisdom" of the world. Instead of living as the body of Christ, Christians too often conform their lives to partisan ideologies and identities, or to the routines of a consumer culture. We are often asked to put other allegiances before what we owe to God and the community of faith; and all too often, our churches seem willing to subordinate the Gospel to the imperatives of economic and political powerholders and institutions.

And yet, we are called not to be conformed to this world, but to be transformed, by the renewing of our minds, so that we might discern the will of God—what is good, and acceptable, and perfect (see Romans 12:2). We speak of the Church as "the body of Christ" because we believe that Christians are called to make present the reality of Jesus Christ in the world. Hence, to "be the Church" is to declare that our allegiance to the God of Jesus Christ always takes priority over the other structures that compete for our attention during every hour of every day of our lives.

Christians from many walks of life feel the tensions among these competing allegiances, and recognize that accommodation and compromise are woefully inadequate responses. Some find themselves frustrated by the modern university and its various guilds, within which the Christian intellectual life is no longer recognized as a viable subject of conversation. Others are concerned that many people who describe themselves as Christians do not know the central stories of the Christian faith, let alone allow their lives to be shaped by those stories. Still others are anxious about the challenges of raising children in the Christian life, in the midst of a culture increasingly driven by consumerism and violence. What holds all these concerns together is the common conviction that the Christian family should play the decisive formative role in our day-to-day lives. And it is clear that many Christian universities, local churches, and believers are unwilling or unable to play this role if it means resisting certain powerful aspects of the existing order.

To offer but one example: at one time, universities provided at least some "free and ordered space" within which the claims of the Christian life could be imagined, criticized, and supported—even in the midst of the competing, often dominant, claims of the state, empire, and economy. But the increasing secularization of the modern university has made it, in most cases, a hostile environment for conversations about the Christian life. And yet, such conversations desperately need to take place if we hope to work toward a greater integration of Christian convictions and Christian practices, and if scholars are to explore what Christianity might mean to their fields of study and their various intellectual vocations. Without space for Christian scholarship and reflection, and without conversations among Christians in the universities, in the workplaces, and in local congregations, the entire church is enfeebled.

From the time of the earliest gatherings of the disciples of Jesus, Christians have recognized that God fashions the Body of Christ to be a visible presence in the world. We are "called out" from the world, as suggested by the original Greek word for church: *ekklesia*. We understand this "calling out" to be the work of the Holy Spirit, who redeems the lives of believers not as isolated individuals, but as members of an alternative community— a resource of resistance to the social and political structures of the age.

Carrying out this communal work requires a common vision and a good deal of mutual support. This is part of the mission of the local church, to which all Christians must remain committed. But congregations and other Christian organizations find it difficult to live a life of discipleship in the midst of competition from the thousands of objects, images, and ideals that vie for our allegiance and attention on a daily basis. Living the Christian life in the midst of such competition requires nourishment and strengthening from the Holy Spirit, carried out through *koinonia* (communion, fellowship) with other persons who find themselves similarly called.

Therefore, we have formed a network of mutual support for the life of Christian discipleship—support that, sadly, is lacking in many local congregations. We believe that we can help one another to narrow the gaps between what we Christians profess and how we live. We call this The

Ekklesia Project, in recognition of the fact that we are "called out" of the world into a different mode of life.

The Ekklesia Project is not a church, nor is it an alternative to existing local churches. It intends to celebrate and make known the work of those congregations and groups whose allegiances to God and the Body of Christ make discipleship a lived reality in the world. The Project also intends, in the spirit of "fraternal correction" (see Matthew 18:15–16), to challenge communities and practices that have minimized or diluted the church's obligation to be a "light to the nations" (see Isaiah 49:6) and a foretaste of the promised Kingdom of God. Those of us who have created The Ekklesia Project hope and expect to be held to the same level of accountability by our brothers and sisters in Christ.

Our principles are simple and straightforward:

1. We believe that the triune God is the origin and ultimate goal of all things; and that, through Jesus Christ, we are called to give our allegiance to God and to make the Church our true dwelling place. We believe that the claims of Christ have priority over those of the state, the market, race, class, gender, and other functional idolatries. "You shall have no other gods before me" (Exodus 20:3).

2. We believe that communal worship is the heart of the Christian life. We seek the guidance of the Holy Spirit to bring our everyday practices into greater conformity with our worship, such that our entire lives may be lived to glorify God. Similarly, we pledge to give and receive counsel about how we might better embody the Gospel in its individual and communal expressions. "Praise the Lord! Praise the name of the Lord; give praise, O servants of the Lord" (Psalm 135:1).

3. We believe that the church undercuts its own vocation when it compromises with the institutions, allegiances, and assumptions that undergird the "culture of death" in our world. We remind all Christians that, in rejecting the sword and other lethal means to advance His goals, Jesus set an example for all of us who seek to follow Him. While accepting rather than imposing death may still be foolish and scandalous in the eyes of non-Christians (see 1 Corinthians 1:23), it remains central to what it means to follow a crucified and risen Messiah. We believe that the process of renewing the church in our day requires Christians to rethink all those values and practices that presume a smooth fit between killing and discipleship—no matter how disturbing or divisive this reappraisal may be (see Matthew 10:34–38). Jesus said, "I have come that they may have life, and have it abundantly" (John 10:10).

213

4. We do not accept the ultimacy of divisions imposed on the Body of Christ—whether they be national borders, denominational divides, cultural and social stereotypes, or class divisions. We seek to restore the bonds of ecclesial unity and solidarity that are always under threat from the powers and principalities of the present age. "For I am convinced that neither death, nor life, . . . nor anything else in all creation, will be able to separate us from the love of God in Christ Jesus our Lord" (Romans 8:38–39).

We seek to embody these principles through an ongoing critical conversation about the Christian life. We expect this to include regular gatherings and retreats at the local, regional, and national levels; a wide variety of publications, in both paper and electronic form, for a variety of audiences (academic, ecclesial, and popular); and an ongoing network of communication (including a regular newsletter). Additionally, the members of The Ekklesia Project pledge that they will maintain vital prayer lives, participate in the worship life of their local churches, perform the traditional works of mercy (e.g., feeding the hungry, clothing the naked, sheltering the homeless, welcoming the stranger, instructing the uneducated), and observe a daytime fast every Friday as a form of prayerful resistance to the idolatrous practices of our culture. We will hold one another responsible for these covenantal practices and those that the Spirit may lead us to accept at a later time.

We invite all Christians from all walks of life to join us. We ask for your prayers and participation; we ask for your commitment of time and money; and we ask you to add your name to the membership of The Ekklesia Project.

ENDORSERS

(* indicates founding members)

Wesley Avram
*Frederick C. Bauerschmidt
Michael Baxter
*Daniel Bell
Norman Bendroth
Margaret Lamberts Bendroth
John Berkman
Albert Borgmann
*Robert Brimlow
Walter Brueggemann

*Michael L. Budde
*Michael Cartwright
*William Cavanaugh
*Rodney Clapp
Randy Cooper
*David Cunningham
*Inagrace Dietterich
Tim Emmett
Stephen Fowl
*Barry Harvey

*Stanley Hauerwas
Thomas Heilke
Murray Jardine
*Kelly Johnson
Philip Kenneson
Brent Laytham
*D. Stephen Long

Christine Lundt
*David McCarthy
Kent McDougall
Sandra Mize
Elizabeth Newman
*Edward Phillips
*Vincent Rocchio

NOTES

INTRODUCTION

1. John Howard Yoder, *For The Nations: Essays Public and Evangelical* (Grand Rapids: Eerdmans, 1997), p. 6.

2. I am indebted to Alex Sider for suggesting this title to me.

3. Francis Cardinal George, "Catholic Christianity and the Millennium: Frontiers of the Mind in the 21st Century," p. 2. I am using a manuscript copy of the archbishop's speech I received from a friend. I assume that the text is widely available and will soon be published, but I have no details about where that may be. It is my understanding that the Library of Congress is in the process of finding a publisher for this series of lectures. The paginations refer to the manuscript copy I have.

4. Ibid.

5. Ibid.

6. Ibid.

7. Ibid., p. 4.

8. Ibid., p. 5.

9. Ibid.

10. Ibid. With Rev. Michael Baxter I have argued in a similar vein in our "The Kingship of Christ: Why Freedom of 'Belief' Is Not Enough," in my *In Good Company: The Church As Polis* (Notre Dame, Ind.: University of Notre Dame Press, 1995), pp. 199–216.

11. For Cardinal George's further reflections on the nature of liberalism and its effect on Catholic theology, see his "How Liberalism Fails the Church," *Commonweal* 126, no. 20 (November 19, 1999): 24–29.

12. Francis Cardinal George, "Catholic Christianity and the Millennium," p. 6.

13. Ibid., p. 8.

14. Ibid., p. 11.

15. Ibid., pp. 11–12.

16. Ibid., p. 12.

17. Stanley Fish, *Doing What Comes Naturally: Change, Rhetoric, and the Practice of Theory in Literary and Legal Studies* (Durham, N.C.: Duke University Press, 1989), p. ix. Fish notes the other objection would be that the essays collected in his book do not constitute a book, dealing as they do with topics as diverse as Milton, Freud, the law, professionalism, formalism, teaching of composition, irony, speech acts, change, rhetoric, blind submission, the uses of theory, and literary history. He rejects this characterization. I might compile a similar list of quite different topics that make up *A Better Hope*, but I would, like Fish, deny that such a list means this is not a book. Like Fish (no doubt without his élan), I use diverse subjects and literatures to develop an ongoing argument—an argument that admittedly may always seem to be about the same thing, that is, what truthful worship of God entails.

18. For my explicit reflections on Reinhold Niebuhr see chapters 2 and 3 of my *Wilderness Wanderings: Probing Twentieth-Century Theology and Philosophy* (Boulder, Colo.: Westview, 1997). My most thorough analysis of Niebuhr's theology will appear in my Gifford Lectures, *With the Grain of the Universe*, in 2001.

19. Francis Cardinal George, "Catholic Christianity and the Millennium," p. 11.

20. I owe this way of putting the matter to Richard Church.

CHAPTER 1

1. "A Tale of Two Stories: On Being a Christian and a Texan," in my *Christian Existence Today: Essays on Church, World, and Living In Between* (Durham, N.C.: Labyrinth, 1988), pp. 25–45.

2. I recently received a letter from a friend that nicely expresses my own ambivalent reactions to the latest U.S.A. My friend is not a Christian but a committed Aristotelian:

"I flew to L.A. with my father for my brother's wedding. The ceremony in my brother's back yard was one of the weirdest I ever attended, performed by an 'ordained minister' in a strange California New Age group that my new sister-in-law is involved in called 'The Movement for Spiritual Inner Awareness.' I had to bite my lip to keep myself from laughing. On reflection, however, there's something seriously wrong with a culture that can abide this sort of crap. It was an object lesson in how right Harold Bloom was in marking gnosticism as 'the american religion.' It also reinforced my commitment to philosophy as an important hedge against gnosticism, since even the most die-hard Plotinian anti-materialist will be constrained to arguing his or her point rather than assuming it is pneumatically self-evident. Bah.

"You can probably garner from the above that I am not in a particularly jovial mood. Certain circumstances surrounding the wedding have depressed and soured me, and a great number of the guests at the wedding had characters that bothered me no end. America is a civilization that makes it very difficult indeed to take one's life seriously, and while I hate being haughty (or crabby), I find most of my fellow countrymen and women rather hard to take of late. I am far too much of a tight-ass (and proud of it, too) to feel terribly comfortable here. I admire the reticence and lack of ostentatious self-display you find in most Europeans and Asians as much as I disdain the shallowness and 'fun-loving' mindset of many of my compatriots. (I always thought 'fun-loving' to be a disguised insult.) The plane ride home was a bit of an epiphany, because the weather was clear from L.A. to N.Y. and I spent most of my time just scanning the amazingly diverse and astonishingly beautiful landscape: the aspens were turning gold in the Rockies, the maples and oaks were bright red in the Alleghenies, and I had bird's-eye views of both L.A. and N.Y.C., the latter being especially beautiful at 20,000 feet. What you have in America is almost unbearably intense scenic beauty, virtually everywhere, combined with an almost equally intense social, political, cultural and moral ugliness. (Well, maybe not 'ugliness' but emptiness.) My wife is always quick to point out the perils of this 'grass is always greener' attitude I am apt to fall into, and she's surely right about it. Nevertheless I don't think I'm entirely wrong either."

3. For a more developed account of this theme see my "Why Christian Ethics Is Such a Bad Idea," in *Beyond Mere Health: Theology and Health Care in a Secular Society*, ed. Hilary Regan, Rodney Horsfield, and Gabrielle McMullen (Melbourne: Australian Theological Forum, 1996), pp. 64–79; and see also chapter 5 below.

4. It is not just that Niebuhr had no or little role for the church in his thought, but it is by no means clear what the status of his theological claims is. In an extraordinary paragraph in the preface to the 1964 edition of *The Nature and Destiny of Man* (Louisville: Westminster John Knox, 1996), Niebuhr observes about his book: "I placed a special emphasis on the eschatology of the New Testament with its special symbols of the Christ and anti-Christ, taking them as symbols of the fact that both good and evil grow in history, and that evil has no separate history, but that a greater evil is always a corruption of a greater good. I believe that the perils of a nuclear age substantiate this interpretation much more vividly than I expected when I presented the thesis. But I am now not so sure that the historic symbols will contribute much to the understanding by modern man of his tragic and ironic history with its refutation of the messianic and utopian hopes of the Renaissance and Enlightenment" (p. xxvi). That Christ only stands on the edge of history was always clear in Niebuhr's work, but that you may not need even the "symbol" is something else again. Interpreting as charitably as possible, one can only assume that this observation is not about Christ but rather the "understanding by modern man."

5. See for example Edmund Santurri, "Rawlsian Liberalism, Moral Truth, and Augustinian Politics," *Journal for Peace and Justice Studies* 8, no. 2 (1997): 1–36. Santurri argues that Christians have a stake in a Rawlsian political strategy to the extent the latter can be saved from Rorty-like skepticism by providing an Augustinian justification. Yet the truth Santurri thinks Augustine supplies is that "order is better than disorder." I find it hard to understand why Augustine is thought necessary to sustain that "truth." Santurri's article is followed by commentaries by David Dawson, Jean Elshtain, Timothy Jackson, Gilbert Meilaender, and Michael White.

6. Nicholas Wolterstorff, "From Presence to Practice: Mind, World, and Entitlement to Believe," the Gifford Lectures for 1994–1995 at the University of St. Andrews. I am indebted to Professor Wolterstorff for making his manuscript available to me. The quote appears on p. 353 of the manuscript.

7. Ibid., p. 358.

8. Martin Marty, *The One and the Many: America's Struggle for the Common Good* (Cambridge, Mass.: Harvard University Press, 1997). For example, in Marty's *Religion and Republic* (Boston: Beacon, 1987), he confesses that the book is meant to celebrate "pluralism." The totalitarian powers of the twentieth century tried to abolish pluralism by attacking religion; tribal forces use their bonds of religion-culture-ethnicity-race to defeat the politics of pluralism. The nineteenth-century attempt at Christian

America often resulted in trying to stifle pluralism. But according to Marty, there is a good pluralism and a bad pluralism. The latter refers to the mere variety of religious-cultural groupings coexisting in a time and place. The former is taken to include a polity that assures freedom for such diverse groups to coexist creatively. America is obviously characterized today by the good pluralism, since it knows neither totalist nor tribalist extremes. Marty writes to reinforce that pluralism—that is, to help develop "publicly accessible theories and theologies by which pluralists can ground their particular faiths in some sort of universal ways by which they can relate their peculiarities to something general. Otherwise there will be only tribal soliloquies and solipsism and the death of the *communitas communitatum*." For all his sophistication, Marty, like Christian ethicists, still stays wedded to the project of writing church history to show what kind of Christianity will be good for America.

It would make a fascinating study to compare Marty's story of religion in America to younger evangelical scholars such as Marsden, Hatch, and Noll. The latter seem not to have quite the same stake Marty does in underwriting "the public," yet they find it hard to free themselves from the structure of the narrative well set by Protestant liberals. For example, in *Religion and the American Culture* (New York: Harcourt Brace Jovanovich, 1990), George Marsden observes, in commenting on the different assessments of the 1900s by Henry Adams and religious leaders, that the two sides reflect the "essential paradox in American civilization: it is both intensely spiritual and intensely materialistic. In part this combination is an inevitable one which can be found in all so-called 'Christian' civilizations throughout the ages. The spiritual dimensions never cut as deep as some of the public expressions of the civilization would suggest. This is true even of medieval Western civilization, of which Henry Adams held a somewhat romanticized view. The paradox in Western civilization reflects a paradox deep in human nature" (p. 101). The last line is, of course, right out of Reinhold Niebuhr.

Mark Noll's work makes particularly interesting reading from this perspective. His *A History of Christianity in the United States and Canada* (Grand Rapids: Eerdmans, 1992) not only has the virtue of dealing with Canada as part of the story but also displays a profound ambivalence over whether the passing of "Christian Canada" and "Christian America" is a blessing or a tragedy. While I am sympathetic with Noll's suggestion that Christianity may find a new birth by being freed from American messianism, I find it interesting that he, with Marsden, writes as if he is telling the story for "anyone." The very presumptions of "objectivity" continue to be operative, even for these professed evangelicals, in the reproduction of the idea that America is the primary agent of history. For Noll's more explicit reflections on the relation of Christianity and politics, see his *One Nation under God? Christian Faith and Political Action in America* (San Francisco: Harper & Row, 1988). The primary theme of this book is that politics is complex; that is, it admits of few black-and-white solutions because humanity is complex. Accordingly, "Christians do well to approach political issues with careful analysis, with a distrust of their first impressions, and with a commitment to explore as many sides of an issue as possible" (p. 89). Noll, like Marsden, proves that he has learned well the lessons taught by Niebuhr, particularly that the Christian contribution to politics comes primarily through insights about human nature. How those insights are in any way dependent on more determinative theological practices is left obscure.

9. Marty, *The One and the Many*, pp. 71–72.

10. Ibid., p. 22.

11. Ibid., pp. 74–76.

12. Ibid., pp. 120–29.

13. Ibid., p. 154.

14. Ibid., p. 225.

15. Alasdair MacIntyre, "How to Be a North American," Publication 2–88, Humanities Series: Federation of State Humanities Councils, 1987, p. 16.

16. I originally thought I might use this essay to explore the difference between the hyphens, that is, the difference between what it means to be, for example, a German-American and a Christian-German and/or American. That America alienates us from our story of origin is not unique because so does Christianity. Indeed I suspect one of the problems for Christians in America is the temptation to confuse those two quite different alienations.

17. Alasdair MacIntyre, "The American Idea," in *America and Ireland, 1976–1996: The American Identity and the Irish Connection,* ed. David Noel Doyle and Owen Dudley Edwards (Westport, Conn.: Greenwood, 1980), pp. 58–59. This article as well as "How to Be a North American" needs to be more widely known, as they would make easy dismissals of MacIntyre's philosophical arguments much more difficult.

18. MacIntyre, "The American Idea," p. 61. I should note that MacIntyre makes clear that what he calls the American idea is not a single or unitary reality but presents very different aspects from different points of view and at different times.

19. Ibid., p. 66. MacIntyre cites as "successes" the increase of the number of Americans who graduate from high school, the number of African-Americans who graduate from college, and the availability of health care to the poor.

MacIntyre is also particularly critical of those forms of anti-Americanism characteristic of Europeans that seek to make America the scapegoat for the sins of Western modernity. Such anti-Americanism is a sign of failure to recognize that in the "democracies of the West you cannot reject America because in the end, if you are honest, America is you. Every American has two nationalities, his own and that from which his or her ancestors originally sprang, whether in Europe, Asia, Africa, or in North America itself. But the counterpart to this is that free persons anywhere also have two nations, whether they like it or not—their own and the United States" (p. 68). MacIntyre is not suggesting, I think, that this is a "good thing," but that this is the way things are. As I suggested above, the way America alienates us from our origin is quite interestingly compared to how becoming a Christian alienates us from our past. I think the difference is quite simple—the church is not a utopian possibility but a concrete community across time.

20. Ibid., p. 61.

21. The "we," of course, needs to be specified. MacIntyre maintains that the boundaries of a culture cannot be identified with political boundaries. This is particularly important for Americans, since we must realize that "there is no adequate way of telling our common story unless we understand how to relate to Mexican understandings of Mexican history and to Canadian understandings of Canadian history, whether of Quebeçois or of English-speaking Canadians" ("How to Be a North American," p. 14).

22. For a fascinating argument to reclaim history as a moral enterprise, see David Harlan, *The Degradation of American History* (Chicago: University of Chicago Press,

1997). Harlan notes that "American culture cannot be thought of as a single conversation carried on by a limited number of distinct and autonomous voices. It is not, as the champions of multiculturalism contend, that American culture has become too pluralistic and diversified to carry on such a conversation—as if we had become a collection of isolated, marginalized, and exotically distinct subcultures, each one speaking its own private language. In fact, it is pretty much the opposite, for all those putatively distinct subcultures have actually been commingling in the night, combining and coalescing with an unrelenting ferocity. . . . This is the point at which Eliot and even Oakeshott fail us. If we are to have the predecessors we need, we must find them ourselves—find them and arrange them such that we can see ourselves as the latest in a long sequence or tradition of such thinkers" (pp. 206–7). That is the task of history according to Harlan. He is quite pessimistic that history as a social science is capable of such a role.

23. MacIntyre, "How to Be a North American," p. 18. MacIntyre is surely right to praise the Vietnam War Memorial, but I think much more can be said about the monument's significance. That the monument pulls us into itself while we see ourselves reflected in the black marble is surely a representation of how we were drawn into the war. Most of us were spectators to the deaths of those whose names are now on the wall. It is right therefore to see ourselves reflected in their deaths. Moreover the long, slow path out of Vietnam mimics the long, slow path into the war. That the monument is, moreover, a slash into the earth is not accidental. The blood spilled in Vietnam by American and Vietnamese surely cries out to us from the ground itself. It is the voice of Abel. Of course such a reading of the memorial is made possible by the Bible. MacIntyre has no reason to resist such a reading, though others might.

24. Ibid.

25. Some no doubt would assume that the war in Vietnam constitutes such a wrong, but I do not. The way the United States exited that war may well constitute such a wrong. Slavery and the genocide against the Native Americans are certainly places to begin to think about such wrongs.

26. Thomas E. Jenkins, The Character of God: Recovering the Lost Literary Power of American Protestantism (New York: Oxford University Press, 1997), p. 21.

27. Ibid., pp. 137–38.

28. William James, The Varieties of Religious Experience (New York: Mentor, 1958), p. 425.

29. Jenkins, Character of God, p. 169.

30. James (in his quite wonderfully obtuse restraint) observes when considering the character of what "over-beliefs" one might hold, "It would never do for us to place ourselves offhand at the position of a particular theology, the Christian theology, for example, and proceed immediately to define the 'more' as Jehovah, and the 'union' as his imputation to us of the righteousness of Christ. That would be unfair to other religions, and, for our present standpoint at least, would be an over-belief" (Varieties of Religious Experience, p. 431).

CHAPTER 2

1. Nicholas Boyle, Who Are We Now? Christian Humanism and the Global Market from Hegel to Heaney (Notre Dame, Ind.: University of Notre Dame Press, 1998), p. 318.

I have followed Boyle's use of capitalization and hyphenation ("Post-Modernism") in this quote, but when I am writing in my own voice I will use neither.

2. That I have been associated with the postmodernist has always seemed to me a mistake deriving from those who fail to understand Wittgenstein's influence on how I work. Stanley Fish is certainly a friend and I have learned from his work, but I have no idea what it would mean to say that Fish is a postmodernist. Philosophically I have learned more from Alasdair MacIntyre, who, exactly because of his appreciation of Nietzsche, is anything but a postmodernist. I suppose my attack on the National Association of Scholars in *After Christendom?* ([Nashville: Abingdon, 1991], pp. 140–52) may have led some to think I am a "relativist," but even if I were a relativist, which I am not, that would not make me a postmodernist. If MacIntyre is a nonfoundationalist, I suppose I must also be such, but again a MacIntyrian nonfoundationalism does not entail the kind of skepticism thought to be at the heart of postmodernism.

By a "playful use of postmodernism," I mean how I have used the "atheism" of postmodernism against the humanism of modernism, for I assume that postmodernism is the only atheism that modernity could produce. Modernism is the rejection of God, or at least a parody of the Christian God, in the interest of a kind of divinization of the human. Postmodernists, seeking to be thorough in their atheism, deny such humanism. See, for example, chapter 11, "No Enemy, No Christianity: Preaching between Worlds," in my book *Sanctify Them in the Truth: Holiness Exemplified* (Edinburgh: T & T Clark, 1998), pp. 191–200. For a powerful account of modernity as a project to build "the city of man," see Pierre Manent, *The City of Man,* trans. Marc Le Pain (Princeton, N.J.: Princeton University Press, 1998). Like Boyle, Manent locates modernity with the discovery of "history" and, in particular, how such history is displayed through the sociological and economic viewpoints.

3. David Toole, *Waiting for Godot in Sarajevo: Theological Reflections on Nihilism, Tragedy, and Apocalypse* (Boulder, Colo.: Westview, 1998).

4. Ibid., pp. 269–70.

5. Terry Eagleton, *The Illusions of Postmodernism* (Oxford: Blackwell, 1996), p. vii. Eagleton's account of postmodernism as a general intellectual style is, I think, about as good a characterization as one can get. I confess, however, that I remain extremely suspicious of whether any coherent postmodern position exists.

6. Eagleton notes that postmodernism as a style of culture allegedly reflects an epochal change characterized by "a deathless, decentred, ungrounded, self-reflexive, playful, derivative, eclectic, pluralistic art which blurs the boundaries between 'high' and 'popular' culture, as well as between art and everyday experience. How dominant or pervasive this culture is—whether it goes all the way down, or figures just as one particular region within contemporary life—is a matter of argument" (ibid., pp. vii-viii). How to understand the relation between postmodernism as an intellectual position and as a cultural movement is not clear to me. For my "use" of modernism against itself, see my "No Enemy, No Christianity: Preaching between Worlds," in my *Sanctify Them in the Truth,* pp. 191–200.

7. Boyle, *Who Are We Now?* p. 82. The problem, I think, is not that postmodernism might not have been present in earlier times but that the unclarity about what postmodernity is makes such judgments arbitrary. Significant thinkers are bound to be ambiguous in terms of "periodizations." Thus Descartes is increasingly read as a late

223 ∎

medieval thinker and Kant, or at least the Kant of the third *Critique*, as a harbinger of Romanticism.

8. Boyle, *Who Are We Now?* p. 290. How Christians must "take history seriously" without becoming Hegelians is one of the great intellectual challenges before contemporary theology. The influence of Deleuze on Milbank I think must be interpreted in this light.

9. Michael Gillespie observes that "nihilism is not the result of the death of God but the consequence of the birth or rebirth of a different kind of God, an omnipotent god of will who calls into question all of reason and nature and thus overturns all eternal standards of truth and justice, and good and evil. This idea of God came to predominance in the fourteenth century and shattered the medieval synthesis of philosophy and theology, catapulting man into a new way of thinking and being, a *via moderna* essentially at odds with the *via antiqua*. This new way was in turn the foundation for modernity as the realm of human self-assertion" (*Nihilism Before Nietzsche* [Chicago: University of Chicago Press, 1995], pp. xii-xiii).

10. Philip Blond, "Introduction: Theology Before Philosophy," in *Post-secular Philosophy: Between Philosophy and Theology*, ed. Philip Blond (London: Routledge, 1998), p. 6. Blond notes prior to this observation that modern theologians and philosophers who have attempted to resist skepticism in theology have done so by means of natural theology—that is, they have "attempted to discern, or infer, the nature of God from a secular construal of the nature of the world" (p. 5). To do this, a correspondence between cause and effect necessitated that some term be given due proportion to both creatures and Creator because it was assumed that mutual knowledge depends on the classical notion that "like knows like."

11. For a much more detailed account of Scotus's position as well as critique, see Catherine Pickstock, *After Writing: On the Liturgical Consummation of Philosophy* (Oxford: Blackwell, 1998), pp. 121–40. Pickstock's book is an extraordinary account of the theological and philosophical developments that created the possibility of modernity and postmodernity correlated with social and political developments. Anyone acquainted with her work will recognize how much I have learned from her as well as her and Blond's teacher, John Milbank. I confess I am insufficiently schooled to evaluate their claims about Scotus.

12. Blond, "Introduction: Theology Before Philosophy," p. 6. When "being" is assumed to be univocal, analogical predication becomes a "theory." Thus the importance of David Burrell's work in freeing Aquinas from those who falsely assume the centrality of analogy in Aquinas means that Aquinas must have had a theory of analogy.

13. Robert Jenson, "How the World Lost Its Story," *First Things*, no. 36 (October 1993): 19–24.

14. Boyle, *Who Are We Now?* pp. 289–90.

15. Boyle suggests that in postmodernity a history that refers to the past has come to an end in favor of history that only names an unrealized future (ibid., p. 81). Boyle argues that Heidegger is the great representative of this understanding of history, since he believed so firmly in our power to make our future that he made that power the source of our historicity. "We make the continuity, and so the history, of our existence by choosing our hero, choosing a tradition and inheritance that we have in common with others. We create our past in the image of our future, of the projection of our existence forward to its

limit in death. We have a fate (*Schicksal*) because, like Nietzsche, we are a fate. Out of the contingencies of that 'fate' Existence chooses its particular destiny (*Geschick*), the events it willingly shares with 'its collectivity, its people.' The flaw in this account is its ignoring of the extent to which our 'destiny,' the historicity of our existence (and indeed of existence itself), is a gift from others, and the extent therefore to which the temporality of existence derives from pastness as well as futurity" (ibid., p. 223). Boyle, I believe rightly, identifies Heidegger's denial of the past with his refusal to understand our existence as the result of an act of love. "Behind Heidegger's reluctance to see historicity as a gift, and not only a construct, lies a general—but, as his analysis of the presuppositions of selfhood shows, not necessarily fundamental—hostility to givenness" (ibid., p. 198).

16. Ibid., pp. 80–81. Boyle's use of the shopping mall as the image for postmodernism is anticipated by James Edwards in his *The Plain Sense of Things: The Fate of Religion in an Age of Normal Nihilism* (University Park: Pennsylvania State University Press, 1997), pp. 47–50.

17. Marx no doubt deserves the credit for the discovery of the significance of money for the transformation of the market. David Harvey provides a wonderfully clear and incisive account of Marx's analysis of money in his *The Condition of Postmodernity* (Oxford: Blackwell, 1990), pp. 99–105. Harvey observes how Marx saw that with the advent of a money economy, the bonds and relations of traditional communities could not help but be dissolved so that money became the real community. This creates the "fetishism of commodities" as money "masks" the social relations between things. Boyle also emphasizes the significance of money for the transition to modernity. But he credits Max Weber, not Marx, with the discovery that the true revolution was not with the invention of capitalist modes of production but with the invention of money as the means to define capital itself (*Who Are We Now?* pp. 104–5).

18. Fredric Jameson, *Postmodernism: Or, The Cultural Logic of Late Capitalism* (Durham, N.C.: Duke University Press, 1991), pp. 1–55. I have changed "late" to "advanced" to indicate my sense that, at least as far as capitalism is concerned, it is not clear how late his "late" is.

19. Harvey, *Condition of Postmodernity*, p. 63.

20. Boyle, *Who Are We Now?* p. 234.

21. Terry Eagleton observes that capitalism deconstructs the difference between system and transgression, because capitalism is the mind-bending paradox of a system whose margins are installed at its center (*Illusions of Postmodernism*, p. 62).

22. Harvey, *Condition of Postmodernity*, p. 105.

23. Boyle, *Who Are We Now?* pp. 153–54.

24. Ibid., p. 152.

25. Eagleton, *Illusions of Postmodernism*, p. 9. I am not sure what connection, if any, there may be between the rise of postmodernism as a movement in university cultures and the end of the Cold War, but I think the loss of a clear "enemy" must have some relation to the lack of seriousness on the part of many intellectuals.

26. Ibid., p. 27. For Richard Rorty's book, see *Achieving Our Country* (Cambridge, Mass.: Harvard University Press, 1998).

27. Rorty, *Achieving Our Country*, p. 97. One of the few things about which Rorty is adamant is that any future politics must leave Christianity behind and, in particu-

lar, any "vocabulary built around the notion of sin" (p. 32). It is unclear to me on what basis he can be so dogmatic, but I find his dislike for Christianity rather charming. He has not, however, given up entirely on religion, urging us not to discard the hope shared by Alison, Bloom, and Matthew Arnold—"the hope for a religion of literature, in which works of the secular imagination replace Scripture as the principal source of inspiration and hope for a new generation" (ibid., p. 136). Rorty identifies this religion of literature with Whitman's and Dewey's hope that America, which is a term convertible with democracy, would be the place where people come to see the ultimate significance of the finite, human, historical project. They both hoped America would be where a religion of love would replace a religion of fear, where the traditional link between the religious impulse to stand in awe of something greater than oneself and the infantile need for security would be broken. They wanted to put hope for a casteless and classless America in the place of the will of God. "They wanted that utopian America to replace God as the unconditional object of desire" (pp. 17–18). Rorty, I suppose, is to be commended for being so candid about his faith in America. Interestingly enough, he critiques the theories of Hegel and Marx, as well as the "rationalizations of hopelessness" like Foucault's and Lacan's, for attempting to satisfy the urges that theology used to satisfy. Such urges, according to Rorty, are what Dewey hoped Americans might cease to feel (p. 38).

28. Ibid., p. 98.

29. Ibid., p. 48.

30. Ibid., p. 105. In some ways Rorty's book is an extended attack on Fred Jameson. But his criticism of Jameson, I fear, is at best inept and at worst stupid.

31. Michel Foucault provides an extraordinary account of the development of this understanding of the state's function in his extremely important article "Governmentality" in The Foucault Effect: Studies in Governmentality, ed. Graham Burchell, Colin Gordon, and Peter Miller (Chicago: University of Chicago Press, 1991), pp. 87–104. Foucault distinguishes the governmentality of the modern state from sovereignty by noting that the former has no interest in disposing things to lead to the common good, but rather the role of government is "to ensure that the greatest possible quantity of wealth is produced, that the people are provided with sufficient means of subsistence, that the population is enabled to multiply, etc." (p. 95). Crucial for the development of this understanding of government is the displacement of the family as the analogical paradigm for government in favor of that new entity called population. "Governmentality" does not mean that the state is any less inclined to go to war but that wars fought by such states, as Hegel says, become ends in themselves. That is, war having no end other than itself becomes the reason for the state to exist.

These are extremely complex matters, obviously, since in Boyle's understanding the effects of globalization are uneven. Globalization complements the workings of a strong state like the United States that is also still captured by the myth of being a savior nation. States such as France and Germany more perfectly fit Foucault's understanding of governmentality. It is, for example, quite interesting to wonder if states such as France and Germany now could initiate a war in the name of their self-interest, whether such interest be understood in terms of honor or of economic well-being. Wars, at least in Europe, increasingly will be police actions initiated by regional alliances. I am indebted to Ken Surin and Reinhard Hütter for pressing me on this point.

32. This contradiction, of course, Rorty shares with people like Margaret Thatcher, who failed to see that nations are growing obsolete not as a matter of fashion but as the

result of the operation of the same economic trends she otherwise endorsed. Boyle wonderfully analyzes this contradiction in the first chapter of his book, "After Thatcherism" (*Who Are We Now?* pp. 13–67). Rorty acknowledges the tension between concern with the inequality of wealth between nations and thinking one's responsibility is to the least advantaged in one's own nation. He confesses he has no idea how this dilemma is to be resolved (*Achieving Our Country*, pp. 88–89). In an interesting manner Martha Nussbaum exemplifies the same tension in her book *Cultivating Humanity: A Classical Defense of Reform in Liberal Education* (Cambridge, Mass.: Harvard University Press, 1997). Nussbaum, who would usually be considered on the other side of the postmodern divide from Rorty, wants to train students at once locally and for world citizenship. This works well as long as she is thinking of white males but proves embarrassing once she turns to African-Americans. Should African-Americans, in the interest of being world citizens, a citizenship of nowhere, become as she recommends "philosophical exiles from our (their) own way of life"? (p. 58). It is hard to be politically correct and a universalist at the same time. Nussbaum does not feel the tension since, like Rorty, she is confident that education for world citizenship has been most fully embraced in the United States (p. 9).

33. Eagleton, *Illusions of Postmodernism*, p. 76.

34. Actually, a place where they have to go is the university, which has become for them a safe haven that serves as well as a quasi-church. Indeed Rorty favorably quotes Eisenach's observation that "progressive intellectuals turned American universities into what he calls 'something like a national "church"—the main repository and protector of common American values, common American meanings, and common American identities'" (*Achieving Our Country*, p. 50).

35. Robert Jenson, *Systematic Theology: The Triune God* (New York: Oxford University Press, 1997), 1:63.

36. John Howard Yoder, *The Politics of Jesus: Vicit Agnus Noster*, 2d ed. (Grand Rapids: Eerdmans, 1994), p. 246.

37. John Howard Yoder, "Armaments and Eschatology," *Studies in Christian Ethics* 1, no.1 (1998): 43–61.

38. See, for example, John Howard Yoder's "Firstfruits: The Paradigmatic Public Role of God's People," that now is the first chapter in his *For the Nations: Essays Public and Evangelical* (Grand Rapids: Eerdmans, 1997), pp. 15–36. Commenting on Barth, Yoder notes that "the order of the faith community constitutes a public offer to the entire society" (p. 27). I have no doubt such a characterization describes Yoder's own views.

39. I am extremely grateful to Professor Schlabach for his permission to use his characterization of my position. Schlabach's account, however, does raise some interesting questions about the differences between Yoder and me. Yoder in style and substance was always more willing to work within the world as he found it than I have been. For example, I will polemically try to expose what I take to be the contradictions in a position by forcing those that would defend just-war theory in the name of democracies to see that they cannot do so with consistency. In contrast Yoder would assume it is a good thing to believe that war should be limited and try to help those with that belief to live accordingly. The difference may be a matter of style, but I believe it may also be due to what might be described as my lingering longing for Christendom. For example, the strategy of argument I use in this paper, I suspect, would be quite foreign to Yoder's way of thinking about postmodernism.

227 ■

40. Boyle, *Who Are We Now?* p. 8.

41. Ibid., p. 91.

42. Ibid., pp. 91–92.

43. Ibid., p. 92. For this reason Boyle thinks that the moral authority of the church in the future will lie more with the college of bishops than with the papacy. It will be the bishops who will have the authority to challenge the claim of the global market to express and exhaust the human world. Already the church has produced the glorious examples of the martyred Bishops Oscar Romero and Juan Geraldi Conedera, who could understand what was going on in their little countries of El Salvador and Guatemala much better than could John Paul II (hindered as he has been by his Polish fear of communism, though now we've seen him changing regarding Cuba). I owe this Central American reminder to Sarah Freedman.

44. Dan Bell makes this observation in his remarkable dissertation "The Refusal to Cease Suffering: The Crucified People and the Liberation of Desire" (Duke University, 1998).

45. See, for example, Ephraim Radner's extraordinary account of the effects of our division on the church in his *The End of the Church: A Pneumatology of Christian Division in the West* (Grand Rapids: Eerdmans, 1998). It would be fascinating to compare Boyle's more Hegelian account of history with Radner's. Both maintain that Christians owe the world an account of the history of the world, but Radner argues such an account can never lose its "figural," that is biblical, character. According to Radner, the division of the sixteenth century resulted in a limitation on pneumatic accounts of history that require repentance. As a result "modern historical consciousness" was created, which was but the cultural adaptation of a straitened Christian consciousness due to the incapacitation of the figural reading of history by multiple ecclesial referents (p. 301).

46. Boyle, *Who Are We Now?* p. 93. The careful reader who checks my use of this quote from Boyle will discover that I did not follow Boyle's appeal, which begins the quote, to the "Catholic belief that we are but creatures, and the creatures of a wholly unknowable God," which he believes safeguards us from self-worship. I do not know whether Boyle and I are in fundamental disagreement on the matter of knowledge of God, but it is clear to me, as Blond puts it, that "negative theology requires a positive discourse about God, if, that is, this form of negation is to be recognizably about God at all" ("Introduction: Theology Before Philosophy," p. 5).

47. Besides those mentioned earlier, I am indebted to Abraham Nussbaum, Joel Shuman, and Michael Cartwright for their criticisms and, as usual, Jim Fodor.

CHAPTER 3

1. This paper was written for a book of essays by Methodists who dissent from the Methodist position on homosexuality but wish to stay loyal to the church. My essay was judged not sufficiently "on target" and was therefore not used.

2. Nicholas Boyle, *Who Are We Now? Christian Humanism and the Global Market from Hegel to Heaney* (Notre Dame, Ind.: University of Notre Dame Press, 1998).

3. Ibid., p. 59.

CHAPTER 4

1. I am indebted to Richard Church for integrating material from an unpublished essay on the development of Christian ethics into this essay.

2. Max Stackhouse, "Religious Ethics," *Council on the Study of Religion Bulletin* (December 1978): 128–31.

3. Jack Reeder, "Religious Ethics As a Field and Discipline," *Journal of Religious Ethics* 6, no. 1 (spring 1978): 32–53.

4. Stackhouse, "Religious Ethics."

5. William Everett, "Vocation and Location: An Exploration in the Ethics of Ethic," *Journal of Religious Ethics* 5, no. 1 (spring 1977): 91–114.

6. Alasdair MacIntyre, "Theology, Ethics, and the Ethics of Medicine and Health Care," *Journal of Medicine and Philosophy* 4, no. 4 (December 1979): 434–40.

7. John Howard Yoder, *The Politics of Jesus* (Grand Rapids: Eerdmans, 1972).

8. I have not tried to correct the mistakes I made in this account by revising the text, because I thought the mistakes instructive. That I so characterized Yoder "back then" shows how much I had to learn from him.

9. Vernard Eller, *War and Peace from Genesis to Revelation* (Scottsdale, Penn.: Herald, 1981).

10. George Forell, *History of Christian Ethics*, vol. 1 (Minneapolis: Augsburg, 1979).

11. Richard Mouw, *Politics and the Biblical Drama* (Grand Rapids: Eerdmans, 1976).

12. I was tempted to rewrite this sentence because I am embarrassed not only by the "put yourself up against" phrase but even more by the confident use of "you." I simply assume the "you" names all of us out of the Protestant mainstream who go to the AAR. We owe an inestimable debt to those who have represented liberationist themes for many things, not the least their making easy presumptions about the "you" problematic.

13. I am most remiss, perhaps, in not including Boston University, which had and has a deep and abiding influence on the developing of Christian ethics in this country. I do so partly because I have little knowledge of the kind of training being done at Boston. I generally associate Boston with a continuing commitment to the working out of the commitments of the social gospel in a quite different social context. I realize, however, that the story is no doubt much more complex. (This and footnotes 14 and 16 were part of my original paper.)

14. Alasdair MacIntyre has suggested it is a mistake to interpret the central thrust of Ramsey's position as deontological. MacIntyre observes, however, that the perpetrator of this misunderstanding is Ramsey. In contrast MacIntyre contends that "Ramsey's notion of fidelity to a covenant is at least a partial specification of what can be taken to be the telos of human life. Such fidelity is a virtue understood very much as Aristotle understood virtue." MacIntyre contends further that it is difficult to see how any theologian could be a genuine deontologist. "A consistent deontologist would have to reject the view that what we ought to do derives its point and purpose from the fact that God created us for a particular telos. Deontology, with its emphasis on the logical independence of the realm of value from the realm of fact, can scarcely find a place within any theological framework, although Christian deontologists, most notably Kant, have sometimes sought with ingenuity rather than faith to find it such a place" ("Theology, Ethics, and the Ethics of Medicine and Health Care," pp. 437–39).

15. For a fascinating account of this process see the article by J. David Hoeveler, Jr., "The University and the Social Gospel: The Intellectual Origins of the 'Wisconsin Idea,'" *Wisconsin Magazine of History* (Summer 1976): 282–98. Hoeveler concentrates his analysis on John Bascom, Richard Ely, and John R. Commons, all Protestant liberals and social-gospel advocates. Hoeveler argues that these men set out to reshape

university education according to the vehicle of their ideal—namely, the creation of the Christian state. Bascom became the fifth president of the University of Wisconsin in 1874. According to Hoeveler, "Bascom was literally obsessed with the problem of organizing social power as outlined in [his] *Sociology*. Bascom described for his students an age he judged to be destructive in its use of power, a ruthlessly competitive society with aggregated power in the hands of a few individuals. Such an arrangement of forces was unethical and un-Christian in nature, and ultimately debilitating to society as a whole. When Bascom therefore called for 'harmonious power,' he turned directly to the state, the agency of public power, for its exercise. The state, Bascom wrote in *Sociology*, must create social power, surpassing the work of isolated individuals. Furthermore, the state must give power to the weaker elements in its midst, a concern that suffused most of the reform measures that Bascom endorsed. Bascom was in fact making an important modification of the evangelical format: he now turned to the state as a surrogate for churches and voluntary societies. Modern America could no longer rely on these institutions for the perfection of the nation and must instead look directly to the state for moral leadership and action" (p. 289). Bascom did not hesitate to put the university to the task of advancing the Christian project of furthering the spiritual progress of humankind through state agency.

Bascom represents the general presumption that the emerging social sciences were seen as the natural ally for the attempt to "Christianize" American society. This is not accidental. Not only were many of the early "social scientists" card-carrying members of the social gospel or sons of social-gospel ministers, they also shared a common history. In her extraordinary book *The Origins of American Social Science* (Cambridge: Cambridge University Press, 1991), Dorothy Ross observes "that American social science owes its distinctive character to its involvement with the national ideology of American exceptionalism, the idea that America occupies an exceptional place in history, based on her republican government and economic opportunity. Both this national self-conception and the social sciences themselves emerged from the late eighteenth- and early nineteenth-century effort to understand the character and fate of modern society. The successful establishment of republican institutions and the liberal opportunity guaranteed by a continent of virgin land, Americans believed, had set American history on a millennial course and exempted it from qualitative change in the future. America would forestall the mass poverty and class conflict that modernity appeared to be creating in Britain. Before the Civil War this vision of American exceptionalism drew the social sciences into the national effort to stay the hand of time. Social scientists found fixed laws of history and nature that would perpetuate established national institutions" (pp. xiv–xv). The story Ross tells in her wonderful book of the development and subsequent professionalization of the disciplines of economics, sociology, and political science provides a necessary background for the story I tell of the much less powerful, but no less interesting, development of Christian ethics as a discipline.

16. H. Richard Niebuhr never lost his passion for making the church faithful, but I think it fair to say that the church never was as central for him after *The Social Sources of Denominationalism* and *The Church against the World*. From my perspective, and contrary to the majority views, I regard H. Richard Niebuhr's *The Kingdom of God in America* (New York: Harper & Row, 1937) as a step backward. I am, of course, well aware that Niebuhr wrote in collaboration with Daniel Day Williams and James M. Gustafson *The Purpose of the Church and Its Ministry: Reflections on the Aims of Theological Education* (New York: Harper and Row, 1956), but it is by no means clear the difference that

230

book made for the position Niebuhr developed in *The Responsible Self: An Essay in Christian Moral Philosophy* (New York: Harper and Row, 1969).

17. See James Gustafson, "Theology Confronts Technology and the Life Sciences," *Commonweal* 16 (June 1978): 386–92.

18. David Little and Sumner Twiss, *Comparative Religious Ethics* (New York: Harper, 1978).

19. Ronald Green, *Religious Reason: The Rational and Moral Basis of Religious Belief* (New York: Oxford University Press, 1978).

20. Gene Outka, *Agape: An Ethical Analysis* (New Haven, Conn.: Yale University Press, 1972).

21. Though the theological differences between Gustafson and me are apparent, we remain on the same side to the extent we are each committed to keeping theological ethics theological. We just differ on the theology that keeps ethics theological. I am aware, of course, that there are many different kinds of liberal theology. When I refer to liberal theology I mean to indicate those theologians who think the knowledges produced by modernity render traditional theological claims problematic. They then seek to find a way to redescribe how theological claims work in a manner that can make theology congruent with modernity. This usually results in the assumption that a distinction can be drawn between form and content in a manner that construes theological claims as expressions of a prior content. Some account of morality has been one of the popular ways of identifying that content in modernity. In other words, once you no longer think what Christians claim about God and God's creation can be thought true, such speech can still be used on the assumption that it is important for sustaining something called morality. Christian ethics becomes the way to save what is left for Christian theology after modernity. The heart of my project over the years has been to counter that strategy.

22. Max Stackhouse, "The Continuing Importance of Walter Rauschenbusch," in Walter Rauschenbusch, *The Righteousness of the Kingdom*, ed. Max Stackhouse (New York: Abingdon, 1968), pp. 13–59.

23. Ibid., pp. 20–21.

24. Ibid., p. 23. I question the presuppositions behind Stackhouse's use of Troeltsch's types, but there can be no question of their descriptive usefulness in characterizing the social vision of progressive Protestantism.

25. Robert T. Handy, *A Christian America: Protestant Hopes and Historical Realities* (New York: Oxford University Press, 1971), p. vii. Handy observes: "There is no little irony in the fact that members of a Christian church which confidently established itself as the 'true church' whenever possible could become articulate spokesmen for religious freedom when they lived under someone else's establishment! So Puritans objected to Anglican establishment in Virginia, and Anglicans in New England demanded their rights as Englishmen. Members of churches which in Europe remained solidly committed to state-church patterns on the American scene could find themselves in minority status, resisting establishment as defined by others. As such groups as Dutch Reformed, Swedish and German Lutherans, Roman Catholics, and Scotch-Irish Presbyterians recognized that on the American scene establishment was not a possibility for them, they looked with varying degrees of enthusiasm to other ways of maintaining themselves and making their particular contributions to the

health of Christian civilization" (p. 14). Handy's book is the best single source for the background of the story that I had planned to write.

26. George Marsden, *Religion and American Culture* (New York: Harcourt Brace Jovanovich, 1990), p. 96. Christopher Lasch argues, however, that there was a profound difference between Christian ideas of progress and the general progressivism of secular hopes for America. According to Lasch, "The essence of hope, for Christians, lay in the 'conviction that life is a critical affair,' as Richard Niebuhr once put it, 'that nothing in it is abiding, that nothing temporal is able to bear the weight of human faith,' and yet that life is good and that a conviction of its goodness forbids us 'to give up any part of human life as beyond hope of redemption.'" In contrast the modern conception of progress is "not the promise of a secular utopia that would bring history to a happy ending but the promise of steady improvement with no foreseeable ending at all. The expectation of indefinite, open-ended improvement, even more than the insistence that improvement can come only through human effort, provides the solution to the puzzle that is otherwise so baffling—the resilience of progressive ideology in the face of discouraging events that have shattered the illusion of utopia" (*The True and Only Heaven: Progress and Its Critics* [New York: W. W. Norton, 1991], pp. 46, 47–48). For Lasch, Reinhold Niebuhr becomes one of the heroes of his book for his challenge to the humanistic view of progress as well as his "particularism" (pp. 369ff.). Lasch regrets that Niebuhr increasingly downplayed the latter in his last work, but he still finds him an important challenge to the optimism intrinsic to the American belief in progress. I admire Lasch's narrative, but I think Niebuhr would have appeared even more complex, and more American, in my narrative.

27. I confess that the last generalization is based more on impression than on any close study of the use of H. Richard Niebuhr's book among historians. Yet I think it cannot be denied that Niebuhr's book provided a different perspective for the narration of Christianity in America that went far beyond, just as most of his work did, the strictly "ethical."

28. Reinhold Niebuhr, *The Irony of American History* (New York: Charles Scribner's Sons, 1952). Though this book comes late in Niebuhr's career, history was always the source as well as the means of expression for his theology. For an extremely useful account of the importance of Niebuhr's perspective on the work of American historians, see Richard Reinitz, *Irony and Consciousness: American Historiography and Reinhold Niebuhr's Vision* (Lewisburg, Penn.: Bucknell University Press, 1980). Reinitz nicely shows the irony of Niebuhr's use of irony to provide an apologetic account of American exceptionalism. For example, Reinitz calls attention to Niebuhr's discussion of how the achievement of a greater "degree of social justice than our [American] bourgeois ideology would allow involves the exaggeration of American accomplishments and a degree of blindness to our faults. Although this argument undoubtedly contains an element of truth, its implications are excessively comforting to American self-esteem and, what is more important, it ignores some of Niebuhr's own ironic insights into our relationship to our national wealth and the way we avoid acknowledging social conflict" (p. 97).

29. Martin E. Marty, *Religion and Republic: The American Circumstance* (Boston: Beacon, 1987), pp. 95–123. Marty notes, "Reinhold Niebuhr's thought was grounded in his perception that he was a servant of and, in a sense, a prophet to America-in-*praxis*. He conceived America as a nation of behavers and experiencers and not very often as theorists about their belief. But his reportorial perceptions were never reproduced as ends in themselves. Instead, he turned them into much of the stuff of his the-

ology" (p. 99). I think that the same description could be used, not without justice, to describe Marty's work, as well as many others who think of themselves as "historians," not "ethicists."

30. James L. Ash, Jr., "American Religion and the Academy in the Early Twentieth Century: The Chicago Years of William Warren Sweet," *Church History* 50, no. 4 (December, 1981): 451–52. Mathews was, of course, one of the most sophisticated theologians associated with the social gospel. For an account that does justice to Mathews's in many ways quite complex christological views, see William Dennis Lindsey, "Shailer Mathews' Lives of Jesus: The Search for an Adequate Theological Foundation for the Social Gospel" (Ph.D. diss., University of St. Michael's College, Toronto, 1987).

31. Part of the complexity of the story involves the ever-changing character of the university. That Christian ethicists tried to professionalize the discipline was but a response to the increasing professionalization of the university. No one has told this story better than Barton Bledstein in *The Culture of Professionalism: The Middle Class and the Development of Higher Education in America* (New York: W. W. Norton, 1976). Bledstein's characterization of Richard Ely is particularly telling given Ely's role in the social gospel. Bledstein notes that early in his career Ely's advocacy of socialism embarrassed many of his colleagues. "To protect his own academic career and answer the charge of unprofessional conduct, Ely in the 1890s recanted his earlier views and became a squeamish academic careerist. No accusation more intimidated the youthful, bold professional than that of being unprofessionally enthusiastic. In the process of re-establishing his scholarly credentials, Ely turned to the research topic of rural land economics, a subject that interested a select few, threatened no one, and lent itself to a vast amount of technical detail and minutiae" (pp. 328–29).

32. I have always maintained—but I have seldom been believed—that I could have never appreciated the power of Yoder's work if I had not been trained in this tradition.

33. A version of the overview chapter can be found in my *Against the Nations: War and Survival in a Liberal Society* (Notre Dame, Ind.: University of Notre Dame Press, 1992), pp. 23–50. I have written a number of essays in which I test some of my ideas about this story. For example see my "Why Christian Ethics Is Such a Bad Idea," in *Beyond Mere Health*, ed. Hilary Regan, Rodney Horsfield, and Gabrielle McMullen (Melbourne: Australian Theological Forum, 1996), pp. 64–79. Moreover, very good books like that of Gary Dorrien, *Soul in Society: The Making and Renewal of Social Christianity* (Minneapolis: Fortress, 1995), are now available. Dorrien's book tells the story in a somewhat different fashion from the way I had intended, but I much admire the way he has helped show the interrelation between the social gospel and later developments. Not to be overlooked is Harlan Beckley's fine book *Passion for Justice* (Louisville: Westminster John Knox, 1992).

34. Contingent factors, of course, have also made a difference for my decision not to write the book. I had no idea I would be asked to give the Gifford Lectures in 2001. Even though that gives me a good lead time, I did not think I could do justice to them as well as the book on Christian ethics in America. I plan, however, to subvert some of the work I have done for the book into the Giffords. At least as I am now thinking about the lectures, I will have extensive sections on Reinhold and H. Richard Niebuhr.

35. I focus on Ramsey because of his quite interesting history in relation to the *JRE*. He served as the president of the board of the *JRE* for many years, yet I always wondered what he thought of the general direction of the journal. For example, Ramsey

233 ▪

was adamant that in spite of his regard for Ron Green, the name of the Society of Christian Ethics should not be changed to the Society of Religious Ethics. I always suspected that Ramsey supported the *JRE* because he thought we needed a journal that would provide voice for people from other traditions, but he had deep suspicions about some of the theories some thought necessary to provide a justification for the *Journal*.

36. In his wonderfully done book on Rauschenbusch, Ryan, and Niebuhr, *Passion for Justice*, Beckley observes that Reinhold Niebuhr was right to criticize Rauschenbusch for being overly hopeful about progress toward justice. Beckley also thinks Rauschenbusch overstated the role of Christ and Christianity as the historical source of advances toward justice. Accordingly, Beckley suggests, "we have quite properly abandoned the idea that advancing justice requires that we christianize society. Fortunately, these aspects of Rauschenbusch's thought were not based upon Jesus' redemptive influence inducing a new era in history that transcends the created order. Advancing justice, according to Rauschenbusch's understanding of the kingdom, requires that the social order maximize opportunities for individuals to integrate their natural interests through self-development in solidarity with others" (pp. 345–46). But why, given such an understanding of the ethical task, should ethics be called Christian? I am not suggesting that any account of Christian ethics requires the presumption that the social order must be "Christianized"; rather I am simply asking in what community ethicists are standing when they do their work. One of the other reasons I decided the book I had planned did not need to be written was Beckley's and Dorrien's fine books.

37. Of course the phrase "in the field" begs for clarification. "In the field" can name those who attend the Society of Christian Ethics, where the presence of women and African-Americans has had a decided impact. Yet it is by no means clear how that presence has translated into the work represented in the *JRE*. Which raises a further question of the relation between the developing academic field of Christian or religious ethics and those figures who are not academics but clearly represent impressive moral achievements—e.g., Martin Luther King and Dorothy Day. I had excluded them from the story I planned to tell because I was concerned to provide an account of the development of the discipline. Such an exclusion may but indicate the impoverishment of what it means to be a discipline.

38. One of the ways to think of the ambiguous character of the *JRE* is in terms of its relation to the Society of Christian Ethics and the American Academy of Religion. One often has the sense that many of the people associated with the *JRE* loyalties are much closer to the AAR but yet the primary readership and support comes from the SCE.

CHAPTER 5

1. The social gospel was, of course, an aspect of liberal theology. That it was so is one of the reasons the social gospel is thought to be antagonistic to evangelistic and pietistic forms of Christianity. The work of Timothy L. Smith, however, has helped us see that whatever differences there may be between the social gospel and revivalism, there are deeper continuities. As Smith notes, "The awakening of 1858–59 set the stage for a tremendous advance in interdenominational social and religious work, quickening the pace by which the churches Christianized the land. Old benevolent societies took on new functions, new ones like the Y.M.C.A. and the Christian Labor Union appeared, and for a brief period the churches themselves joined hands and hearts to usher in the kingdom of Christ" (*Revivalism and Social Reform: American Protestantism*

on the Eve of the Civil War [Baltimore: Johns Hopkins University Press, 1980], pp. 43–44). Smith makes explicit the connection between revivalism and the social gospel, observing that "in the postwar period the evangelical ideology of the millennium merged without a break into what came to be called the social gospel. The triumph of Yankee arms restored the faith of even Princeton conservatives that Christianity and civilization were marching forward toward perfection" (p. 235).

2. Dores Robinson Sharpe, *Walter Rauschenbusch* (New York: Macmillan, 1942), pp. 393–94. Sharpe's biography is often dismissed because of its lack of any critical perspective, but it is all the more valuable because of that. As the passage suggests, not only did he know Rauschenbusch, but Rauschenbusch valued him as a friend. His book is an irreplaceable source of information about Rauschenbusch, as he often makes available materials that might otherwise be lost. Moreover, the unembarrassed expression of love by one male for another so unavoidably present throughout Sharpe's book helps us understand the kind of intense male relations that characterized the formation of the Brotherhood of the Kingdom. For an account of the "maleness" of the social-gospel movement, see Janet Fishburn, *The Fatherhood of God and the Victorian Family* (Philadelphia: Fortress, 1981).

3. Sharpe quotes this from the *Rochester Democrat and Chronicle*, January 25, 1913, p. 232. The newspaper article also reports Rauschenbusch's account of writing *Christianity and the Social Crisis* (New York: Macmillan, 1907). He notes, "I decided to write a book on social questions for the Lord Christ and the people. This was a dangerous book and I entered upon my task with fear and trembling. It was part of my Christian ministry, a religious book to me" (p. 233).

4. Max Stackhouse also uses his quote as the "best statement" of Rauschenbusch's early period in his "The Continuing Importance of Walter Rauschenbusch." This essay serves as the introduction to Rauschenbusch's *The Righteousness of the Kingdom*, ed. Max Stackhouse (Nashville: Abingdon, 1968), a book never published by Rauschenbusch which was found in the archives of the American Baptist Historical Society. Stackhouse edited the manuscript. His introduction remains one of the most insightful treatments of Rauschenbusch's work and significance. He notes that *Righteousness of the Kingdom* is more radical than Rauschenbusch's later work, which is probably the reason I think it his best book. In *Righteousness of the Kingdom* Rauschenbusch rightly insists that Christianity is revolutionary insofar as it seeks to make real the kingdom of God on earth. This program includes a twofold aim: "the regeneration of every individual to divine sonship and eternal life, and the victory of the spirit of Christ over the spirit of this world in every form of human society and a corresponding alteration in all the institutions formed by human society" (pp. 110–11).

5. Reinhold and H. Richard Niebuhr also had newspaper experience: they each for short periods aided their older brother Walter, who owned and managed the Lincoln, Illinois, *Courier-Herald*. The influence of Rauschenbusch and the Niebuhrs at least partly derived from their extraordinary skill at "turning a phrase." This skill no doubt came from other sources than their involvement with newspapers, but learning to write for a newspaper certainly was a help to each of them in quite different ways. The paper in which Rauschenbusch's articles appeared was called *For the Right*. The paper's aim was to discuss questions affecting workers from the standpoint of Christian socialism. Paul Minus reports that Rauschenbusch wrote twenty-one articles for the paper, and these fell into two broad groups: (1) articles that sought to convince workers to engage in gradual and nonviolent means of social change and (2) articles that endorsed par-

ticular objectives such as an eight-hour workday, single tax, a city-owned subway, and ownership of utilities (Paul Minus, *Walter Rauschenbusch: American Reformer* [New York: Macmillan, 1988], pp. 67–68).

The importance of newspaper experience should not be limited to their writing. The emergence of "ethics" as a distinct subject from the social gospel has meant that no matter how hard some have tried to make ethics "academic," the journalistic "temptation" is always around the corner. As the story unfolds I hope to show that Christian ethics, at its best, is, in fact, a form of journalism.

6. Minus notes that there is no evidence of how Rauschenbusch felt about the Rockefellers, though there can be no doubt that there was a quite close relationship between Aura Rockefeller and Pauline, sharing as they did a common Baptist piety (ibid., pp. 96–97). Minus also reports that between 1900 and 1918 the Rockefeller family gave Rauschenbusch and his family approximately eight thousand dollars, but these funds were given with no strings attached (ibid., pp. 133–34).

7. For these details of August Rauschenbusch's life as well as what follows I am indebted to Minus, *Walter Rauschenbusch*, pp. 1–18.

8. One of Walter Rauschenbusch's first tasks on returning to Rochester to become head of the German department was to finish his father's uncompleted biography. Minus quotes Rauschenbusch's account of his father's baptism: "It was a step that cost him dear; it cut his family to the quick; it completely alienated many of his friends; it rendered his entire future uncertain; but he followed the truth" (ibid., p. 3). Minus notes that Rauschenbusch admired his father's "following the truth no matter what the cost," but I suspect that such admiration was qualified by an unavoidable knowledge of the unhappiness that characterized his father and mother's marriage.

9. Quoted in ibid., pp. 32–33. The quotes come from a letter to Munson Ford.

10. Rauschenbusch's writing is filled with organic metaphors. One of my favorites is the last paragraph of *Christianity and the Social Crisis*. He has been discussing the slowness of the coming of the kingdom of God. He suggests that things may be speeding up, as the twentieth century could harness and control social forces the way the nineteenth controlled natural forces. Since the Reformation began to free the mind and direct the force of religion toward morality, things have speeded up. Then he says, "Last May a miracle happened. At the beginning of the week the fruit trees bore brown and greenish buds. At the end of the week they were robed in bridal garments of blossom. But for weeks and months the sap had been rising and distending the cells and maturing the tissues which were half ready in the fall before. The swift unfolding was the culmination of a long process. Perhaps these nineteen centuries of Christian influence have been a long preliminary stage of growth, and now the flower and fruit are almost here. If at this juncture we can rally sufficient religious faith and moral strength to snap the bonds of evil and turn the present unparalleled economic and intellectual resources of humanity to the harmonious development of a true social life, the generations yet unborn will mark this as that great day of the Lord for which the ages waited, and count us blessed for sharing in the apostolate that proclaimed it" (p. 422).

11. The best source for an exposition of Rauschenbusch's "piety" is the introduction by Winthrop Hudson to *Walter Rauschenbusch: Selected Writings* (New York: Paulist, 1984). This volume is in the Paulist Press series Sources of American Spirituality. Hudson observes: "For any outward change to have meaning and to endure, Rauschenbusch insisted that attention must be given to the deep wells of personal religious life.

In terms of his own understanding of his vocation, Rauschenbusch was an evangelist in the tradition of the great revivalists, seeking to win people to an experience of Christ and to put them to work in the interests of Christ's kingdom. He entered the ministry with a strong desire to 'save souls' and this, in his own mind, continued to be a constant objective" (p. 4).

12. Rauschenbusch's father returned to Germany in 1888 on his retirement. Caroline, after spending two years with her son, rejoined her husband in Germany in 1890. Rauschenbusch, as far as I know, never left any written record of exactly what caused the discord between his mother and father, but there are indications that his father may have been an alcoholic.

Rauschenbusch, like many of the social gospelers, was unrelenting in his condemnation of the "liquor trade." For the role Prohibition played in the demise of the social gospel as a political force, see Donald B. Meyer's *The Protestant Search for Political Realism, 1919–1941* (Berkeley and Los Angeles: University of California Press, 1961).

13. Minus, *Walter Rauschenbusch*, p. 55.

14. Walter Rauschenbusch, *A Theology for the Social Gospel* (Nashville: Abingdon, 1960), p. 97.

15. Minus, *Walter Rauschenbusch*, p. 61. Of course Rauschenbusch was hardly the first social gospeler. In fact, he is close to the end of the movement, which was primarily known prior to 1900 as "social Christianity." For an extremely useful background essay, see Robert Handy's introduction to his compilation *The Social Gospel in America, 1870–1920* (New York: Oxford University Press, 1966), pp. 3–16. This book contains selections from Washington Gladden, Richard T. Ely, and Rauschenbusch. Handy rightly notes that while the social gospel fell within the general framework of what might be called "evangelical liberalism," many liberals did not become advocates of the social gospel. The actual experience of the pastorate was certainly crucial for Gladden and Rauschenbusch.

16. Rauschenbusch confesses in *Christianizing the Social Order* (New York: Macmillan, 1921) that he owed his "first awakening to the world of social problems to the agitation of Henry George in 1886, and wish here to record my lifelong debt to this single-minded apostle of a great truth" (p. 394). It is not clear from the context what this "great truth" might be, though it is probably George's advocacy of the "single tax." Equally important for Rauschenbusch is the idea, which he attributed to social scientists and economists such as Ely, that "within certain limits human society is plastic, constantly changing its forms, and the present system of social organization, as it superseded others, may itself be displaced by something better" (*Christianity and the Social Crisis*, p. 195). Ely, particularly early in his career, was a committed social-gospel reformer. However, after his move to Johns Hopkins from Wisconsin, he increasingly sounded like a "social scientist" rather than a social reformer. He seemed to understand that if economics was to gain academic respectability as a science, expressions of religious fervor were best left in the background.

17. Rauschenbusch, *Christianity and the Social Crisis*, pp. 244–46. Minus reports that Rauschenbusch was twice hit by streetcars in Rochester as he attempted to ride his bicycle to the seminary. He probably had not heard the cars due to his deafness (Minus, *Walter Rauschenbusch*, p. 135). Rauschenbusch was very active in the civic affairs of Rochester, taking particular interest in the Rochester Railway Company, which, as a "thorn in their flesh," he managed to improve (ibid., p. 124). He also was involved in

public school issues in Rochester as well as working to secure better recreational facilities. He was also, as would be expected, a member of the Anti-Saloon League.

18. Rauschenbusch, *Christianizing the Social Order*, p. 127. Rauschenbusch never seems to have felt any tension between his democratic ideals and the building of social orders that would "make bad men do good things."

19. Minus suggests that this may have been due to the continued degeneration of his hearing (*Walter Rauschenbusch*, p. 69).

20. Rauschenbusch, *Christianizing the Social Order*, p. 93.

21. Ibid.

22. Ibid. Rauschenbusch was certainly influenced by German liberal theology, but that influence was more general than specific. Rauschenbusch was simply not interested in the more technical issues of theology found in someone like Ritschl. He thought that Ritschl's theology lacked "sociological" insight—which is but Rauschenbusch's way of saying that Ritschl's theology remained too socially conservative. As we shall see, Harnack was at least as strong an influence on him as Ritschl.

23 Walter Rauschenbusch, *Dare We Be Christians?* with foreword by Stephen G. Post (Cleveland: Pilgrim, 1993).

24. Ibid., pp. 18–19.

25. Ibid., p. 22. Rauschenbusch was impressed, like many of his contemporaries, with evidence from eugenics. Eugenics, after all, was "science," and "science" promised to be the means to make the world better. Rauschenbusch simply accepted without question that "race" mattered. For example, in *Theology for the Social Gospel* he says that "the impartation of divine life and immortality to the race was accomplished when he was a babe. The atonement might actually have been frustrated if the life effort of Jesus had been successful, for if the Jews had accepted his spiritual leadership, they would not have killed him" (pp. 149–50). Such appeals to race might seem "innocent," but Rauschenbusch used racial theories to underwrite what were generally accepted in his time as progressive positions. Thus he notes, again in *Theology for the Social Gospel*, that "it is essential to our spiritual honesty that no imperialism shall masquerade under the cover of our religion. Those who adopt the white man's religion come under the white man's influence. Christianity is the religion of the dominant race. The native religions are a spiritual bulwark of defence, independence, and loyalty. If we invite men to come under the same spiritual roof of monotheism with us and to abandon their ancient shelters, let us make sure that this will not be exploited as a trick of subjugation by the Empires" (p. 186). Noble sentiments no doubt, but still presuming the superiority of the white race. I am indebted to Kelly Jarrett for her research on the racial characteristic of social progressives at the turn of the twentieth century.

It would be unwise to make too much of Rauschenbusch's genetic theories, but I cannot resist calling attention to his observations about monasticism. In fact his attitude to monasticism was ambiguous, because he recognized that the monasteries did much charitable work. Yet he notes that the energy they ought to have used in making society "normal" they used in making themselves "abnormal." No doubt they served humankind as monks, but they would have served even better if they had remained in the "natural bonds of family and neighborhood." "Monasticism eliminated the morally capable, just as war eliminates the physically capable. God alone knows where the race might be today if the natural leaders had not so long been made childless by their own goodness. The wonderful fecundity of the Protestant parsonage in men of the highest ability and ideality is proof of what has been lost" (*Christianity and the Social Crisis*, pp. 173–74). Such a view is but a motif in Rauschenbusch's more general negative attitude toward Catholicism.

26. This was the eighth aim of the group as set forth in the pamphlet "Spirit and Aims of the Brotherhood," agreed upon in the December 1892 meeting of the group in Philadelphia. I am quoting from Sharpe's useful account of the Brotherhood, *Walter Rauschenbusch*, pp. 121–22. Among members of the group were Leighton Williams, Nathaniel Schmidt, Samuel Zane Batten, George Danna Boardman, and William Newton Clark. A picture of the Brotherhood taken in 1894, which Minus reproduces in his biography, shows twenty-six members. In *Christianizing the Social Order* Rauschenbusch notes that "the organization had been too unselfish to become large, but it was a powerful support and stimulus in those early days of isolation" (p. 94).

27. Sharpe quoting Rauschenbusch's essay "The Brotherhood of the Kingdom" from the *National Baptist* sometime in 1893 (*Walter Rauschenbusch*, pp. 119–20).

28. Rauschenbusch begins *Theology for the Social Gospel* with this remarkable declaration: "We have a social gospel. We need a systematic theology large enough to match it and vital enough to back it" (p. 1). Thus his title for the book reflected his assumption that the social gospel was a movement that preceded its theological articulation. No doubt it may have felt that way to Rauschenbusch and his friends, but it is apparent that the theological presuppositions of Protestant liberalism were shaping the movement from the beginning.

29. For the best account of the formation of the Brotherhood in the context of Rauschenbusch's spiritual life, see Hudson, introduction to *Walter Rauschenbusch: Selected Writings*, pp. 1–41.

30. C. Howard Hopkins wonderfully documents the social gospel as a popular movement in his *The Rise of the Social Gospel in American Protestantism, 1865–1915* (New Haven, Conn.: Yale University Press, 1940). The popularity of Charles Sheldon's *In His Steps* is but an indication of the widespread power of the movement. Hopkins notes that Sheldon's book sold 100,000 copies in the first year.

31. Walter Rauschenbusch, *Prayers of the Social Awakening* (Boston: Pilgrim, 1925), was originally published in 1909 as *For God and the People*. Rauschenbusch organized the book by beginning with more traditional prayers for morning, noon, and night, praise and thanksgiving, but most of the book consisted in prayers for social groups and classes.

Walter Rauschenbusch, *The Social Principles of Jesus* (New York: Association, 1919), was published in 1916 under the auspices of the YMCA. It was meant as a weekly study guide for college students. I discuss it below.

32. Reinhold and H. Richard Niebuhr were men of profound piety, but their piety did not as directly shape their understanding of ethics as Rauschenbusch's piety did. Both Niebuhrs wrote prayers of great power, but it would have occurred to neither of them to publish anything like *Prayers of the Social Awakening*. There is a sense in which Reinhold Niebuhr, like Rauschenbusch, wanted to effect a "movement," but his movement was of a quite different character. That "difference" is not easily characterized, but suffice it to say that while there are hundreds of social-gospel hymns, as far as I know there are no hymns celebrating "Christian realism."

I wrote this paragraph on November 14, 1994. Later that day I received a copy of *Perspectives: A Journal of Reformed Thought* 9, no. 9 (November 1994). On the cover of the issue was this prayer of Walter Rauschenbusch:

Thanks for Creation
O God, we thank you for this earth, our home;
for the wide sky and the blessed sun,
    for the salt sea and the running water,
    for the everlasting hills and the never-resting winds,
    for trees and the common grass underfoot.
We thank you for our senses
    by which we hear the songs of birds,
    and see the splendour of the summer fields,
    and taste of the autumn fruits,
    and rejoice in the feel of the snow,
    and smell the breath of the spring.
Grant us a heart wide open to all the beauty;
and save our souls from being so blind that we pass
    unseeing when even the common
      thornbush
    is aflame with your glory,
O God our creator, who lives and reigns for ever and ever.

I do not know where the editors of *Perspective* found this prayer, but it certainly testifies to the lasting impact of Rauschenbusch that one of his prayers would appear almost a century later on the cover of a Calvinist magazine. Some of the same phrases in this prayer appear in his prayer "For This World" in *Prayers of the Social Awakening* (p. 47).

33. Minus, *Walter Rauschenbusch*, p. 100. Minus relates how his appointment was not without controversy, since several wealthy trustees of the school were concerned about Rauschenbusch's "socialism." Rauschenbusch submitted an article in which he weighed the strengths and weaknesses of socialism which seems to have satisfied the trustees. Yet he was by no means pleased to have had to go that far in defending himself before the trustees, especially as he knew he was in the right.

34. Minus reports that German Baptists from the early years of his New York pastorate had learned to look to Rauschenbusch to defend their interests. Indeed, as part of an appeal in the early 1890s for funds to support the German department, Rauschenbusch displayed the kind of racial consciousness that I highlighted above. He said, "Is the American stock so fertile that it will people this continent alone? . . . Are the whites of this continent so sure of their possession against the blacks of the South and the seething yellow flocks beyond the Pacific that they need no reinforcement of men of their own blood while yet it is time?" He went on to explain: "The Germans . . . are of the same stock as the English, readily assimilated, and a splendid source of strength for America, physically, intellectually, and morally" (Minus, *Walter Rauschenbusch*, p. 105).

Rauschenbusch was certainly happy to be a Baptist. Soon after he returned to the seminary, he published four articles on "Why I Am a Baptist" in which he gave four reasons for his position: hereditary influence; Baptist form of church organization approximately Christian in its essence; the Baptist conception of worship, which is clean of the historically pagan influences that leaked in during the early centuries and were afterward religiously preserved and cherished; and Baptist freedom from creeds and loyalty to the Bible (Sharpe, *Walter Rauschenbusch*, p. 155). The third reason not only suggests but manifests Rauschenbusch's considerable anti-Catholic sentiments.

35. Sharpe, *Walter Rauschenbusch*, p. 141.

36. Minus, *Walter Rauschenbusch*, pp. 116–17.

37. Rauschenbusch, *Righteousness of the Kingdom*, p. 150.

38. Walter Rauschenbusch, "The Influence of Historical Studies on Theology," *American Journal of Theology* 11 (January 1907): 111–27. This article is interesting not only because of its content but also because Rauschenbusch assumes a more "scholarly" tone than is usually the case. In his "The Continuing Importance of Walter Rauschenbusch," Max Stackhouse rightly emphasizes the centrality and significance of history for Rauschenbusch. Stackhouse notes: "The Kingdom of God functions as a discriminating principle as to what is authentically historical and what is destructive of the historical. Thus, for Rauschenbusch, the Kingdom itself is not only normative but refers to some actual dimensions of history that are describable" (p. 31).

39. Stackhouse, "Continuing Importance," p. 12.

40. Rauschenbusch's "only" indicates his deep distrust of any "spiritual" interpretation of the Bible. In *Christianity and the Social Crisis* he suggests that in the Bible the church is always portrayed as having a historical literature that might have opened its eyes to "social facts," but usually the social enlightenment contained in the Scripture "was numbed by the dogmatic and ecclesiastical interest of the Church and by the allegorical method of interpretation. . . . The allegorical method neutralized the social contents of the Bible by spiritualizing everything. For instance, the emancipation of the Israelite tribes from galling overwork and cruelty in Egypt, and their conquest of a good tract of land for settlement, is a striking story of social revolt, but it was turned into an allegory of the exodus of the soul from the world and its attainment of the Promised Land beyond the Jordan of death. It was an ingenious and swift way of getting ready-made spiritual and doctrinal results from the Bible. But like a sleight-of-hand performer taking ribbons and rabbits out of a silk hat, it never took anything out of the Bible that was not already in the mind of the interpreter, and thus it learned nothing new from the Bible" (p. 197). Rauschenbusch continues by observing that the church in this respect shared with all the rest of humanity the "childhood of the world, the lack of historical sense, the inability to understand the facts and laws of social development. The moral intuition awakened by religion made it swifter and bolder to hope for a radical social change than those who travelled by common sense alone; but the prevalent belief in the miraculous and in constant divine interventions counteracted the enlightening effects of its moral vision" (p. 198).

There is a fascinating paragraph in *Theology for the Social Gospel*, however, that indicates that Rauschenbusch was aware of the ideological presuppositions of historical work. It is his conviction that the "professional theologians of Europe," who belong to as well as have a sympathy with the bourgeois classes, are constitutionally incapacitated for understanding Jesus' revolutionary ideas about fraternal ethics of democracy. Instead they overemphasize the ascetic and apocalyptic aspect of Jesus' radical sayings about property and nonresistance (p. 158). Rauschenbusch does not refer to anyone

241 ■

in particular in this passage, but it is hard to believe that he is not aiming it at Albert Schweitzer's *The Quest of the Historical Jesus*, which was published in German in 1906.

41. *Theology for the Social Gospel*, p. 114. The influence of Harnack on Rauschenbusch is evident throughout this essay as well as in all his work. As we shall see, one of the reasons Christianity was distracted from its mission of social regeneration was the encounter with Hellenism and the subsequent concern for dogma.

42. Ibid., p. 115. Though Rauschenbusch certainly had a generous spirit and mind, I think it fair to say that he did not like Catholicism. For example, in this article he notes that "the church was not pure and evangelical up to the conversion of Constantine. The hierarchy, the sacramentalism, and the superstition of Catholics were in full bloom several generations before Christianity became the state religion" (p. 124). Sharpe tells of an incident in 1904 when Rauschenbusch had been asked to write an article for the *Encyclopedia Americana*. The Catholic editor requested that he tone down the article. Rauschenbusch was none too happy about this petition, which in effect amounted to an "emasculation" of his article. In a letter to the managing editor of the *Encyclopedia*, he protested being asked to cut out of his account the evils of the church that caused the Reformation. He continued: "The great church attendance of Catholic churches is often pointed to as proof that religion is dying in Protestant churches. I asserted that Protestantism in its nature is less churchly and makes the individual more independent of church life, and that accounts for the fact to a large extent. But that was cut out" (Sharpe, *Walter Rauschenbusch*, pp. 152–53). One of the oddities of Rauschenbusch's observation is that here we have the great exponent of "social Christianity" praising the individualism of Protestantism. Such a tension characterized not only Rauschenbusch's ecclesiology but his social theory in general.

In *Christianizing the Social Order* Rauschenbusch observed that it is hard to judge what tack the Roman Catholic Church will take relative to the social awakening. Roman Catholicism is a complex mixture of reactionary and progressive forces and, as a international body, is the greatest conservative force in the Western world. He notes that its dogma, theology, philosophy, ritual, and hierarchy could have never come into existence if Christianity had originated in the modern world. Indeed, after a century in America it has still not made any serious concession to democracy. However, "if the entire Catholic Church in America could follow its own Christian and American spirit, unhampered by foreign tendencies and influences, there would certainly be a sudden and splendid spurt toward democracy" (pp. 26–27).

43. Rauschenbusch, *Christianizing the Social Order*, p. 117.

44. Rauschenbusch's praise of the Reformation does not mean he was uncritical of Luther and Calvin. He was, after all, a Baptist. For him the true center of the Reformation was the Anabaptists, because, as Minus puts it, they "recognized the church's failures and courageously sought a restoration of primitive Christianity" (Minus, *Walter Rauschenbusch*, p. 153). Rauschenbusch observes in "Influence of Historical Studies on Theology" that "the anabaptist movement was the most purely religious of all the movements, and that was stamped out because the social classes within which it spread did not command enough political power to protect it. Any theory of religious and moral movements which separates them from the patriotic and social movements of the nations is wholly contradicted by history. The more we comprehend history, the more we see the organic and inseparable unity of life" (p. 123). This will be the last favorable judgment of the Anabaptists in the history of Christian ethics in America until we get to Yoder.

45. Ibid., p. 127.

46. Ibid., p. 158.

47. Ibid., p. 162.

48. Rauschenbusch, *Christianity and the Social Crisis*, p. xxxvii.

49. Rauschenbusch's "profamily" position is most apparent in his critical attitude toward celibacy. He observes: "Even Chrysostom, the sensible, pictures the model husband as the one who lives almost like a monk. Now, marriage is the fundamental social relation. The family is the social cell. It is society in miniature. If this was the attitude of ascetic Christianity toward the most natural and the most loving of all social institutions, what chance of proper treatment did the other social relations have?" (ibid., p. 166).

50. Ibid., p. 217. Rauschenbusch, like many social critics of his and our day, wanted the results of the Industrial Revolution without the side effects. It would be unfair to accuse Rauschenbusch of wishing to return to "simpler" times, but certainly one cannot help but notice that the social model underlying his critique of capitalism looks very much like some kind of guild socialism.

51. Rauschenbusch notes: "Our optimists treat it as a sign of progress that 'so many professions are now open to women.' But it is not choice, but grim necessity, that drives woman into new ways of getting bread and clothing. The great majority of girls heartily prefer the independence and the satisfaction of the heart which are offered to a woman only in a comfortable and happy home" (ibid., pp. 276–77). Such sentiments are today usually expressed by the "religious right," which is but a reminder that the "religious right" may be the last form of Protestant liberalism left.

52. The moralistic character of Rauschenbusch's analysis should not be missed. In particular, he thought the graft that had become prevalent in American culture to be an indication that our civilization was in crisis. He notes that by nature human beings are imitative creatures, which can be a great source of good, but the processes of competitive industry have created a lavishness of expenditure that results in degradation. In fact, the spirit of democracy that wiped out the old class lines is now part of the problem. "In Europe a peasant girl or a servant formerly was quite content with the dress of her class and had no ambition to rival the very different dress of the gentry. With us the instinct of imitation works without a barrier from the top of the social pyramid to the bottom, and the whole process of consumption throughout society is feverishly affected by the aggregation of unearned money at the top. The embezzlements of business men, the nervous breakdown of women, the ruin of girls, the neglect of home and children, are largely caused by the unnatural pace of expenditures. If the rich had only what they earned, and the poor had all that they earned, all wheels would revolve more slowly and life would be more sane" (ibid., p. 268).

53. Ibid., p. 286.

54. The oft-made criticism that the social gospel ignored individual salvation and righteousness in preference to social salvation is manifestly false. Such a criticism resulted from Rauschenbusch's attack on those who stressed individualistic salvation to the exclusion of the social. As he says in *Theology for the Social Gospel*, "The social gospel is the old message of salvation, but enlarged and intensified. The individualistic gospel has taught us to see the sinfulness of every human heart and has inspired us with faith in the willingness and power of God to save every soul that comes to him. But it has not given

243

us an adequate understanding of the sinfulness of the social order and its share in the sins of all individuals within it" (p. 5).

In *Christianity and the Social Crisis* Rauschenbusch argues that "the fundamental contribution of every man is the change of his own personality." What is required is that we realize in ourselves a "new type of Christian manhood" that seeks to overcome evil not by withdrawing from the world but by revolutionizing it. If this new type of religious character multiplies among young "men and women, they will change the world when they come to hold the controlling positions of society in their maturer years" (p. 412).

55. Rauschenbusch in several places notes the deleterious effects of wealth on the ministry. When a church is composed of many wage-earners and a few wealthy families, the departure of a single family may mean the church can no longer pay the minister's salary. Rauschenbusch observes that "such a condition will almost inevitably breed an unwholesome deference at some points and unwholesome jealously at others" (*Christianity and the Social Crisis*, pp. 294–95). He later notes that this results in the lowered spirit of the ministry, because it requires those in the ministry, if they seek "a warm berth," to "get into the right stratum of society. Smoothness and courtly grace count for more than spirituality and earnestness. Prophetic vigor may even be a disqualifying virtue. It is hard to make a comparative judgment of so elusive a thing as the spirit of a profession, but it does seem that a spirit of anxiety, ambition, and self-advancement is gaining ground and sapping one of the noblest of all professions of its power and its happiness. When lawyers, doctors, teachers, journalists, and artists have been 'commercialized' to their inner loss, is it likely that the ministry can escape?" (ibid., pp. 301–2).

56. I will say more below about Rauschenbusch's understanding of salvation as the institutionalization of democracy.

57. The second chapter of *Christianizing the Social Order* begins with the claim "The American churches are part of the American nation" (p. 7). To begin with the reform of the church is but to start the reform of the nation. Thus he later observes that "with true instinct the re-awakened democracy turned its forces on the redemption of the church" (ibid., p. 85).

58. Rauschenbusch, *Christianity and the Social Crisis*, pp. 339–40. No doubt sentiments such as these are what led H. Richard Niebuhr to locate Rauschenbusch in the "Christ of Culture" type in *Christ and Culture* (New York: Harper & Brothers, 1951), pp. 100, 112. Such typing reveals more about the very presumptions of that typology than it does about Rauschenbusch.

59. An indication of the "success" of the social gospel is that most who read this will not think that the very description "social sin" needs defense. That was certainly not the case, however, when Rauschenbusch was writing. Yet the question remains whether the description "social sin" makes sense theologically.

60. Rauschenbusch praises President Theodore Roosevelt, "the most eminent exponent and leader," for his effort to have federal and state control of corporations (*Christianity and the Social Crisis*, p. 386). Rauschenbusch identifies the three great communistic institutions as the family, the school, and the church. He points out, for example, that the public schools are supported on a "purely communistic basis" since even people with no children are taxed for the education of the children in the community. He identifies the modern state as communistic in its very nature, since wel-

fare and military defense, which were formerly private affairs of the nobles, have now become the business of the nation (ibid., pp. 390–91).

61. For a compelling account of the social gospel's appeal see Susan Curtis, *A Consuming Faith: The Social Gospel and Modern American Culture* (Baltimore: Johns Hopkins University Press, 1991). Curtis observes that the "social gospel ideology initially was the product of a minority of writers and ministers within American Protestantism, but its impact on American culture was far-reaching. It was the product of a generation of Protestant men and women searching for certainty and reassurance in a troubled, changing world. The social gospel conferred meaning on modern work and family relations, and it created an agenda of reform that gave anxious middle-class Americans purposeful work. In the end, it helped ease the transition from Protestant Victorianism to a secular consumer society" (p. xv).

62. Rauschenbusch gave literally hundreds of speeches. By 1912 he had to use a speaker's bureau to keep track of his commitments (Minus, *Walter Rauschenbusch*, pp. 173–76). Reinhold Niebuhr followed the same pattern.

63. *Unto Me* (New York: Pilgrim Press, 1912) was a book of only thirty-one pages dealing with the religious quality of social work. Rauschenbusch strikes his characteristic themes in it, suggesting that social work is the fundamental form of Christian service since it deals with the causes of social misery. He does make a quite interesting observation about the kind of people who go into social work, a description that might include himself: "We all have our private religious history, and most of us have suffered in the course of it. As modern men we have passed through the scientific and philosophical doubt of this age of transition. For many of us the pillars that used to support religion in our childhood have crumbled and fallen. The number of educated men and women who have had a time when they saw themselves as non-religious is probably greater than we know. Some social workers have turned from the collapse of their religion to social work as the best things left to them after the wreck, as the worthiest substitute for the beauty of the religion they had lost. But some of them at least are watching the growth of a new religious life in their minds" (pp. 21–22). What is remarkable is Rauschenbusch's acknowledgment that there might be some reasons to doubt the truth of Christianity on scientific and philosophical grounds. This became a major concern for the Niebuhrs, but aside from this comment Rauschenbusch never seems to have considered whether his understanding of Christianity might be false.

Dare We Be Christians? is a lovely meditation on 1 Corinthians 13. It was also published by Pilgrim Press and, as noted above, has recently been reissued in a new edition. Neither of these book sold as well as *Christianity and the Social Crisis*.

64. In *Christianity and the Social Crisis* Rauschenbusch notes that the religious ideal of Israel was theocracy, but "theocracy meant the complete penetration of the national life by religious morality. It meant politics in the name of God. That line by which we have tacitly separated the domain of public affairs and the domain of Christian life was unknown to them" (p. 8). Rauschenbusch clearly wanted theocracy as a social policy without its being a state policy. It seems to have never occurred to him that some might find this distinction hard to draw, much less maintain, in practice.

65. Rauschenbusch, *Christianizing the Social Order*, p. 125. In *Righteousness of the Kingdom* Rauschenbusch had developed at great length the theocratic ideal of Israel as essential for understanding the messianic hope. He suggests that the prophets universalized and gave new spiritual depth to that hope, but he does not explain whether

245 ■

theocracy has been left behind. Nor does it seem that Jesus, who is in continuity with the prophets, challenged their theocratic ideal; rather, it now becomes embodied in his personality. Rauschenbusch simply seems unworried that theocracy might be a problem, since he believed so deeply the form that theocracy takes is democracy.

66. Rauschenbusch, *Christianizing the Social Order*, p. 125.

67. Rauschenbusch, *Righteousness of the Kingdom*, p. 92.

68. Rauschenbusch, *Christianizing the Social Order*, p. 137.

69. Ibid., p. 350.

70. Sharpe, *Walter Rauschenbusch*, p. 360. Sharpe provides a quite good account of Rauschenbusch's position on war, pp. 356–92.

71. Hudson, introduction to *Walter Rauschenbusch: Selected Writings*, pp. 134–35. Sharpe quotes quite a different section of the sermon, in which Rauschenbusch says, "I, too, hate war. . . . But I do not rule God out of war. . . . He is the God of peace and of war, of gentleness and wrath" (Rauschenbusch in Sharpe, *Walter Rauschenbusch*, pp. 358–59). I am not suggesting that Sharpe left out the more jingoistic parts of the sermon on purpose, but they are certainly not there.

72. Rauschenbusch, *Christianizing the Social Order*, p. 18.

73. Minus, *Walter Rauschenbusch*, p. 178.

74. Sharpe, *Walter Rauschenbusch*, p. 379.

75. Ibid., pp. 385–88.

76. Minus, *Walter Rauschenbusch*, p. 193.

77. Rauschenbusch, *Theology for the Social Gospel*, p. 4.

78. As I observed above, the significance of the title *A Theology for the Social Gospel* should not be missed. Rauschenbusch assumed that the "social gospel" was already established as a position and movement. What was needed was a theology to support the social gospel. Yet that way of putting the matter makes it appear as if theology had been somehow absent from his earlier work, which is surely not the case. That he assumed that a "theology" was still needed for the "social gospel" may be one of the locations to help explain the later assumption that "ethics" could or should be distinguished from theology. As we shall see, however, theology and ethics are inseparable in Rauschenbusch.

79. Rauschenbusch, *Christianity and the Social Crisis*, p. 3. Rauschenbusch does not identify what "modern studies" have shaped his views of the prophets, but I think he is either directly or indirectly drawing on the work of Julius Wellhausen. Wellhausen's *Prolegomena to the History of Ancient Israel* was published in 1878. Though Rauschenbusch's description of the prophets' lasting effect is quite different from Wellhausen's, it is interesting that Wellhausen treats the prophets under the general title "Prophetic Reformation." I am using the edition of the *Prolegomena* edited by W. Robertson Smith (New York: Meridian, 1961), pp. 484–92.

80. Rauschenbusch's antipathy toward Catholicism is clearly present in his reading of the prophets and Jesus. He repeats the familiar pattern, assuming that the prophetic critique of ritual and dogma in the name of ethics is rediscovered in the Reformation. Thus the history of Israel reproduces the Protestant understanding, or at least the nineteenth-century Protestant understanding, of the Reformation. The prophets become

the charismatic spirit that is "routinized" by priestly Judaism associated with the temple. Jesus becomes Luther, giving new birth to the originally prophetic inspiration. For a wonderful critique of this pattern see Jon D. Levenson, *The Hebrew Bible, the Old Testament, and Historical Criticism* (Louisville: Westminster John Knox, 1993).

81. Rauschenbusch, *Christianity and the Social Crisis*, p. 7. Rauschenbusch thought that the beginning of personal and priestly religion began in the prophets when Israel lost its national life by foreign conquest. Beginning with Jeremiah the prophets increasingly turned their back on the Jewish nation and produced the Jewish church. Such a step was forced on the prophets by "dire necessity," but even then their insistence on personal religion was a means to an end of social reconstruction (ibid., p. 29).

82. Ibid., p. 9. Rauschenbusch notes that it was only when the national life of Israel was crushed by foreign invaders that the prophets lost the large horizon of life and began to address the individual. Rauschenbusch's tendency to draw rather direct parallels between Israel and America suggests that he supported American power as necessary for a recovery of the corporate understanding of American life.

83. Ibid., p. 12.

84. Ibid., p. 13.

85. Ibid., p. 15. In general, Rauschenbusch shared the general presupposition associated with American progressivism that progress was inevitable. He was quite insistent that obstacles could be erected against progress, so the process was not automatic. Yet he simply assumed that the present time is the best time to live, since it is the most advanced. There is a striking passage in his *Social Principles of Jesus* in which he reflects on people's need to adjust their religious views to their growing powers and intellectual horizons. He continues, "The same problem arises when society passes through eras of growth. Religion must keep pace. The Church must pass the burning torch of religious experience from age to age, transmitting the faith of the fathers to the children, and not allowing any spiritual values to perish. But it must allow and aid religion to adjust itself. Its inspiring teaching must meet the new social problems so effectively that no evil can last long or grow beyond remedy. In every new age religion must stand the test of social efficiency. Is it passing that test in Western civilization?" (pp. 142–43).

86. Rauschenbusch, *Christianity and the Social Crisis*, pp. 26–27.

87. Ibid., p. 48.

88. Rauschenbusch developed these contrasts in several places, but I have paraphrased his summary from *Christianizing the Social Order*, p. 66. Rauschenbusch had a particularly strong animus against apocalypticism, attacking it in numerous contexts. He thought that apocalypticism not only turned the enthusiasm of great historical movements into injurious fanaticism but also was antithetical to the development of a scientific attitude toward social change and organization. He observes that Jesus took his illustrations from organic life, for "Jesus had the scientific insight which comes to most men only by training, but to an elect few by divine gift. He grasped the substance of that law of organic development in nature and history which our own day at last has begun to elaborate systematically. His parables of the sower, the tares, the net, the mustard-seed, and the leaven are all polemical in character. He was seeking to displace the crude and misleading catastrophic conceptions by a saner theory about the coming of the kingdom. This conception of growth demanded not only a finer insight, but a higher faith. It takes more faith to see God in the little beginnings than in the completed results;

more faith to say that God is now working than to say that he will work some day" (*Christianity and the Social Crisis*, pp. 59–60). The irony of Rauschenbusch's association of organic growth with the development of a "scientific attitude" toward society is that the social sciences were increasingly moving to a more mechanistic model of explanation. Accordingly the "scientific task" was not to change society but to understand society.

89. Rauschenbusch, *Righteousness of the Kingdom*, p. 124.

90. Rauschenbusch, *Theology for the Social Gospel*, p. 148. Harlan Beckley observes that "Rauschenbusch differed from the theological liberalism of his day that ignored the evangelical emphasis upon the redemptive work of Christ and the distinctiveness of Jesus' ethic" (*Passion for Justice: Retrieving the Legacies of Walter Rauschenbusch, John A. Ryan, and Reinhold Niebuhr* [Louisville: Westminster John Knox, 1992], p. 37). Beckley's book is so well done I am almost hesitant to disagree with him, but I do not think it quite right to suggest that Rauschenbusch differed from most liberals in his stress on the distinctiveness of Jesus' ethic and even more on the importance of Jesus' personality. The reason is that "most liberals" were, like Rauschenbusch, evangelical liberals. The centrality of Jesus in their work may have lacked intelligibility, but that Jesus was central there can be no doubt. "Liberalism" was, after all, a form of Protestant pietism, as is apparent from Rauschenbusch's own example. Therefore liberals saw no deep discontinuity between their liberalism and their evangelical commitments.

91. Rauschenbusch, *Righteousness of the Kingdom*, p. 126. Rauschenbusch's suggestion that Jesus threw his life into the life "of the race" should not be taken lightly. For example, in *Christianizing the Social Order* he observes that wherever historical investigation has uncovered the early history of the Aryan race it has discovered communities of free men. "Thus the essentials of a righteous social life, justice, property, democracy, equality, cooperation, were embodied in the rude and simple conditions of these communities. Here the social supremacy of the Aryan race manifested itself and got its evolutionary start. Here the traditions of democracy and justice were dyed into the fiber of our breed so that they outlasted ages of despotism and reasserted themselves whenever the grip of tyranny slackened" (p. 376). A few pages later Rauschenbusch observes, "Christianity itself is such a strain of higher social life derived from one of the breeding grounds of righteousness. Israel was one of the unsubdued communities in which the love of freedom and justice was kept alive through all disaster. The social passion for fraternity was enormously intensified through the influence of Jesus himself. With that social impetus derived from the prophets and from Jesus, Christianity entered the Roman world like a young mountain torrent" (*Christianizing the Social Order*, pp. 378–79). Rauschenbusch never suggests how a race transmits its "sense of community," though he does call attention to the sacred writings in Israel.

92. Rauschenbusch, *Theology for the Social Gospel*, p. 154. Rauschenbusch's attitude toward Catholicism shaped his views of Judaism prior to Jesus. The Jews became Catholics prior to Jesus.

93. Ibid., pp. 174–75.

94. Ibid., p. 175.

95. Rauschenbusch, *Righteousness of the Kingdom*, p. 134. This statement of the human condition will appear again in Reinhold Niebuhr and in a different way in H. Richard Niebuhr. The fundamental assumptions of German idealism are obviously at work shaping their anthropologies.

96. Rauschenbusch never "theorized" his assumption that humans possess knowledge of the good and right. In other words, he never provides any account of natural law or common grace, but he seems to have assumed something very much like a natural-law position. For example, in *Christianizing the Social Order* he says: "We have a divine instinct for righteousness within us that acts as a guide. Like a compass needle, it is always quivering and shifting, always liable to deflections and aberrations that have led many a bold captain on the rocks. But it answers mysteriously to the cosmic will of God, and we disregard it at our peril. Many have been ruined by following its lead without scientific intelligence; but more by far have been beached on the mud flats by nailing a gilded stick to the bow and steering by that" (p. 326). Rauschenbusch's language of "instinct" does not immediately suggest Kant as the source of his views, but otherwise his position seems quite similar to Kant's. In *Christianizing the Social Order* he praises Kant (and Herder and Leibniz) for refusing to confine God's saving work to Israel and the church and seeing that Christ educated all humankind by the varied agencies of human institutions. He praises Kant in particular for contemplating the possibility of an ethical commonwealth that is "a duty that the race owes to the race, the duty of realizing its divine destiny." He then suggests, again in a quite non-Kantian manner, that so vast an enterprise cannot be accomplished by human beings; only God can bring it to reality. "But because we feel the duty, we may conclude that the Ruler of the moral universe is behind it and is cooperating with us, and each of us must work for it as if all depended on himself" (ibid., p. 89).

97. No doubt Rauschenbusch saw these as closely connected. Superstition thrives on ignorance, which in turn underwrites ritualism, the latter being the source of priestly power. It is the spirit's democratic character that frees us from superstition and priests, since the spirit teaches us that we need no sacraments to assure us that we are the children of God, nor do we need a "Holy Church" to mediate between us and God (*Righteousness of the Kingdom*, pp. 134–41).

98. Rauschenbusch, *Theology for the Social Gospel*, pp. 190–91. Rauschenbusch first stated this view concerning the importance of historical criticism of the Bible in *Christianity and the Social Crisis*. He observed that we see in the Bible what we have been taught to see there. In the Middle Ages men thought that they found their abstruse scholastic theology and philosophy in the simplicity of the Gospels. Accordingly, the social enlightenment contained in the Bible was hidden by dogmatic and ecclesiastical interests through the allegorical method of interpretation. In this respect, the church shared with all of humanity a childlike view of the world, since they lacked any historical sense and therefore could not understand the facts and laws of social development. However, now the social movement has created the modern study of history. "The new present has created a new past. The French Revolution was the birth of modern democracy, and also of the modern school of history. The Bible shares in that new social reinterpretation" (*Christianity and the Social Crisis*, pp. 45–46, 196–97). Rauschenbusch clearly assumed that such a development was the work of the Spirit for no other reason than that Jesus is now able to talk with us as he did to his Galilean friends, and the better we know Jesus, the better we understand the social character of his message of the kingdom.

99. Rauschenbusch, *Theology for the Social Gospel*, p. 194.

100. Ibid., p. 195.

101. Rauschenbusch, *Theology for the Social Gospel*, p. 97.

102. Ibid., p. 14.

103. Friedrich Schleiermacher is, of course, the great exemplification of this theological style. Schleiermacher does treat God-consciousness prior to consciousness of sin, but sin is the first "doctrine" he addresses. Though Rauschenbusch seldom refers to Schleiermacher, it is hard to believe that he had not read *The Christian Faith*. Sharpe quotes from a letter Rauschenbusch wrote to William Gay Ballantine in 1912 that suggests he had more than a passing acquaintance with Schleiermacher: "I have to confess to you that I am not a theologian and never shall be. The trinitarian conception that has come nearest to satisfying me has been the modified Sabellianism of Schleiermacher and Bushnell. God and Christ may differ for my analytic intellect, but for my religious life they are convertible terms. The God of the stellar universe is a God in whom I can drown. Christ with the face of Jesus I can comprehend, and love and assimilate. So I stick to him, and call him by that name. Let others do differently if they are differently made. I prefer to superimpose the two concepts on each other and get more out of each" (quoted in Sharpe, *Walter Rauschenbusch*, p. 322). Reinhold Niebuhr claimed not to be a theologian for much the same reasons.

104. Rauschenbusch, *Theology for the Social Gospel*, p. 31.

105. Reinhold Niebuhr will mount an all-out critique of Rauschenbusch's view of sin, but Niebuhr remains, like his predecessor, a liberal theologian. Indeed Niebuhr is in many ways more determinatively liberal just to the extent that he assumes that theological discourse begins and ends in anthropology.

The overall structure of Rauschenbusch's work is properly characterized as "optimistic," but he certainly had a sense of the "tragic." What he meant by "tragedy" is no doubt different from the way Niebuhr used that term to describe the very character of history, but at times Rauschenbusch can sound Niebuhrian. For example, in the chapter "The Consciousness of Sin" in *Theology for the Social Gospel* he says, "By our very nature we are involved in tragedy. In childhood and youth we have imperious instincts and desires to drive us, and little knowledge to guide and control us. We commit acts of sensuality, cruelty, or dishonour, which nothing can wipe from memory. The weakness or the stubbornness of our will and the tempting situations of life combine to weave the tragic web of sin and failure of which we all make experience before we are through with our years" (p. 32).

106. James Gustafson rightly does not use the language of sin as grammatically primary for the description of our sense of the wrong we do. Rather, he suggests that "the capacity for fault is part of our human nature" (*Ethics from a Theocentric Perspective* [Chicago: University of Chicago Press, 1981], 1:293–317).

107. Rauschenbusch, *Theology for the Social Gospel*, pp. 35–36.

108. Ibid., p. 50. It is interesting that Rauschenbusch talks little about pride as the first among sins. Pride is the source of sin for Reinhold Niebuhr.

109. Ibid., p. 52.

110. Ibid., p. 99.

111. Ibid., p. 142.

112. Ibid., p. 143. The trick, of course, is how that might be done without the use of force or coercion. Rauschenbusch's failure to specify how to get from where we are to this kind of unity is the reason, I suspect, that many found and continue to find him "too optimistic." He is certainly open to that kind of critique, but I think the difficulty goes deeper than the charge of optimism suggests. The problem, moreover, is not pecu-

liar to Rauschenbusch but is also inherent in the work of Reinhold Niebuhr and Paul Ramsey. Quite simply, they each assume the presupposition of liberal social theory that "social problems" are solved by securing cooperation between individuals. To criticize Rauschenbusch for being too optimistic, or Niebuhr for being too pessimistic about the achievement of such cooperation, fails to see that the problem resides in their assumption about the problem.

113. Ibid., p. 90. Rauschenbusch's account of sin no doubt draws on his pastoral experience; one cannot help but be reminded of his story of the manager of the streetcar company in New York, told in *Christianity and the Social Crisis*. Moreover, why he thought societies must be so constructed as to make bad men do good things is more intelligible given this account of sin.

114. Rauschenbusch, *Theology for the Social Gospel*, p. 66.

115. Ibid., p. 62.

116. Ibid., pp. 248–58. Rauschenbusch does not specify whether *graft* means (1) the acquisition of wealth by unfair means or (2) the dishonest paying off of elected officials. I suspect he means both.

117. Ibid., p. 260.

118. Ibid., p. 271.

119. Ibid., p. 119.

120. Ibid., p. 122. In his chapter on the church, Rauschenbusch praises Schleiermacher and Ritschl for rediscovering that our consciousness of salvation must be mediated by a social organism called the church. Equally interesting is his discussion of Josiah Royce's book *The Problem of Christianity* (Chicago: University of Chicago Press, 1968) and the latter's development of a philosophy of loyalty. Rauschenbusch, though generally quite sympathetic with Royce, criticizes him for slighting Jesus in favor of the importance of the church. In contrast, Rauschenbusch maintains that if the church is to have saving power it must embody the personal life of Christ (*Theology for the Social Gospel*, pp. 125–28).

121. Rauschenbusch, *Theology for the Social Gospel*, p. 137.

122. Ibid., p. 14.

123. Ibid., p. 142.

124. Beckley, *Passion for Justice*, pp. 25–26. Beckley's "discovery" is a nice illustration of how dominant Reinhold Niebuhr's reading of the social gospel has been for people trained in Christian ethics. Niebuhr seldom mentioned Rauschenbusch, yet it has been assumed that Rauschenbusch was the representative of Niebuhr's characterization of "liberal Christianity." According to Niebuhr, liberal Christianity accommodated itself to the ethos of the age, thereby sacrificing its most characteristic religious and Christian heritage "by destroying the sense of depth and the experience of tension, typical of profound religion. Its Kingdom of God was translated to mean exactly that ideal society which modern culture hoped to realize through the evolutionary process. Democracy and the League of Nations were to be the political forms of this ideal" (*An Interpretation of Christian Ethics* [New York: Living Age, 1960], p. 23).

125. Beckley rightly observes that "if Rauschenbusch was naively optimistic, it was due to a misreading of the social forces of his time and place, not to an overestimation of the power of ideals to effect justice" (*Passion for Justice*, p. 70).

126. Rauschenbusch, *Christianizing the Social Order*, pp. 332–40.

127. Beckley, *Passion for Justice*, p. 69. Beckley rightly observes that there is no basis in Rauschenbusch for "universal principles of justice derived from the eternal law of God implanted in the natural order. The principles of justice are distinctively Christian. They become universal only as the kingdom advances, that is, as the world is christianized" (ibid., p. 83).

128. Rauschenbusch, *Theology for the Social Gospel*, pp. 174–75.

129. Ibid., p. 165.

130. Ibid., pp. 112–13.

131. Rauschenbusch was not naive about the politics of America. For example, he was particularly concerned with the effect of economic inequalities for political life. He observed that "genuine political democracy will evidence its existence by the social, economic, and educational condition of the people. Generally speaking, city slums, a spiritless and drunken peasantry, and a large emigration are corollaries of class government. If the people were free, they would stop exploitation. If they cannot stop exploitation, the parasitic interests are presumably in control of legislation, the courts, and the powers of coercion" (ibid., p. 75). In *Christianity and the Social Crisis* he has an extensive discussion of the effect of economic inequality on political democracy. As he puts it, "A class which is economically strong will have the necessary influence to secure and enforce laws which protect its economic interests" (pp. 253–54; this section runs from p. 253 to p. 264). As noted above, Rauschenbusch was also acutely aware of how inequality of income works to lower the spirit of the ministry.

132. Rauschenbusch, *Christianizing the Social Order*, pp. 128–56. Rauschenbusch confesses to some misgivings regarding the suggestion that politics has been Christianized, since it has only been on the "thorny path of sanctification" for a century and a half (p. 148). Moreover, democracy as the cooperative idea of Christianity applied to politics is the battleground between the Christian principles of liberty and equality and the mammonistic principle of business life. So the results are not yet fully in.

In this context, Rauschenbusch observes that just as Christianity is more than the church, so democracy is not equivalent to Christianity; but in politics "democracy is the expression and method of the Christian spirit" (ibid., p. 153).

133. Ibid., p. 158.

134. Ibid., p. 235. Dores Sharpe includes in his biography an unpublished talk Rauschenbusch gave at the Labor Lyceum of Rochester in 1901 on socialism. In it Rauschenbusch distinguished between dogmatic and practical socialism and clearly identified himself with the latter. Dogmatic socialists, according to Rauschenbusch, expect socialist aims to be realized at once through a social catastrophe. Practical socialists believe in immediate social reforms that move society gradually toward the social ideal. He criticized Marx for reducing all social ills to a single cause, which he attributed to his philosophical training. In particular Rauschenbusch thought dogmatic socialists concentrated too much on the exploitive character of labor and not enough on land. Rauschenbusch was quite critical of the dogmatic socialist avoidance of reform efforts aimed at making the current system more tolerable. The reforms he recommended are (1) appropriation of economic rent by taxation, (2) appropriation of chief sources of profits by municipal ownership of natural monopolies such as water, gas, electricity, (3) extension of industrial machinery to allow people to control commu-

nications such as the telegraph and the post office, (4) more support for education, libraries, museums, parks, playgrounds, baths, (5) breaking up accumulations of capital through inheritance taxes, (6) organization of labor for social management of industry, and (7) labor legislation to shorten the workday, improve sanitary conditions of labor, prevent child and female labor. Such was Rauschenbusch's socialism (Sharpe, *Walter Rauschenbusch*, pp. 203–16).

135. Rauschenbusch, *Christianizing the Social Order*, pp. 355–56.

136. Ibid., p. 163.

137. Ibid., p. 173. Rauschenbusch did not condemn the profit motive as such, noting that profit is the fair reward a society owes for useful labor and service. The problem is when profit is gained without productive labor, at the expense of others, and without willing consent (ibid., p. 226). It is interesting that Rauschenbusch never attacks the market mechanism as such.

138. Ibid., pp. 169–79.

139. Ibid., p. 185. Rauschenbusch is quoting Ruskin's account of the economic man of capitalism. That he does so is interesting because Ruskin was in many ways more radical in his critique of capitalism than Rauschenbusch; Ruskin—enamored as he was by a craft society—refused to accept many of the basic premises of a capitalist social order. Certainly that kind of radicalism is always "just around the corner" in Rauschenbusch. For a fascinating account of Ruskin from this perspective see John Milbank, *Theology and Social Theory: Beyond Secular Reason* (Oxford: Blackwell, 1990), pp. 197–200.

140. Rauschenbusch, *Christianizing the Social Order*, p. 204.

141. Ibid., p. 205.

142. Ibid., pp. 210–11. Rauschenbusch is clearly drawing on Max Weber's *The Protestant Ethic and the Spirit of Capitalism*, which was published in German in 1905, but he does not indicate he knows Weber.

143. Rauschenbusch, *Christianizing the Social Order*, p. 221. In appealing to honor, Rauschenbusch interestingly again quotes Ruskin.

144. I am not suggesting that Niebuhr was actually influenced by Rauschenbusch in this manner, as there were no doubt many influences that made Niebuhr such an able practitioner of the art of journalism. What is important is not the direct influence but that Niebuhr desired to narrate the world in a manner not unlike Rauschenbusch's, though the content of his narrative of course was quite different.

For an interesting comparison of Rauschenbusch and Reinhold Niebuhr, see Christopher Lasch, "Religious Contributions to Social Movements: Walter Rauschenbusch, the Social Gospel, and Its Critics," *Journal of Religious Ethics* 18, no. 1 (spring 1990): 7–25. Lasch argues that Rauschenbusch has a much clearer understanding of the self-perpetuating character of injustice than the hard-boiled realist who rejected his approach to social reform as moralistic. Yet Lasch also observes that by tying itself to the humanitarianism of the Enlightenment, the social gospel lost the chance to address the needs of modern society on a deeper level. According to Lasch, Rauschenbusch could not explain "why victims of injustice should submit to the authority of a democratic God who shared their own standards of right and wrong yet presided over a world in which those standards were consistently flouted and betrayed" (p. 21).

145. Hopkins's *Rise of the Social Gospel in American Protestantism* remains one of the best narratives of the rise and fall of the social gospel. Meyer's *Protestant Search for Political Realism* is a good continuation of the story that documents some of the reasons for the social gospel's "decline." Paul Carter's *The Decline and Revival of the Social Gospel: Social and Political Liberalism in American Protestant Churches, 1920–1940* (Ithaca, N.Y.: Cornell University Press, 1954) continues as one of the most important accounts of the history after Rauschenbusch.

Whether the social gospel "declined" or was "absorbed" is a pivotal question with no easy answer. From the perspective of the story I am telling, the social gospel was more absorbed than defeated. That may even be true when the social gospel is considered as a political movement. It became irrelevant not so much because its advocates did not get what they wanted as because much of what they wanted came to pass, and as a result they were simply no longer needed. What could be sadder for "prophets" than to get what they want?

146. The most recent *Methodist Hymnal* (Nashville: United Methodist Publishing House, 1989) has few classical social-gospel hymns—John Haynes Holmes, "The Voice of God Is Calling," and Frank Mason North, "Where Cross the Crowded Ways of Life," being the most notable. North's hymn reflects the "city" character of the social-gospel movement with lines like "O tread the city's streets again." James Russell Lowell's "Once to Every Man and Nation" has been left out. Lowell's hymn explicitly assumes that there will be "new Messiahs," but I do not know if it was Lowell's social vision or his theology that led to this hymn's exclusion from the new hymnal.

147. *The Methodist Hymnal* (Nashville: United Methodist Publishing House, 1964), hymn 191. The masculine emphasis no doubt disqualified this hymn from being included in the new hymnal. One might have wished that the "statism" embodied in the hymn might have made it equally questionable.

Some social-gospel hymns used what can only appear as "subversive" language. For example, *The Church School Hymnal for Youth* (Philadelphia: Westminster, 1934), hymn 285, used this hymn by John Haynes Holmes:

> My Master was a worker,
> With daily work to do,
> My Master was a comrade,
> A trusty friend and true.
>
> And he who would be like Him
> Must be a worker too.
> And he who would be like Him
> Must be a comrade too;
>
> Then welcome honest labor
> And honest labor's fare
> In happy hours of singing,
> In silent hours of care.
>
> For where there is a worker,
> The Master's man is there.

Where goes a loyal comrade,
The Master's man is there.

148. Hopkins, *Rise of the Social Gospel in American Protestantism*, p. 143.

149. Ibid., p. 144. It is easy to satirize Sheldon, but such satire too often fails to appreciate the considerable power of his and other such novelists' work. For example, Jane Tompkins provides an extraordinary rereading of *Uncle Tom's Cabin* in her *Sensational Designs: The Cultural Work of American Fiction, 1790–1860* (New York: Oxford University Press, 1985), pp. 122–46. Tompkins notes that *Uncle Tom's Cabin* is a conservative book because it advocates a return to an older way of life, such as the household economy, but Stowe's reliance on such patterns of living and traditional beliefs gives her novel revolutionary potential (pp. 144–45). I suspect the same kind of "conservativism" also accounts in large part for the power of Sheldon's (and Rauschenbusch's) work.

150. Rauschenbusch, *Christianizing the Social Order*, p. 46. There may be an implied criticism of Sheldon in Rauschenbusch's praise, as he may have feared that Sheldon's approach was too concentrated on changing the life of individuals and then, only subsequently, the social order.

151. Minus, *Walter Rauschenbusch*, p. 167.

152. Rauschenbusch, *Prayers of the Social Awakening*, p. 20 (this was the title given the book by Rauschenbusch for the 1912 edition). Rauschenbusch says that the rest of the petitions in the prayer deal with "spiritual needs," such as the need for forgiveness. He seems never to have questioned the distinction between the social and the spiritual, assuming that they were closely interrelated. The very distinction, of course, often was produced by the kind of social practices he was against.

153. Ibid., pp. 139–41.

154. Ibid., pp. 65–66.

155. His prayer "For All True Lovers" ends, "Grant them with sober eyes to look beyond these sweet days of friendship to the generations yet to come, and to realize that the home for which they long will be part of the sacred tissue of the body of humanity in which thou art to dwell, so that they may reverence themselves and drink the cup of joy with awe" (ibid., p. 95).

156. Minus, *Walter Rauschenbusch*, p. 168.

157. Rauschenbusch, *Social Principles of Jesus*, p. 2.

158. Ibid., pp. 3–4.

159. Ibid., pp. 8–9. We see again Rauschenbusch's "natural law" position not only in this passage but in the structure of *Social Principles of Jesus*. He begins with what he takes to be undeniable—that we each have a "social instinct"—and then suggests in what ways Jesus and Christianity have given fresh reality to that instinct.

160. Ibid., p. 12. Rauschenbusch observes that "prostitution is the worst form of contempt for personality" (p. 12).

161. Ibid., p. 13.

162. Ibid., pp. 14–16.

163. Ibid., p. 152.

164. Hopkins provides a quite useful account of the development of the Federal Council of Churches, and in particular the social gospel's role in the formation of the Council (*Rise of the Social Gospel in American Protestantism*, pp. 302–27).

165. Hopkins quoting the Inter-Church Conference on Federation, *Church Federation*, edited by Elias Sanford (New York, 1906), p. 305.

166. The relation between the social gospel and social work is a story that is still to be told. As noted above, Rauschenbusch's pamphlet *Unto Me* was an address originally delivered before social workers.

167. Hopkins, *Rise of the Social Gospel in American Protestantism*, pp. 316–17. This "Social Creed" closely followed that of the Methodists, which was adopted by the Baltimore General Conference in 1908. A report of the conference can be found in Hopkins, *Rise of the Social Gospel in American Protestantism*, pp. 290–91. The Methodists in many ways became the "social gospel" denomination. Why they did so would make a fascinating study. At least part of the explanation is the peculiar "American" character of Methodism. Though Methodism had its roots in England, it was hewn from the frontier and shaped by revivalism, with the result that it acquired a distinctively "practical" character. Methodism also became the home, particularly at Boston University, of Protestant liberal theology. That Protestant liberalism found a home in Methodism may seem odd, but there is in fact a close historical and conceptual relation between pietist religious expression and Protestant liberalism. Both assume an immediate relation between the individual and God that does not require mediation by a church. Such factors at different times and ways no doubt played a role in the hospitality for the social gospel by Methodists, but surely also at work was the middle-class nature of both movements, particularly in the last part of the nineteenth century and the twentieth. For a good overview of Methodist thought see Thomas Langford, *Practical Divinity: Theology in the Wesleyan Tradition* (Nashville: Abingdon, 1983).

168. Of course one of Rauschenbusch's problems is his assumption that Christianity is intelligible without a church. He assumed *Christianity* names a set of beliefs and practices that find their most intense exemplification in the church, but Christianity as such was for him intelligible without its church.

169. No doubt philosophical and theological issues contribute to rendering Rauschenbusch's assumption that rather clear ethical injunctions follow from Christian belief, but more significant are the changing social circumstances of Christians in America. Protestants have, of course, lost their ability to dominate the cultural discourses of American social and political life, but equally important, they have lost their confidence as Christians that they should want to. This may be due to the vague process usually called "secularism," but I think the problem has always been there in the liberal political presumptions that have increasingly shaped American practices. Those liberal presumptions, which of course shape most American Christians as much as if not more than any Christian practices, require Christianity to be understood as a set of privatized beliefs. Some argue such beliefs can or should have "public" significance, but to so argue already accepts liberal political arrangements as normative.

170. For a fascinating comparison of Rauschenbusch and John Howard Yoder, see Reinhard Hütter, "The Church: Midwife of History or Witness of the Eschaton?" *Journal of Religious Ethics* 18, no. 1 (spring 1990): 27–54.

CHAPTER 6

1. Walter Abbott, *The Documents of Vatican II* (New York: Guild, 1996). *Dignitatis Humanae Personae* appears on pages 675–96.

2. John Courtney Murray, preface to *Dignitatis Humanae Personae*, p. 673.

3. I wish I could provide the documentation to support this claim. At the time of the debates surrounding *Dignitatis* I was studying at Yale, where I had the benefit of learning about the council's work from George Lindbeck. At the time I was doing extensive work on John Courtney Murray, and I had a much more favorable assessment of this work then than I now do. I remember at the time I was surprised that Lindbeck was somewhat suspicious of Murray's contribution, exactly because Lindbeck better understood what was theologically at stake between Murray and the French. It was from Lindbeck I learned of the importance of "the French" in the debates. I assume by "the French" he meant people like Congar and de Lubac who would have obviously understood the problematic character of Murray's neoscholastic presumptions about the relation of nature and grace.

4. *Dignitatis Humanae Personae*, p. 688.

5. Ibid. p. 678.

6. For a devastating account of the development of this modern understanding of rights, see Pierre Manent, *The City of Man* (Princeton, N.J.: Princeton University Press, 1998), pp. 124–55. Manent notes that once the notion of rights is freed from any ontological moorings, it cannot help but appear arbitrary. As a result, claims about rights become but a way to describe wants. "If man has a right to life, he also has a right to die, or at least a death with dignity; if he has a right to work, he also has a right to leisure; if he has right to live in his country, he also has the right to travel; if a woman has a right to a child, she also has the right to an abortion; if she has a right to respect, she also has a right to pleasure, even to orgasm; in short, since it is time to stop, there is nothing under the sun or moon that is not susceptible of becoming the occasion and matter of a human right. This verifies the expansive force of the tautology linking man to the rights of man" (p. 139).

7. *Dignitatis Humanae Personae*, p. 680.

8. Ibid., p. 681.

9. For my defense of such a focus on the body see my chapter "The Sanctified Body: Why Perfection Does Not Require a 'Self,'" in my *Sanctify Them in the Truth: Holiness Exemplified* (Edinburgh: T & T Clark, 1998), pp. 77–92.

10. *Dignitatis Humanae Personae*, p. 681. That "religion" transcends terrestrial and temporal affairs may be true for Hinduism, but one can hardly associate such a view with Christianity. What could it possibly mean for a faith that worships Jesus Christ to say that our God "transcends temporal" affairs. As Robert Jenson observes, the God we find revealed in Scripture does not have immunity from time but rather is the One alone capable of taking time into his very life without ceasing to be. As Jenson puts it, "God is not eternal in that he adamantly remains as he began, but in that he always creatively opens to what he will be; not in that he nags on, but in that he gives and receives; not in that he perfectly persists, but in that he perfectly anticipates" (*Systematic Theology: The Triune God* [New York: Oxford University Press, 1997], 1:217).

11. *Dignitatis Humanae Personae*, p. 685.

12. Ibid.

13. Ibid.

14. Ibid., p. 686.

15. Ibid., p. 683.

16. Ibid., pp. 689–90.

17. Ibid., p. 690.

18. Ibid.

19. Ibid., p. 691.

20. I am following Oliver O'Donovan's description of liberation theology as "Southern" in his *The Desire of the Nations: Rediscovering the Roots of Political Theology* (Cambridge: Cambridge University Press, 1996). Given my criticism of liberation theology, it may seem disingenuous for me to use it in this context. Yet my criticisms of liberation theology have always been informed by the presumption that we share far more in common than we differ.

21. John Howard Yoder, *The Politics of Jesus* (Grand Rapids: Eerdmans, 1972). Yoder's revision of *The Politics of Jesus* appeared in 1994.

22. I am obviously drawing on John Milbank's extraordinary analysis in *Theology and Social Theory: Beyond Secular Reason* (Oxford: Blackwell, 1990).

23. *Dignitatis Humanae Personae*, p. 693.

24. Ibid., 675.

CHAPTER 7

1. I have obviously "borrowed" this title from John Milbank's essay "Only Theology Overcomes Metaphysics," in his *The Word Made Strange: Theology, Language, and Culture* (Cambridge: Blackwell, 1997), pp. 36–52. Jenson has expressed great appreciation for Milbank's *Theology and Social Theory* in Robert Jenson, *Systematic Theology: The Works of God*, vol. 2 (New York: Oxford University Press, 1999).

2. Jenson, *Systematic Theology*, 2:209.

3. Ibid.

4. Robert Jenson, *Systematic Theology* (New York: Oxford University Press, 1997), 1:32.

5. Ibid., 1:63.

6. Ibid., 1:20. Jenson praises Barth's attempt in the *Church Dogmatics* "to interpret all reality by the fact of Christ; indeed, it can be read as the first truly major system of Western metaphysics since the collapse of Hegelianism. One need not adopt all Barth's characteristic theologoumena to take the massive work as a model and challenge in this respect" (ibid., 1:21). In his *Essays in Theology of Culture* (Grand Rapids: Eerdmans, 1995), Jenson reflects on why his two theological heroes— Jonathan Edwards and Karl Barth—should both come from a different theological tradition from his own. "It is, I think, because both are ruthless in refusing to be confined within or protected by a special epistemological 'compartment' called 'theology'" (ibid., 1:222).

7. Ibid., 1:215.

8. Ibid., 1:217.

9. Ibid., 1:46.

10. Jenson quite rightly observes that the concept of reason is fundamentally an ethical concept involving a set of commands. Those commands are, he suggests, the two sides of the enterprise of becoming human—its task-character and its mutuality (*Essays in Theology of Culture*, p. 31).

11. Ibid., p. 35.

12. Ibid.

13. Ibid., p. 141.

14. Jenson, *Systematic Theology*, 2:79. Jenson's understanding of politics is but a development of his quite extraordinary account of the significance of conversation for God's identity as well as our identity. With his usual economy he puts the matter exactly, noting, "I am who and what I am precisely in conversation with those who offer me my self" (ibid., 2:104).

15. Ibid., 2:79–80.

16. For this use of "theological politics" in distinction to "political theology," see Arne Rasmusson's *The Church As Polis: From Political Theology to Theological Politics As Exemplified by Jürgen Moltmann and Stanley Hauerwas* (Notre Dame, Ind.: University of Notre Dame Press, 1995).

17. Jenson, *Systematic Theology*, 2:81–82. In *Essays in Theology of Culture*, Jenson puts the matter this way: "Right polity holds itself open to prophecy. Right polity will, as the traditional political ethics of the church have always said, open and guard a space for the public speech and reception of the community's speakers of godly promise" (p. 142). Jenson, I think, is suggesting something close to Barth's contention that at a minimum a just society must allow for the free preaching of the gospel. So the very existence of the church is a significant sign that a polity has at least the beginnings of justice. The difficulty, of course, is whether the gospel the church preaches is the gospel.

18. Jenson, *Systematic Theology*, 2:91.

19. Ibid., 2:86. Some may well think that I must be reading Jenson's mail: I often seem to be saying what he has already said before I knew he had said it. But I confess I did not know Jenson was going to develop the significance of the Ten Commandments in the second volume of the *Systematic Theology* when Will Willimon and I began our Sunday school book *The Truth About God: The Ten Commandments in Christian Life* (Nashville: Abingdon, 1999). In this little book we argue just as Jenson does that the commandments are not simply negative prohibitions but cohere by positive virtues shaped in and to the course of their history. So the history of Israel and the church provides the positive meaning of the commandments that is not apparent in the text—at least not apparent if the text of the commandments is divorced from the narrative in which they are reported.

20. Jenson, *Systematic Theology*, 2:87.

21. Jenson provides the following example: "Historicist nihilism manifests itself most democratically as sheer inability to reason ethically. I choose an instance that notably infests the academic, reminiscently 'liberal' community. A Minnesota poll recent as of this writing (1990) reported that most Minnesotans believe (1) that abortion is the tak-

ing of personal human life and (2) that folk should have 'the right' to abort as they freely choose. The evil to which I here call attention is not the number of abortions that *Roe vs. Wade* has produced, terrifying as this is. The subtler, more demonic evil appears in our ability simultaneously to entertain the two referenced opinions. The nihilism is the escape of 'choice' from community. It is freedom that consists in excuse from responsibility for the other and for the story line of my life so far, freedom that occurs on a horizon of sheer temporal sequentiality with no plot at all" (*Essays in Theology of Culture*, pp. 187–88).

22. Ibid., p. 133. While Jenson shares the moral and cultural concerns of many who identify themselves as neoconservatives, he is anything but one of them. He is not because he understands that capitalism is at the heart of the Enlightenment dream that produced America. Indeed the retreat into the "family" is exactly the strategy a capitalist economy desires, so that the family becomes an end in itself rather than an institution in service to a common good. For example, he observes that those who would celebrate the lack of conscience of the market fail to see that the inevitable result is for the market to become a communal good in its own right in which the moral vacuum it creates drains the community of moral and aesthetic substance (*Systematic Theology*, 2:315–16). For Jenson, nothing indicates immorality more clearly than ugliness. To be sure, the inequities produced by capitalism are terrible, but finally the problem with economic and political life produced by capitalism is they are so ugly. Thus I confess I was tempted to write on Jenson's ethics as an attempt to reinscribe the significance of beauty in the moral life.

23. Ibid., 2:204–5.

24. Ibid., 2:207.

25. Ibid., 2:207–8.

26. Ibid., 2:296. Jenson's strong claims in this respect make me wonder if he is not, secretly to be sure, a Methodist.

27. Ibid., 2:302.

28. Ibid., 2:289.

29. Jenson, *Essays in Theology of Culture*, pp. 65–66. Jenson often makes clear that no matter how justified or beneficial the Constantinian settlement may have been, we are now well rid of the Christian accommodation to the state. The separation between the church and the culture that was once Christian is a long and drawn-out affair which cannot help but create for Christians deep ambiguity. That churches are tempted to accommodate "seekers" or incompetent members is but the way to apostasy. In this time of "uncertain boundaries, the church must not dilute or estrange her sacramental culture but instead train would-be believers in its forms, not dispense from God's *torah* but instead reform would-be believers' moral structure, not succumb to theological relativism but teach would-be believers the doctrine of Trinity." In short, the church now finds itself returned to a situation in which the catechumenate was born. Those who have inculcated the metaphysical mechanism and moral relativism of the alien culture that surrounds us cannot help but be initially shocked and puzzled by the church's life (*Systematic Theology*, 2:305).

30. Jenson, I think, quite rightly refuses to locate human significance in any one attribute that allegedly distinguishes us from the animals. Rather he maintains that our "specificity in comparison with the other animals is that we are the ones addressed by God's moral word and so enabled to respond—that we are called to *pray*. If we will, the odd creature of the sixth day can after all be classified: we are the praying animals" (ibid., 2:58–59).

Such a view seems quite congruent with Alasdair MacIntyre's account in his *Dependent Rational Animals: Why Human Beings Need the Virtues* (Chicago: Open Court, 1999).

31. Jenson, *Systematic Theology*, 2:210.

32. Despairing of the overly abstract discussions of the relation of nature and grace, I have largely ignored addressing the question of their relation. However, for my attempt to address why an account of nature is theologically unavoidable, see my *Sanctify Them in the Truth: Holiness Exemplified* (Nashville: Abingdon, 1998), pp. 37–60.

33. Jenson, *Systematic Theology*, 2:210.

34. I have tried to suggest in this essay why ethicists must read Jenson, but I think there is one "ethicist" Jenson needs to read: John Howard Yoder. Of course Jenson may well have read Yoder and sees no reason he needs to engage his work, but if that is the case Jenson has made a mistake. For example, as rich as Jenson's christological reflections are, I think he has not dealt sufficiently with Jesus' teachings. In that respect Jenson would find Yoder a wonderful resource for reflection on why and how Jesus the teacher (Jesus the prophet) and Jesus the crucified are necessarily understood as the one Word of God. Unfortunately Yoder's most systematic reflections on these topics are in his never-published book "Preface to Theology: Christology and Theological Method." The contents of the "Preface" are his lectures in systematic theology at Associated Mennonite Biblical Seminary and can be obtained from Cokesbury Bookstore at the Divinity School, Duke University.

35. Jenson may think something like a just-war position can be theoretically justified, but he certainly cannot think that the United States is a polity capable of conducting a just war. So even if he is theoretically a just warrior, in fact he is a pacifist—at least in terms of his being a resident of the United States.

36. Jenson, *Essays in Theology of Culture*, p. 41. "Violence As a Mode of Language" was first published in the *Bulletin of Lutheran Theological Seminary* 51 (1971): 33–42.

37. Jenson, *Essays in Theology of Culture*, p. 44.

38. Ibid., p. 45.

39. Ibid., p. 47. This is the source of Jenson's challenge to my account of nonviolence in his "Review of Stanley Hauerwas' *After Christendom?*" *First Things*, no. 25 (August/September 1992). I tried to respond in an essay on John Milbank's work that can now be found in my *Wilderness Wanderings: Probing Twentieth-Century Theology and Philosophy* (Boulder, Colo.: Westview, 1997), pp. 188–98.

40. Jenson, *Essays in Theology of Culture*, p. 48.

41. Indeed, Jenson's theology rightly stresses the analogical character of our descriptions, which includes, of course, violence. He therefore needs to provide examples of the disciplined use of the language of violence in order to prevent violence from describing anything and everything. I am indebted to Alex Sider for pointing this out to me. I am also indebted to Prof. Reinhard Hütter and Richard Church for critically responding to this essay.

CHAPTER 8

1. John Howard Yoder, *The Politics of Jesus* (Grand Rapids: Eerdmans, 1972). A second edition was published in 1994. Yoder "updated" the scholarship by adding "Epilogues" to some of the chapters. My references are to the first edition.

2. John Howard Yoder, *The Priestly Kingdom: Social Ethics As Gospel* (Notre Dame, Ind.: University of Notre Dame Press, 1984), p. 7.

3. Yoder, *Politics of Jesus*, p. 132.

4. Ibid., p. 105.

5. Yoder, *Priestly Kingdom*, p. 9.

6. Yoder, *Politics of Jesus*, p. 101.

7. John Howard Yoder, "Karl Barth and Christian Pacifism" (work paper No. 4 prepared for peace section of the Mennonite Central Committee, 1966).

8. Yoder's "pamphlet" later became Yoder's *Karl Barth and the Problem of War* (Nashville: Abingdon, 1970).

9. John Howard Yoder, *The Christian Witness to the State* (Clewton, Kan.: Faith and Life Press, 1964).

10. For those interested, that paper is included in my *Vision and Virtue: Essays in Christian Ethical Reflection* (Notre Dame, Ind.: Fides Press, 1974), pp. 197–221. I have given the book's first publication date to indicate how much I owe to Fides Press. Where else was I going to get my distinct point of view published? I am, of course, indebted to the University of Notre Dame Press, and in particular to Jim Langford, for republishing the book in 1981.

11. See, for example, E. P. Sanders, *Jesus and Judaism* (Philadelphia: Fortress Press, 1985).

12. Fredric Jameson, *Post-modernism Or The Cultural Logic of Late Capitalism* (Durham, N.C.: Duke University Press, 1984), p. 390.

CHAPTER 9

1. "This conference" was the tenth annual conference sponsored by the Evangelical Contribution on Northern Ireland. These Protestant Christians are committed to furthering reconciliation with Catholics. I am indebted to them, and particularly to their director David Porter, for providing me with the opportunity to address the conference.

2. For anyone wanting to get a start on understanding Northern Ireland, I found John White's *Interpreting Northern Ireland* (Oxford: Clarendon, 1990) indispensable. Tim Pat Coogan's *The IRA: A History* (Niwot, Colo.: Reinhardt, 1994) was also extremely informative. James Leyburn's *The Scotch-Irish: A Social History* (Chapel Hill: University of North Carolina Press, 1962) and James Lydon's *The Making of Ireland: From Ancient Times to the Present* (New York: Routledge, 1998) were invaluable for providing background. On the way back from Ireland I read Robert McLiam Wilson's wonderful novel *Eureka Street* (London: Minerva, 1996), which probably should be required reading for everyone whether they are interested in Northern Ireland or not.

3. Michael Ignatieff, *The Warrior's Honor: Ethnic War and the Modern Conscience* (New York: Henry Holt, 1997), pp. 53–54. Ignatieff notes that it is hardly "secular myopia" to observe that after fifty years of the official secularism of the communist regime, combined with the more effective secularization made possible by economic modernization, the hold of organized religion had been eroded in the Balkans. None of the militiamen he talked to said they were defending their faith, but rather that they were defending their families. Indeed Ignatieff suggests that Huntington's argument that the Balkans represent the continuing significance of religious difference shows

exactly the opposite. "It is precisely because the religious differences were fading away that they triggered such an exaggerated defense. It was not because religion triggered deep feelings, but because it triggered unauthentic ones, that it helped to unleash such a tumult of violent self-righteousness" (p. 55). John White observes, however, that the Catholic and Protestant communities of Northern Ireland are not mirror images of one another, since the Protestant community is more fragmented than the Catholic (*Interpreting Northern Ireland*, p. 49).

4. Wendell Berry, *The Hidden Wound* (New York: North Point, 1997), p. 78. Miroslav Volf provides a profound analysis of this process in his *Exclusion and Embrace: A Theological Exploration of Identity, Otherness, and Reconciliation* (Nashville: Abingdon, 1996). Volf observes, "Exclusion can entail cutting of the bonds that connect, taking oneself out of the pattern of interdependence and placing oneself in a position of sovereign independence. The other then emerges either as an enemy that must be pushed away from the self and driven out of its space or as a nonentity—a superfluous being—that can be disregarded and abandoned. Second, exclusion can entail erasure of separation, not recognizing the other as someone who in his or her otherness belongs to the pattern of interdependence. The other then emerges as an inferior being who must either be assimilated by being made like the self or be subjugated to the self. Exclusion takes place when the violence of expulsion, assimilation, or subjugation and the indifference of abandonment replace the dynamics of taking in and keeping out as well as the mutuality of giving and receiving" (p. 67).

5. Aquinas observes, quoting Aristotle, that "those things are most to be feared which when done wrong cannot be put right . . . or for which there is no help, or which are not easy." Aquinas rightly understands such matters to be about fear, for they remind us that to be so "caught" is to be completely out of control. Thus Aquinas comments that "those evils which, after they have come, cannot be remedied at all, or at least not easily, are considered as lasting for ever or for a long time: for which reason they inspire fear." They do so, I think, because we know the acknowledgment of how such evils constitute our lives is but another name of damnation (*Summa Theologica*, trans. Fathers of the English Dominican Province [Westminster, Md.: Christian Classics, 1948], 1–2.42.6).

6. Berry, *Hidden Wound*, p. 6.

7. Ibid., p. 3. Greg Jones has addressed these issues in a wonderful paper (yet unpublished) entitled "Healing the Wounds of History." I am in Jones's debt for his probing of these issues.

8. Ibid., p. 8.

9. Ibid., p. 92.

10. Whether racism produced slavery or slavery produced racism is a fascinating but, I believe, unresolvable question. Berry argues that Africans were not enslaved because they were black but because their labor promised to free us from economic necessities. In short, Africans were enslaved because they could not prevent themselves militarily from being enslaved. Berry thinks it likely, therefore, that what we now call racism came about as a justification for slavery after the fact. "We decided that blacks were inferior in order to persuade ourselves that it was all right to enslave them" (pp. 112–13). Such a development becomes a vicious circle as the presumed inferiority of the workers inevitably infects the quality of the work they do, which then only confirms the racist presumptions of the overlords.

C. Eric Lincoln argues that racism in America is not the "lingering memorabilia of the slavery. That is a misconception, the recognition of which uncovers new and unplumbed possibilities for its eradication. The truth is that slavery was merely the political institutionalization of a preexisting ideology. It was an *existing* racism that redefined Indians and Africans alike for ambitious economic and social convenience of Europeans bent on the maximization of a new world of opportunities they were unprepared to confront with their own labor." Lincoln argues that recognizing that racism preceded slavery is critically important if we are not to be held hostage to the past. For to believe that racism is an aftermath of slavery tempts us to think that with time it will recede from our consciousness and wither from our institutions. Slavery was ended and we assumed that time would do the rest. Such an assumption has obviously been shown wanting (C. Eric Lincoln, *Coming Through the Fire: Surviving Race and Place in America* [Durham, N.C.: Duke University Press, 1996], pp. 132–33). The extent that Lincoln and Berry actually disagree is not easily determined.

11. Lincoln, *Coming Through the Fire*, p. 133.

12. Ibid., pp. 133–34. For a philosophical exploration that argues that the historian cannot let the dead be left behind, see Edith Wyschogrod, *An Ethics of Remembering: History, Heterology, and the Nameless Other* (Chicago: University of Chicago Press, 1998).

13. Lincoln, *Coming Through the Fire*, p. 157. In a similar fashion Amos Elon argues, "I have lived in Israel most of my life and have come to the conclusion that where there is so much traumatic memory, so much pain, so much memory innocently or deliberately mobilized for political purposes, a little forgetfulness might finally be in order. This should not be seen as a banal plea to 'forgive and forget.' Forgiveness has nothing to do with it. While remembrance is often a form of vengeance, it is also, paradoxically, the basis of reconciliation. What is needed, in my view, is a shift in emphasis and proportion, and a new equilibrium in Israeli political politics between memory and hope" ("The Politics of Memory," *The New York Review of Books* 40 [October 7, 1993]: 5).

14. Ignatieff, *Warrior's Honor*, p. 186.

15. Ibid. Ignatieff's reference to Joyce is to the famous reply of Stephen Dedalus in *Ulysses:* "History is a nightmare from which I am trying to awake."

16. Ignatieff, *Warrior's Honor*, p. 188. At the very time I was writing this paper Augusto Pinochet was arrested in Britain. Duke is fortunate to have Ariel Dorfman on our faculty. Dorfman is a novelist and playwright who had been an aide in Salvador Allende's government and subsequently had to flee for his life when Pinochet took over. Dorfman is obviously a very sophisticated intellectual, which makes his response to Pinochet's arrest all the more interesting. He said, "To see the man that betrayed [Allende] and devastated my life and took the lives of so many people I love, to see that man confronted with his crimes, unable to leave his hospital room, is for me, to restore a cosmological balance to the universe." Dorfman's comment appears in an article by Jason Wagner, "Humbling of a Dictator," *The Chronicle* (Duke University student newspaper) 94, no. 45 (November 2, 1998): 1, 13. Vengeance is not a disposition to be found only among the uneducated. In a subsequent article Dorfman notes that the trial of Pinochet will not be easy for Chileans, because such a trial means they must confront those whom Pinochet tortured and murdered. As Dorfman puts it, "Do we want a nation that does not care about those thousands and is willing to forget them in order to have an uneasy and erratic

peace? Or are we strong enough to begin the difficult task of finally, at long last, living in a world without Pinochet?" ("Chile's Strange Relationship with Pinochet," *Duke University Dialogue* 13, no. 24 [December 11, 1998]: 7). For an extraordinary theological account of Chile under Pinochet, see William Cavanaugh, *Torture and Eucharist: Theology, Politics, and the Body of Christ* (Oxford: Blackwell, 1998).

17. Ignatieff, *Warrior's Honor*, p. 190. My friend Michael Quirk rightly reminds me that, contrary to the liberal assumption that justice and vengeance are opposites, justice is a "purification" of the moral impetus behind vengeance. Vengeance schooled by justice no longer takes delight in the harm it must do.

18. George Will, "Race Advisory Report Immune to Time's Passage," *The Herald Sun* (Durham, N.C.), September 27, 1998, p. A17.

19. George Will, "Scalia Missed Point but Made Right Argument on Separation of Religion," *Durham Morning Herald*, April 22, 1990, sec. F. I discuss Will's column in *After Christendom?* (Nashville: Abingdon, 1991), pp. 30–31. A second edition of *After Christendom?* was published in 1999.

20. "Peace in Northern Ireland?" *PeaceWatch* 4, no. 5 (August 1998): 4–5.

21. Finnan O'Toole comments on the same process in his *The Lie of the Land: Irish Identities* (London: Verso, 1997). He notes that Leopold Bloom's observation in *Ulysses* that a nation is the same people living in the same place or in different places no longer holds. The reason is that the Irish face the disappearance of that Ireland under the pressures of economics, geography, and the collapse of the religious monolith. "We live in different places, but are we the 'same people'? Only if we can understand sameness in a way that incorporates difference, that brooks contradictions, and that is comfortable with the idea that the only fixed Irish identity and the only useful Irish tradition is the Irish tradition of not having a fixed identity" (p. xv). He continues, "The paradox of the Republic of Ireland in the aftermath of the British Empire—its national independence is underwritten by transnational corporations and by a supra-national European Union. Its sovereignty is a power that can be exercised mostly by giving it up" (pp. xvi–xvii). In short, O'Toole is recommending that Ireland learn to enjoy globalization because, like it or not, Ireland is already lost in that process.

22. I am aware that this seems an exaggerated claim, but I think there is a correlation between history as science, which turns out to be a form of forgetting, and capitalism. For an exploration of these issues, see chapter 2 of this book; my *Sanctify Them in the Truth: Holiness Exemplified* (Edinburgh: T & T Clark, 1998), pp. 206–14; and my "The Christian Difference: Or Surviving Postmodernism," *Cultural Values*, 3, 2 (April, 1999) pp. 164–81.

23. Some may discern the influence of Alasdair MacIntyre shaping the argument of this section. I should certainly like to think MacIntyre has taught me how to think about these matters. This may seem odd since MacIntyre is anything but a pacifist. For my attempt to explore the difference between MacIntyre's perspective on these issues and my defense of nonviolence see chapter 10, "The Nonviolent Terrorist: In Defense of Christian Fanaticism," in *Sanctify Them in The Truth*, pp. 177–90.

Michael Quirk warns me against romanticizing Irish poverty, noting that while their poverty prevented them from acquiring the rapaciousness and affluent unconcern that plagues Americans, it is nonetheless the case that the Irish way of dealing with poverty was emigration. Emigration was, he suggests in a letter, devastating to Ireland because it fomented a strain of passive-aggressive resentment at home and a kind of forgetfulness, disguised as romanticism among the "wild geese," about the mother country. Quirk acknowledges that Irish poverty tempered any illusions they may have had about being a "universal" or "savior" culture, but on the other hand it put a crimp in their natural good cheer that encouraged a kind of self-loathing that authors as diverse as Joyce and McCourt describe and exemplify.

24. Volf, *Exclusion and Embrace*, p. 135.

25. Ibid.

26. Ibid., p. 136. Volf is responding to Gregory Jones's argument in his *Embodying Forgiveness: A Theological Analysis* (Grand Rapids: Eerdmans, 1995) that it is a mistake to forget. As Jones puts it, "the judgment of grace enables us, through the power of the Holy Spirit, to remember well. When God promises to 'blot out [Israel's] transgressions' and 'not remember [Israel's] sins' (Isaiah 43:25; see also Jeremiah 31:34), God is not simply letting bygones be bygones. Rather, God is testifying to God's own gracious faithfulness. Moreover, such forgiveness provides a way to narrate the history of Israel's sinfulness with the context of God's covenant of grace. To be sure, such a narration makes it possible, and even necessary, to forget the sin. But the past itself, the history, is and needs to be remembered so that a new and renewed future becomes possible" (p. 147).

27. Volf, *Exclusion and Embrace*, p. 138.

28. Gregory Jones, "Healing the Wounds of Memory," unpublished lecture, p. 9. Jones continues in this lecture to explore the profound set of reflections of the relation between memory and forgiveness he began in *Embodying Forgiveness*.

29. Robert Jenson, *Systematic Theology* (New York: Oxford University Press, 1997), 1:217–18. I left out a paragraph in Jenson's text that is not essential to my argument but extremely important. Jenson notes, "There is something Barth did not say that must be said, and with emphasis. Simply that source and goal are real in God would not make his eternity a 'duration,' a *temporal* infinity. He is *temporally* infinite because 'source' and 'goal' are present *and* asymmetrical in him, because he is primarily future to himself and only thereupon past and present for himself. It is in that he is Spirit that the true God avoids—so to speak—the timelessness of mere form or mere consciousness. Therefore such paired denials and affirmations as the following must always be to hand: God is not eternal in that he adamantly remains as he began, but in that he always creatively opens to what he will be; not in that he hangs on, but in that he gives and receives; not in that he perfectly persists, but in that he perfectly anticipates."

30. Jones, *Embodying Forgiveness*, p. 173.

31. Christian Duquoc, "The Forgiveness of God," *Concilium* 184 (1986): 40–41. Earlier in the article Duquoc had observed that "terror results from the combination of violence and the idea," which means no account of violence is adequate that fails to understand that, in the words of Robespierre, "terror is the emanation of virtue." Thus the wish for a utopia, of a world without corruption, unleashes a world of limitless violence. It is against this background that the politics of God's forgiveness can be seen: God's forgiveness breaks the link, as Duquoc puts it, between "violence and the idea" (p. 39).

32. Ibid., p. 42.

33. Jones, *Embodying Forgiveness*, p. 173.

34. Jones, *Embodying Forgiveness*, p. 179.

35. "French Bishops' Declaration of Repentance," *Origins* 27, no. 18 (October 16, 1997): 303. For an informative article that surveys the objections against the current pope's penchant for such confessions, see Avery Dulles, "Should the Church Repent?" *First Things*, no. 88 (December 1998): 36–41.

36. A fascinating comparison, I suspect, remains to be made between the Truth and Reconciliation Commission in South Africa and President Clinton's recent Advisory Committee on Race in America. The latter floundered in the therapeutic culture of blame and counterblame, victim and victimizer. Part of the difficulty is the American sense that we are not part of histories that constitute our moral identities. Therefore most whites in America simply do not believe that we have any history of which we should feel ashamed.

37. Christian Duqouc ends his article with these words: "Forgiveness is, of course, gratuitous, God does not ask for compensation, but it opens up a new era. Forgiveness would be abstract if this era remained purely interior. This is the sense in which the forgiveness of God, revealed by the person who was victim of a crime, does not stop meaning that God is working in solidarity with the victims of history towards a world renewed, and this not simply by means of reversing the situation but by creating new relationships. The forgiveness of God is the proclamation of the kingdom: it comes about by conversion and not by substituting power for power. The God of Jesus does not impose himself; he is the one who, by dint of a patience that is often insulted, reveals a face quite other than the one our games of violence and our idolatry of power invite" (pp. 43–44).

38. Timothy Garton Ash, "True Confessions," *The New York Review of Books*, July 17, 1997, pp. 33–38.

39. Ibid., p. 37.

40. Ibid. Ash is quite right about the importance of *ubuntu* for Tutu. See, for example, Michael Battle's fine study *Reconciliation: The Ubuntu Theology of Desmond Tutu* (Cleveland: Pilgrim, 1997). Tutu has now written his own account of the commission's work in his book *No Future without Forgiveness* (New York: Doubleday, 1999). His own account of the importance of *ubuntu*, which he describes as the view that "my humanity is caught up, is inextricably bound up in yours," is found on pp. 30–32. He also describes the work of the commission as the work of memory. General amnesty, according to Tutu, is really amnesia, which results in the "heart" returning to hold the present and future hostage (p. 28). He therefore refuses to accept Ash's claim that the TRC is utopian, noting that "it is ultimately in our best interest that we become forgiving, repentant, reconciling, and reconciled people because without forgiveness, without reconciliation, we have no future" (p. 165). Of course Tutu does not deny that his Christian convictions shape his understanding of the process.

41. Paul Ricoeur has explored these issues in a marvelous essay, "Reflections on a New Ethos for Europe," *Philosophical and Social Criticism* 21, nos. 5–6 (1998): 3–13. Ricoeur argues that what prevents cultures from allowing themselves to be recounted differently is the influence perceived over the collective memory of what may be called "founding events." Memory of such events tends to freeze history in a manner that makes that history incommunicable. Ricoeur does not try to suggest why this process occurs, but surely one of the reasons is the assumption that we need to keep faith with the dead. The challenge before Europe, according to Ricoeur, is to acquire the "ability to recount the founding events of our national history in different ways" through an exchange of

cultural memories. Such an exchange is possible only through forgiveness, by which we renarrate our specific narrative identities. As Ricoeur puts it, forgiveness enables a "mutual revision in which we are able to see the most valuable yield of the exchange of memories. Forgiveness is also a specific form of that mutual revision, the most precious result of which is the liberation of promises of the past which have not been kept" (p. 9). Ricoeur argues that forgiveness in the full sense exceeds political categories, since it belongs to the order of charity. That may be true for "politics," but it cannot be true of that politics we call church.

Ricoeur provides a compelling account of the relationship among memory, narrative, and forgetting in "Memory and Forgetting," in *Questioning Ethics: Contemporary Debates in Philosophy*, ed. Richard Kearney and Mark Dooley Gardner (London: Routledge, 1999), pp. 5–11. All the essays in the first section of *Questioning Ethics* are relevant for what I have tried to do in this paper. Richard Kearney's "Narrative and the Ethics of Remembrance" is particularly important. Kearney observes that fundamentalism arises when a nation forgets its own narrative origins, which suggests that any "solution" to the Northern Ireland problem may require the willingness of the British and Irish nationalists to exchange memories. He observes, "Genuine amnesty does not and cannot come from blind forgetfulness (amnesia), but only from a remembering which is prepared to forgive the past by emancipating it from the deterministic stranglehold of violent obsession and revenge. Genuine pardon, as Ricoeur observes, does not involve a forgetting of the events themselves but a way of *signifying* a debt to the dead which paralyzes memory—and, by implication, our capacity to recreate ourselves a new future" (p. 27).

42. I have a hunch that Italy would be a fascinating study for how forgiveness works for the building of a culture. Stories matter, and the stories that shape a people matter even more. That Alessandro Manzoni's *The Betrothed* (London: Penguin, 1972) is the novel taught to every Italian schoolchild has to make a difference even in a society that was surely once one of the most violent in the world.

43. After I had finished this essay I was kindly sent a book that attempts to explore the relation of memory, forgiveness, and the reconciling of histories for Northern Ireland. The book contains wonderful essays I highly recommend. See *Reconciling Memories*, edited by Alan Falconer and Joseph Liechty (Blackrode, Ireland: The Columba Press, 1998).

CHAPTER 10

1. The quotation marks around *liturgy* suggest the unfortunate and still all too common Protestant assumption that "liturgical" churches are Catholic. Often the worship shaped by the experience of Protestant revivalism is not thought to be liturgical.

2. Of course one of the ironies of this view is that the "Sunday morning worship service" thought too "formal" for effective evangelism is the result of past evangelistic form. For example, it is not uncommon in Methodist services that the offering is taken up before the sermon. This order is the result of revivals in which it was assumed that following the sermon some would respond and be "saved." You would not want an offering intruding between the sermon and the response of those needing to be saved. Such an intrusion would mean you might miss the emotional moment, thus letting the sinner escape. Edward Phillips notes that the revival had three distinct liturgical movements: (1) preliminaries, involving hymn singing, special music, testimonies, love offer-

ings, (2) the message, and (3) the altar call. This pattern, he observes, "became embedded in the Protestant mind as the pattern of church meeting. The problem is that it became the pattern, not just for revivals, but for Sunday worship. Sunday morning was turned into an evangelistic service" ("Creative Worship: Rules, Patterns, and Guidelines," *Quarterly Review* 10, no. 2 [1990]: 14).

3. Julian Hartt, *Toward a Theology of Evangelism* (New York: Abingdon, 1955), p. 9. Hartt's book remains one of the finest accounts of evangelism we have. Hartt's influence at Yale Divinity was everywhere during the years we studied there.

4. Augustine, *The City of God*, trans. David Knowles (Harmondsworth, England: Penguin, 1972), p. 890 (19.23).

5. The reason I am a theologian is that I never was able to get "saved." I understood I was a member of the church, but I also knew that I was supposed to be saved at a Sunday night service—Sunday night services were what we did between summer tent events. I wanted to be saved, but it just never happened. I finally decided somewhere around fourteen that if God was not going to save me I would "dedicate my life to Christian service" by becoming a minister. So during the sixteenth singing of "I Surrender All"—a relatively short altar call, as altar calls went on Sunday nights—I dedicated my life to God by declaring I would become a minister. That never happened, but it did result in my majoring in philosophy in college, going to seminary, doing a Ph.D. in theology, and as they say, the rest is history.

6. The effect of the loss of eloquence in worship is a moral loss. Our lives morally depend on our being able to describe that which we do and do not do truthfully. When the language used in worship is degraded, so are our lives. For example, consider the word *just*. Often those who pray extemporaneously say, "Lord, we would ask you just to do X or Y." Not only is the use of *just* in that context ugly, but theologically it suggests, "Lord, we are really not asking for all that much given your power." I realize that often the use of *just* is meant to suggest humility, but such humility cannot help but sound like a pose. Eloquence, of course, is not achieved by using "archaic" language but by the constant attention necessary to put basic matters simply.

7. I mention the Psalms in particular because of Saliers's work to ensure their inclusion in the 1989 edition of the *United Methodist Hymnal*. It is my belief that this hymnal is the most important development in Methodism in the last fifty years. Theologians often think that what is important is what other theologians think, but much more important is what the church does. It is to Saliers's great credit that he has understood this. The time he has dedicated to help the church sing is not wise if you want a successful academic career, but he has rightly understood that such a career is a very small thing indeed compared to the glory of praising God.

8. This is particularly the case if you are, like me, a convinced Aristotelian. For Aristotle, what and how we "feel" when we do the virtuous thing is as important as our doing it. Aristotle says moral virtue "is concerned with emotions and actions, and it is in emotions and actions that excess, deficiency, and the median are found. Thus we can experience fear, confidence, desire, anger, pity, and generally any kind of pleasure and pain either too much or too little, and in either case not properly. But to experience all this at the right time, toward the right objects, toward the right people, for the right reason, and in the right manner—that is the median and the best course, the course that is a mark of virtue" (*Nicomachean Ethics*, trans. Martin Ostwald [Indianapolis: Bobbs-Merrill, 1962], 1106b.15–24). I take it that those concerned with help-

ing us worship God rightly do so as Aristotelians—which is to say, it is not enough that we do what we do but that we do what we do rightly. It is, of course, crucial to remember that we do not worship alone, which means that sometimes I must rely on my fellow worshipers to feel rightly for me.

9. Ed Phillips had to tell me that "In the Garden" was written not by Fanny Crosby but by Austin Miles. The problem with this beloved hymn is not, as is often suggested, the hymn's barely repressed sexual longing. There is nothing wrong with desire even if it is confused. Rather the problem with hymns like "In the Garden" is that their lyrics and music are shallow. A steady diet of worship formed by such hymns and prayers not only reflects a shallow church but also produces a shallow people. I know this seems like a harsh judgment that can also betray a "high culture" arrogance that disdains "popular religion." I have nothing but profound respect for the "country churches" that thought "In the Garden" the best hymn they sang. The problem, however, is that hymn and the worship that was shaped by it proved incapable of preparing those who sang it to recognize, much less resist, the world that increasingly made their Christian commitments unintelligible. I am well aware that many churches whose hymns and prayers are richer are often equally unprepared to challenge the world. Yet hymns like "A Mighty Fortress" have the potential to help mount a resistance that "In the Garden" can never muster.

In a letter to me about this hymn Ed Phillips—a church historian and liturgist who teaches at Garrett Theological Seminary—notes that "the last stanza subverts the entire text and makes it, actually, more interesting than you might at first notice: 'I'd stay in the garden with him though the night around me be falling, but he bids me go; through the voice of woe his voice to me is calling.' In other words, we might *want* to remain 'in the garden' all day long, but Jesus says, 'Get out there where the suffering is!'"

10. Marva Dawn, *Reaching Out without Dumbing Down* (Grand Rapids: Eerdmans, 1995), pp. 75–104.

11. I may have been among the last in this society to learn that Willow Creek is the paradigm of churches that use modern marketing methods to sustain church growth. The best way to think about such "churches" is to compare them to a shopping mall where periodically the customers are gathered for a common event. Such churches seek to be full-service institutions providing athletic activities, clubs, and childcare. If such churches were more centered around determinative liturgies that were recognizably Christian they might be usefully compared to medieval cathedrals. The latter were often centers for carnival, trade, and politics, and I see no reason to be critical. The problem with churches like Willow Creek is not that they are the center of so many activities but that those activities do not require for their intelligibility the Mass. I realize such a comment will invite the charge I am romanticizing the medieval life, but I am more than willing to take that risk. For an arresting account of the vitality of religious life in late medieval culture see Eamon Duffy, *The Stripping of the Altars: Traditional Religion in England, c. 1400–1580* (New Haven, Conn.: Yale University Press, 1992), as well as David Aers's criticism of Duffy for failing to provide an adequate account of the complex social, political, and military factors shaping "religion": David Aers, "Altars of Power: Reflections on Eamon Duffy's *The Stripping of the Altars*," *Literature and History* 3, no. 2 (autumn 1994): 90–105.

12. That this invitation is particularly directed at a person's marital status is but an indication of the privatization of Christianity in liberal cultures. The church gets to

claim its own peculiar jurisdiction, in this case something to do with the family, because the family is "private." Such an invitation would have been interesting if it had said, "Whether you are rich or poor, in debt or not, just out of prison or on the street, you are welcome." Such an invitation would have indicated some recognition of how class divides our churches, but to acknowledge class is even more threatening for most churches than the acknowledgment of homosexuality or racial divides. I have noticed the "higher" a church's liturgy, the more likely some recognition of class is possible. I have no strong evidence to support this generalization, nor am I sure, if it is true, why it is so. Of course, this is true mainly of Roman Catholic churches. That farm workers, for example, appear at Catholic masses predominantly populated by middle-class people is open to many explanations. But such explanations surely must involve an account of how the liturgy offers some challenge to the power that class has over our lives.

13. To attract large numbers of people presupposes that they are coming to worship without their coming requiring fundamental change in their own lives. There is nothing wrong in itself with worship being entertaining, but the difficulty is the kind of entertainment necessary to attract large numbers. If worship must, as is often alleged, compete with TV, then TV will always win. Our only hope is that some will find the demanding character of the worship of God so enthralling they will be drawn to it time and time again.

14. For an account of Wesley's views on these matters, see Ole Borgen, *John Wesley on the Sacraments* (Grand Rapids: Francis Asbury Press/Zondervan, 1986).

15. The worship service at Pleasant City had no confession of sin. Since the service from which I extracted the bulletin quote was a Fourth of July service, there were pledges made to the United States flag, the Christian flag, and the Bible. Sin was mentioned in the last pledge: "I pledge allegiance to the Bible, God's Holy Word, and will make it a lamp unto my feet, a light unto my path, and hide its words in my heart that I may not sin against God."

16. Of course, that sin names the powers does not mean that we do not sin. We confess our sins as those who have willingly sinned, but our willingness names complicity. I often think the closest paradigm we have to what it means to confess our sin is the alcoholic's confession at AA: "My name is X and I am an alcoholic." It may be that alcoholism is a power that possesses someone in such a manner that they can never remember "choosing" to be an alcoholic. Only as I confess that alcoholism is "me" is there any hope of recovery. Sin may not always be something I have "done," but it is nonetheless mine.

17. For an extraordinary account of our current sacrificial system we call America, see Gil Bailie, *Violence Unveiled: Humanity at the Crossroads* (New York: Crossroads, 1995). Bailie's analysis draws on the remarkable work of René Girard.

18. For an account of the way I teach Christian ethics at Duke Divinity School, see my *In Good Company: The Church As Polis* (Notre Dame, Ind.: University of Notre Dame Press, 1995), pp. 153–68. I confess I have no idea how much I have stolen over the years from Donald Saliers, *The Soul in Paraphrase: Prayer and Religious Affections* (New York: Seabury, 1980), but I know it is more than I have acknowledged. For example, everything I have said in this essay could be and, hopefully, will be read as a commentary on his claim that "prayer is a logically required context for the utterance of theological truths" (p. 82).

19. I am indebted to Kelly Johnson and Jim Fodor for their criticism of an earlier draft of this essay.

CHAPTER 11

1. For an analysis of Aristotle's account of friendship see Stanley Hauerwas and Charles Pinches, *Christians among the Virtues: Theological Conversations with Ancient and Modern Ethics* (Notre Dame, Ind.: University of Notre Dame Press, 1997), pp. 31–54.

2. Rowan Greer, *Broken Lights and Mended Lives: Theology and Common Life in the Early Church* (University Park: Pennsylvania State University Press, 1986), pp. viii–ix.

3. George Marsden, *The Outrageous Idea of Christian Scholarship* (New York: Oxford University Press, 1997).

4. Ibid., pp. 45–46.

5. Ibid., p. 47.

6. Ibid., p. 91. For a similar view see Grant Wacker, "Understanding the Past: Reflections on Two Approaches to History," in *Religious Advocacy and American History*, ed. Bruce Kuklick and D. G. Hart (Grand Rapids: Eerdmans, 1997), pp. 159–78. One of the difficulties with the way Marsden and Wacker make their case is that they continue to state the "problem" in terms that assume the legitimacy of liberal practices. For example, Marsden says that anyone teaching religion should not "proselytize" (p. 53), but it is hard to imagine any course about matters that matter in which the teacher does not want to change the lives of the students. Or as Wacker puts the question: "Should historians impose value judgments on their narratives above and beyond the layers of evaluation that are already present in everything that they do?" (p. 162). The problem is not with the answer Wacker gives to this question but that any answer one gives is a mistake because the question is wrongly put. "Impose" implies the historian has some further judgment to make that is more determinative than how the story is told in the first place. What Marsden and Wacker fail to see is the game is up as soon as you use the language of "values." The issue is what descriptions, which often may not appear "value laden," are determining how the story is told and for whom.

7. Friedrich Nietzsche, *On the Advantage and Disadvantage of History for Life*, trans. Peter Preus (Indianapolis: Hackett, 1980), p. 14.

8. Why, for example, do we teach courses in divinity schools called "American Church History," rather than "The Church's Story of America"? Often those who teach "American Church History"—which, of course, is increasingly under pressure to become "American Religious History"—do so appealing to Augustine's two cities as a justification for writing "secular" history of the church in America. Yet such a view betrays Augustine, who, if he followed the same mode he used in the *City of God*, would write to help Christians see why that entity called America is a blip on God's radar screen.

It is, of course, quite a different matter for secular historians. For example, Joyce Appleby, Lynn Hunt, and Margaret Jacob in their book *Telling the Truth about History* (New York: W. W. Norton, 1994) note that historians influenced by postmodernist literary approaches have become more aware that their supposedly matter-of-fact choices of narrative techniques and analytical forms have social and political ramifications. They try to go beyond "current negative or ironic judgments about history," however, by accepting the impossibility of total objectivity and completely satisfying causal explanations in order to have history serve a more intellectually alive democratic community. The latter they identify as the "kind of society in which we would like to live" (pp. 228–29). It simply does not occur to them that Christians might have a problem with that "we."

9. This does not mean that the Christian theologian cannot learn from or use the work of those who are not Christian. God, in Aquinas's phrase, works through secondary causes, inadequate as they are. Indeed it may well be possible that some "secular" historians may provide better accounts of God's work through Israel and the church than those who work explicitly as Christians. For example, see Michael Baxter's enlightening critique of accounts of the Catholic Church in America by Catholic historians in "Writing History in a World without Ends: An Evangelical Catholic Critique of United States Catholic History," *Pro Ecclesia* 5, no. 4 (fall 1996): 440–69.

10. Greer, pp. 17–18.

11. Ibid., p. 75.

12. I am not suggesting that Rowan alone is working in this fashion. For example, George Huntston Williams wrote wonderfully illuminating articles helping us see how issues involved in the Arian controversy were inseparable from questions of the status of the emperor in relation to the church. See his still classic article "Christology and Church-State Relations in the Fourth Century," *Church History* 20, no. 3 (September 1951): 273–328. The works of Robert Wilken and of Peter Brown have been invaluable for helping us to imagine our forebears' struggles to lead less broken lives. See in particular Robert Wilken, *Remembering the Christian Past* (Grand Rapids: Eerdmans, 1995). Wilken observes, "If love is no virtue and there is no love of wisdom, if religion can only be studied from afar and as though it had no future, if the passkey to religious studies is amnesia, if we can speak about our deepest convictions only in private, our entire enterprise is not only enfeebled, it loses credibility. For if those who are engaged in the study of religion do not care for religion, should others?" (p. 23).

There has been a rebirth of work dealing with the so-called Middle Ages that is enriching the Christian imagination in a similar fashion. I am thinking in particular of the work of Eamon Duffy, David Aers, Sarah Beckwith, Miri Rubin, John Bossy, and Frederick Bauerschmidt. I am not suggesting these authors are all in agreement, as they obviously have quite different views about their subjects, but what such work so helpfully does is aid us in recovering a sense of the embodied character of Christianity which we have largely lost today.

13. Greer, p. 171.

14. Ibid., p. vii.

15. One of the delightful aspects of Rowan's work is his ability to avoid current theological divisions by simply forging ahead, confident that what he has learned through years of reading the Fathers makes sense. For example, many of us avoid the language of "experience" like the plague, assuming that any appeals to experience cannot help but reproduce the anthropological reductions of Protestant liberalism. Lindbeck's strictures in *The Nature of Doctrine* (Philadelphia: Westminster, 1984) against the "experiential-expressive" model of religious language only increased our dis-ease with any appeals to experience. Yet in a few short paragraphs in *Broken Lights and Mended Lives* Rowan provides an extraordinary account of experience by using Clement's account of Eunomos and the Pythic grasshopper in the latter's *Exhortation to the Heathen*. It seems that Eunomos was competing in a lyre contest at Delphi when one of his strings broke. A grasshopper flew to his lyre, supplying the missing note. The Greeks regarded this as a tribute to Eunomos's excellence as a musician, but Clement saw the grasshopper as the divine song that transforms and completes the human song. This latter song, according to Clement, is the word of God that "composed the universe into melodious order,

and tuned the discord of the elements to harmonious arrangement, so that the whole world might become harmony." Rowan observes that Clement identifies this new song with God's agent in creation and redemption and that Clement appeals both to scriptural witness to the Redeemer and to Christian experience of redemption as a vision of the new freedom and a transformed moral life (p. 9). I cannot imagine how theology can do without such an appeal to that kind of experience.

16. For a similar perspective, see Frederick Norris, *The Apostolic Faith: Protestants and Roman Catholics* (Collegeville, Md.: Liturgical, 1992). It is no accident, of course, that Norris is also Rowan's student. James Reimer, a Mennonite, argues along the same lines in his "Trinitarian Orthodoxy, Constantinianism and Theology from a Radical Protestant Perspective," in *Faith Decreed: Ecumenical Perspectives on the Affirmation of the Apostolic Faith in the Fourth Century*, ed. S. Mark Heim (Grand Rapids: Eerdmans, 1991), pp. 129–61.

17. Actually the title *Resident Aliens* was suggested by my wife, Paula Gilbert. It came to her while reading the manuscript because of the recurring observation in the book about Christians as aliens. We had probably stolen that phrase from Rowan, but then Paula had also read *Broken Lights and Mended Lives* not long before reading Will's and my book. Thus the tangled path of "influence."

18. Greer, p. 141.

19. Ibid., p. 149.

20. Ibid., pp. 156–57.

21. Ibid., p. 157.

22. Ibid., pp. 165–66.

23. Ibid., p. 170.

24. Ibid., p. 206. Rowan, like Peter Brown, possesses the extraordinary ability to find the particular exemplar for explicating complex historical developments—e.g., his use of Galla Placidia to help us understand that the "fall of the West" to the barbarians was not exactly a clear case of "us" against "them." I reread these pages in *Broken Lights and Mended Lives* (pp. 189–92) just after I had finished Brown's *The Rise of Western Christendom* (Oxford: Blackwell, 1996). Brown's account may in certain respects be more "complete," but I was struck again by how much I had learned about the story Brown tells from Rowan's account in *Broken Lights*.

25. Greer, p. 196.

26. Ibid., p. 205–06.

27. For a more extended discussion of the theological implications of being so "placed," see my *Wilderness Wanderings: Probing Twentieth-Century Theology and Philosophy* (Boulder, Colo.: Westview, 1997). I suspect one of the reasons some have difficulty "pinning me down" (why won't he act like the "sectarian" he clearly must be?) is that I find many of the vestiges of "Constantinianism" so useful for Christians in this time between times. Forms of Christian "rule" inherited from the past can become quite useful forms of resistance now that Christians no longer rule.

28. This kind of objection to the general characterization "Constantinianism" has been developed by Nicholas Wolterstorff in a review of John Howard Yoder's *The Royal Priesthood: Essays Ecclesiological and Ecumenical*, ed. Michael Cartwright (Grand Rapids: Eerdmans, 1994) in *Studies in Christian Ethics* 10, no. 1 (1997): 142–45. Wolterstorff

challenges Yoder's alleged assumption that Constantinianism names the pattern of identifying the church with the world. Wolterstorff asks, "Is it true that Constantine's revolution amounted to the church *identifying* itself with the [secular] power structure? It's true that the company of the baptized became pretty much coterminous with the subjects of the state in the Holy Roman Empire; and it's true that the emperors saw themselves as responsible for many aspects of church life which Yoder and I both think the state ought to keep out of. But did anybody really think of church and state as *identical?* As Yoder acknowledges, the history of late antiquity and the middle ages is full of instances of bishops standing up to princes. Wouldn't everybody at the time have regarded these conflicts as church-state conflicts, not as conflicts between two different bureaus of one organization?" (p. 144). Yoder is perfectly capable of answering such questions, but I think it worth observing in the context of this chapter that Yoder's account of Constantinianism has never denied the point Wolterstorff is making. Yoder's concern is rather with recovering for the church practices that can make possible the kind of discriminating judgments about the church's relation to the social orders in which it finds itself for which Wolterstorff seems to be calling. *Constantinianism* at the very least names the assumption that there is something called "the state" that requires theological legitimation and as a result Christians are made less able to make the discriminations necessary to maintain their tension with the world.

29. I have focused on Paulinus of Pella as the paradigm of how to respond to a collapsing empire because Rowan identifies the response of Paulinus with his own. But one should not forget Rowan also treats Sidonius and Cassiodorus as deserving our respect for their quite different responses to the collapse of the West. Christianity for Sidonius was simply part of the landscape, so being a bishop was not different from being a civil servant. Rowan notes that no matter how accommodated Sidonius's account of Christianity might have been, it is nonetheless the case that his commitment to the church enabled him to take an active part in helping his people adapt to life under barbarian rule. Cassiodorus responded by forming a double monastery committed to the study of Scripture, because for him "to study the Scriptures is to participate in the age to come, and in this way the monks have withdrawn from this age. On the other hand, Cassiodorus insists that the monastery has an obligation to be active in caring for the stranger and for the neighboring people. Baths have been built conducive to the healing of the sick, and the monastery exists in part to be sought by others. 'The peasants must be instructed in good morals,' and they may not be burdened 'with the weight of increased taxes.' The comment is interesting because it presupposes a dependence of the local people on the monastery" (p. 203). I am aware that the response of Cassiodorus looks more like the kind of ecclesiology for which I have argued and there is certainly truth to that. But I am equally aware that Sidonius and Paulinus also have to exist and, even more important, be remembered by us.

30. Greer, p. 211.

31. Ibid., p. 208.

CHAPTER 12

1. Tracy Kidder, *Old Friends* (New York: Houghton Mifflin, 1993), pp. 83, 109.

2. Ibid., pp. 83–84.

3. Ibid., p. 235.

4. Ibid., p. 214.

5. Some readers may object to our drawing on the writings of a twelfth-century monk, because his world seems so distant from our own. And in many ways this is true. It was not, however, a more idyllic world; human envies, hates, and disputes were not only present in a monastic setting, but intensified, partly because "autonomy" was simply not an option. The brothers and sisters had to learn how to negotiate such antagonisms in the light of a common telos that transcended the individual. That learning is what we hope to implement here.

6. Aristotle, *Nicomachean Ethics*, trans. Martin Ostwald (Indianapolis: Bobbs-Merrill, 1962), 1156a.20–24. For an extended discussion of Aristotle's account of the interrelation of happiness, virtue, and friendship, see Stanley Hauerwas and Charles Pinches, *Christians among the Virtues: Conversations with Ancient and Modern Ethics* (Notre Dame, Ind.: University of Notre Dame Press, 1997), pp. 3–51.

7. Aristotle, 1156b.5–10.

8. Ibid., 1157b.17–20.

9. We do not mean to imply that Aristotle had an "abstract" account of friendship. He was acutely aware that friendship requires for its specification a wider politics. Yet he thought he lived at a time when such a politics was absent. Accordingly character friendship became for him an end in itself. In the last book of the *Nicomachean Ethics* Aristotle writes sorrowfully that "with a few exceptions, Sparta is the only state in which the lawgiver seems to have paid attention to upbringing and pursuits. In most states such matters are utterly neglected, and each man lives as he pleases, 'dealing out law to his children and his wife' as the Cyclopes do. Now, the best thing would be to make the correct care of these matters a common concern. But if the community neglects them, it would seem to be incumbent upon every man to help his children and friends attain virtue. This he will be capable of doing, or at least intend to do" 1180a(25–32). This passage surely explains why Aristotle devoted two books of his ethics to friendship. Friendship became, in the absence of any good politics, the only place that a school for virtue might exist. One cannot help but feel he is not just describing his time but ours. For Christians, however, no account of friendship can be justified that is not shaped by the more fundamental community we call the church.

10. Aelred of Rievaulx, *Spiritual Friendship*, trans. Mark F. Williams (Scranton, Penn.: University of Scranton Press, 1994), 2.14.

11. Ibid., 2.9.

12. Ibid., 1.46.

13. Ibid., 1.10.

14. Ibid., 2.52.

15. Ibid., 3.101.

16. Ibid., 2.68.

17. Ibid., 3.79.

18. Ibid., 3.127.

19. Paul Wadell, *Friendship and the Moral Life* (Notre Dame, Ind.: University of Notre Dame Press, 1989), p. 139.

20. Aristotle, *Nicomachean Ethics*, 1166a.23–27.

21. Alasdair MacIntyre, *After Virtue* (Notre Dame, Ind.: University of Notre Dame Press, 1984), pp. 79–84.

22. Aelred, *Spiritual Friendship*, 1.63.

23. "Waiting" and "witnessing" do not mean "preserving the status quo." They mean testifying to the truth of Christ's kingdom in the midst of the world, without expecting that we humans can enact that kingdom ahead of its appointed time.

24. Ibid., 3.82.

CHAPTER 13

1. Karl Menninger, *Whatever Became of Sin?* (New York: Hawthorn, 1973), p. 48.

2. For an extensive critique of liberal accounts of sin see "Salvation Even in Sin: Learning to Speak Truthfully about Ourselves," in my *Sanctify Them in the Truth: Holiness Exemplified* (Edinburgh: T & T Clark, 1998), pp. 61–76.

3. For reflection on the patience that should be required of Christian patients see Stanley Hauerwas and Charles Pinches, *Christians among the Virtues: Theological Conversations with Ancient and Modern Ethics* (Notre Dame, Ind.: University of Notre Dame Press, 1997), pp. 166–78.

4. This is the issue I tried to explore in *God, Medicine, and Suffering* (Grand Rapids: Eerdmans, 1994). The original title was *Naming the Silences*.

5. I am indebted to my colleague and friend Richard Hays for reminding me that "sinsick" is used in the hymn "There Is a Balm in Gilead." This proves the description was not peculiar to Texas, because Richard is from Oklahoma.

6. Thomas Aquinas, *Summa Theologica*, trans. Fathers of the English Dominican Province (Westminster, Md.: Christian Classics, 1948), 1–2.85.5.

7. Ibid., 1–2.84.2.

8. Ibid., 1–2.8.1.

9. Ibid., 2–2.164.1.

10. Ibid., 2–2.163.1–2.

11. Ibid., 2–2.164.1.

12. Ibid., 2–2.164.1, 4.

13. Ibid., 2–2.164.2.

14. Ibid., Q.80, Art.1, Supplement.

15. Ibid., Q.81, Art.1, Supplement.

16. Ibid., Q.80, Art.2, Supplement.

17. This subhead is a play on the title of James Alison's *The Joy of Being Wrong: Original Sin through Easter Eyes* (New York: Crossroad Herder, 1998). It will become obvious how much I owe Alison's quite extraordinary presentation for the general argument of this paper.

18. Alison discusses this passage in ibid., pp. 120–25.

19. Ibid., p. 3.

20. Ibid., p. 123.

21. I cannot here develop Alison's quite extraordinary Christology except to say I am in deep sympathy with his insistence on the historical and bodily character of salvation. Alison rightly assumes the salvation wrought by God in Christ is contingent, which means "that salvation works precisely at the level of producing a different social other, through contingent historical acts and texts, with physical relations, signs and so on. This, of course, places us on a somewhat different course from any transcendental anthropology, which sees, as a matter of philosophical truth, the human being as imbued with a somehow experienced orientation toward grace and glory and therefore the concrete, contingent, historical acts of salvation (the prophets, the coming of Christ, the existence of the Church, the sacraments) as merely making explicit the universal availability of grace." Following this claim Alison notes he does not want to deny that all humans are by the fact of being human called to participate in the divine life. "However, it seems to me that this *theological* doctrine is an important human discovery made in the light of the death and resurrection of Jesus of Nazareth and is part of a discovery that we are, in fact, quite different from what we normally think we are. That is to say, the doctrine of the universal vocation to *theiosis* is itself part of the discovery of salvation as a difficult process worked out in hope, in which we hope to become something which we are not, or are scarcely, now" (pp. 42–43).

22. Ibid., p. 261.

23. Ibid., p. 262.

24. Ibid., p. 263.

25. Ibid., p. 170. One cannot help but to think of Reinhold Niebuhr as the strongest example of such a use of original sin. For Niebuhr original sin became a generalized anthropological description used to justify lesser-of-two-evil arguments. Accordingly any account of holiness was undercut by the oft-made Niebuhrian presumption that when all is said and done we are all sinners. Of course it is true we are all sinners. The problem is when that becomes a covering law explanation to justify the way things are.

26. Ibid., p. 300. While I find Alison's account persuasive, I am not convinced his contrast of the New Testament with the Old is right. I simply do not know how Jews may or may not understand how sin shapes our lives.

27. Ibid., p. 181. This quote comes from a section of this chapter called "Excursus: The Particular Overcoming of Particularity."

28. Ibid., p. 184.

29. Of course, this does not mean there will not be similarities between how Christians and non-Christians understand as well as care for the sick. But what appears as a "sickness" in the world (i.e., growing old) cannot be so understood by Christians. Nor can Christians invest the power in medicine "to relieve the human estate" so characteristic of modern medicine.

CHAPTER 14

1. Ronald Knox, "A Detective Story Decalogue," in *The Art of the Mystery Story*, ed. Howard Haycraft (New York: Carroll and Graf, 1992), p. 194.

2. G. K. Chesterton, "A Defence of Detective Stories," in *The Art of the Mystery Story*, p. 4.

3. Arthur Upfield, *An Author Bites the Dust* (New York: Collier, 1948), p. 73.

4. Chesterton, "Defence," p. 4.

5. Ibid., p. 5.

6. My wife, Paula Gilbert, who is a much more accomplished reader of detective fiction than I can claim to be, discovered that one of the best ways to prepare to go to a new place is reading murder mysteries. That is how we became readers of Arthur Upfield, as no one provides a better introduction to Australia than Upfield. Of course detective fiction is an introduction not only to countries but also cultures and institutions. Oxford always seems different after I have read a new Colin Dexter.

7. Laura Yordy pointed out to me that good detectives are right (more often than not) not because they "reason" perfectly but because they astutely understand the fallibility of practical reason. It is interesting, for example, how good detectives depend on the work of others. Watson is no longer "dumb"; the detective requires others to help her or him see the obvious. I am grateful to Laura Yordy, a theologian who reads mysteries, for her criticism of this paper.

8. Chesterton, "Defence," pp. 5–6. That Chesterton uses the language of "conspiracy" to describe how "law and order" may embody our deepest moral convictions is a reminder of how "order" may also be a form of violence. Thus the "detective" often acts "outside the law" exactly because the law has become disorder. More on this below.

9. This observation might well seem to commit me to a view of natural law closer to McInerny's account than my more determined arguments about the distinctiveness of the Christian ethic. My views on these matters have, I fear, been often misunderstood, as I have never denied that all people are anything less than God's good creation and thus gifted with God's law sufficient to live well. My argument against advocates of natural law has been against those who think, in the interest of showing that Christians can be good democratic citizens, that Christians as Christians cannot have anything morally distinct to say about the way we should live. That is to put the matter too simply, but nonetheless suggests the heart of the matter. The fundamental questions, of course, are christological.

10. Dorothy Sayers, "The Omnibus of Crime," in *The Art of the Mystery Story*, p. 74. Sayers duly acknowledges her indebtedness to E. M. Wrong's essay "Crime and Detection" as the influence behind her account. Wrong's essay can also be found in *The Art of the Mystery Story*, pp. 18–32. One of the reasons, I suspect, that writers of detective mysteries often try, and often quite successfully, to return to the past as a setting is to show that in fact the "discovery" that the crime novel suggests is anything but new. Indeed the success of these endeavors can be used to justify a kind of natural-law account of morality. Eco's *The Name of the Rose* is obviously one of the most exemplary forms of the renarration of the past using the form of mystery. I suspect it is not accidental that his mystery depended on the forms of life shaped by monasticism—i.e., it takes monastics to exemplify the law that should shape life outside the monastery. In other words, monasticism is the institutional form of Aquinas's claim that charity is the form of all the virtues.

11. Sayers, "Omnibus," p. 76.

12. Dorothy Sayers and Jill Paton Walsh, *Thrones, Dominations* (New York: St. Martin's, 1998), was recently published through the good efforts of Walsh as a coauthor of the unfinished manuscript. This, of course, presents the problem of whether in

fact the book represents Sayers's views or those of Walsh. I think any reader of Sayers, however, will find the following quotes quite characteristic of Sayers's perspective.

13. Ibid., p. 131.

14. Ibid., pp. 151–52. The rise of Germany under Hitler and the outbreak of World War II hover in the background of *Thrones, Dominations*.

15. McInerny makes much the same point commenting on what makes Chesterton's Father Brown mysteries Catholic—classified "perhaps generically as Christian, maybe even as religious (and, if you are Socrates or Plato, as philosophical). *The consequences of action reach beyond time and the span of earthly life.* This enhances the importance of fleeting deeds; it puts an enormous premium on what we do here and now. Religion was once dismissed as pie in the sky, but the pie, or its withholding, is the just desserts of what one does on earth. The moral dimension of human action is included in the religious, but not vice versa, and that is why the first mark is, as Flannery O'Connor suggests, universal to imaginative literature" ("Saints Preserve Us: The Catholic Mystery," in *The Fine Art of Murder: The Mystery Reader's Indispensable Companion*, ed. Ed Gorman, Martin Greenberg, Larry Segriff, with Jon Breen ([New York: Carroll and Graf, 1993], p. 149).

16. P. D. James, "The Baroness in the Crime Lab: Interview by Martin Wroe," *Books and Culture* 4, no. 2 (March/April 1998): 15. James, in the same interview, observes rightly, I think, that the classical detective story is not primarily concerned with violence. "It is concerned with bringing order out of disorder, with exploring human nature under the impact of this unique crime" (p. 14). In *Thrones, Dominations*, Harriet explains to Peter that "murder is the only crime for a detective story. It has true glamour. Anything less is liable to strike the reader as Perrier to champagne" (p. 222). Raymond Chandler comes as close as anyone to explaining why murder is the singular crime of mysteries when he observes that "murder, which is a frustration of the individual and hence a frustration of the race, may, and in fact has, a good deal of sociological implications" ("The Simple Art of Murder," in *Art of the Mystery Story*, p. 223). "A good deal of sociological implications" is, to say the least, an understatement.

17. Of course when I was first tempted by McInerny to read mysteries I was not a pacifist. That was the result of another Notre Dame colleague—John Howard Yoder. I suspect that Yoder was not a reader of mysteries.

18. This was the argument of Paul Ramsey, who insisted that just war not only provided a casuistry for thinking about war but was also a theory of statecraft. See, for example, his *Speak Up for Just War or Pacifism* (University Park: Pennsylvania State University Press, 1988), with an epilogue by me.

19. As a pacifist I am quite committed to trying to think what is necessary to allow a Christian committed to nonviolence to consider performing police functions. I refuse to accept the presumption that the police function must be understood as controlled violence. Rather, I assume most of what police officers do is nonviolent response to violence. After all, police officers are called peace officers. Indeed I think one of the most interesting challenges before pacifists and just-warriors is to think together about what would be required to have a society in which the police would not be required as part of their task to use lethal weapons.

20. Some pacifists do write murder mysteries—Irene Allen and Chuck Fager are Friends who have done so. I confess I know of no Mennonite who has written a murder mystery. I particularly commend Allen's *Quaker Silence* (New York: Villard, 1992).

21. McInerny, "Saints Preserve Us," p. 149. Crime does not equal that which is immoral or sin, which is why Aquinas maintained that an immoral law cannot and should not be obeyed. The difficulty, given the contingent character of law (and morality), is discovering when a law is immoral. For example, a law may be moral in one context and become something less in changing social contexts. I am thinking in particular of laws that structure economic relations. Perhaps one of the reasons that murder is *the* crime in mysteries is that the law against murder is less open to injustice.

22. Sarah Freedman pointed out to me that in this way the great Dostoyevski does go beyond the mystery genre (beyond crime and punishment!) by exploring how such redemption is possible

23. Sayers and Walsh, *Thrones, Dominations*, pp. 302–3.

24. One of the issues I have not addressed in this essay is whether murder mysteries are inherently conservative literature in that detection of crime always favors the status quo. There is, of course, some truth to that generalization, but interestingly enough murder mysteries often provide ways to explore in what ways such a generalization is wrong. They do so not only by helping us understand the desperation and loneliness of those who murder but also by positioning the "detective" on the edges of established society. The work of Anne Perry is particularly interesting in this respect: the class nature of Victorian England is at once reinforced and challenged by her accounts.

An even more powerful objection to mysteries as a genre than their conservative bias has been raised by Oliver O'Donovan in a letter to me (of July 30, 1998) responding to this essay. Oliver observes that the detective story trades upon and reinforces our sense of justice, "but does its modernity not lie precisely in the isolation of criminal justice from relational justice, in which we are all involved not just as witnesses but as perpetrators? The essential modernity of the genre, as I see it, lies in its identification of the justice-moment as the *exceptional moment*, and its location of the justice-act in the *exceptional individual*, i.e. the detective who alone construes the world and its testimonies coherently. The detective is certainly a hero. But making justice the prerogative of heroes reflects a curiously *gesellschaftlich* view of social relations. The knight in armour in the Arthurian romance contributed a certain skill (i.e. at arms) to the performance of justice in which other people were in other ways, by their commonplace virtues, involved. But the detective works in a moral vacuum—and must do so, for one rule of the detective mystery which you have not articulated is the sceptical canon: *All must be suspect!* There is no place in a detective story for a character who is simply too good to have committed a murder."

I wish I had a good response to O'Donovan's point, but I do not. I can say that I think the murder mystery genre, given that the story is often so contextually located, at least suggests that the justice being enacted is—to use O'Donovan's term—"relational."

INDEX

283